HUMANIZING OUR GLOBAL ORDER:
ESSAYS IN HONOUR OF IVAN HEAD

Ivan Leigh Head

Humanizing Our Global Order

Essays in Honour of Ivan Head

*Edited by Obiora Chinedu Okafor
and Obijiofor Aginam*

UNIVERSITY OF TORONTO PRESS
Toronto Buffalo London

© University of Toronto Press Incorporated 2003
Toronto Buffalo London
Printed in Canada

ISBN 0-8020-8736-1

Printed on acid-free paper

National Library of Canada Cataloguing in Publication

Humanizing our global order : essays in honour of Ivan Head /
   edited by Obiora Chinedu Okafor and Obijiofor Aginam.

   Includes bibliographical references.
   ISBN 0-8020-8736-1

   1. Globalization.   2. International relations.   I. Head, Ivan, 1930–
   II. Okafor, Obiora Chinedu   III. Aginam, Obijiofor, 1969–

   JZ1318.H84 2003   303.48'2   C2003-900838-X

Grateful acknowledgment is made to the International Development Research
Centre for funding to assist with the publication of this volume.

The University of Toronto Press acknowledges the financial assistance to its
publishing program of the Canada Council for the Arts and the Ontario Arts
Council.

University of Toronto Press acknowledges the financial support for its publishing
activities of the Government of Canada through the Book Publishing Industry
Development Program (BPIDP).

Contents

Foreword

I am very pleased to write this foreword in appreciation of Ivan Head and his singular career in service to Canada and the world. The hallmark of that service has been Professor Head's belief that to serve the world is truly to serve Canada and that the resolution of global problems is fundamental to sustaining our own prosperity and well-being. In the pursuit of international peace and cooperation, he has given all of us a deeper understanding of the links these issues have to our own country and to our own lives.

I first met Ivan in the early 1970s when he was a foreign policy adviser to Prime Minister Pierre Trudeau. This was a time of ferment in our thinking about the role of Canada in the world. The test that each policy had to pass was not whether a narrow, national self-interest was being advanced, but whether the policy was likely to lead to a better world from which our country would inevitably benefit. We were encouraged to view our country as an 'effective power,' one that was ready to attack real problems and contribute to solutions that bettered the situation of all members of the international community.

Out of this philosophy grew the dedication of both Pierre Trudeau and Ivan Head to addressing the urgent problems that afflict developing countries and their billions of citizens. They believed that it was essential for Canadians to dedicate themselves to the cause of Third World development, not only because it was just and right, but because it was fundamental to ensuring global peace and security.

Ivan's assumption of the presidency of the International Development Research Centre in 1978 was a natural extension of his involvement with issues that had preoccupied him from his time as a junior foreign service officer in Malaysia through to his work at shaping and executing Canadian foreign policy at the highest levels. It fell to Ivan to consolidate and advance the already enviable reputation of the IDRC as a force for innovation and excellence in supporting research by developing country scholars and institutions into problems they had identified as important to the development of their countries and their regions. In doing so, he combined a natural sympathy and understanding of their circumstances with an unfailing interest in and commitment to their work. A scholar himself, he appreciated that there was no substitute for basing policy and technological choices on well-reasoned research that took into account not only scientific principles but also the social and political circumstances in which those choices were to be implemented. Throughout his tenure at the IDRC he was an articulate advocate for the belief that there must be continuing national engagement with developing countries and their unique problems, and for a policy of providing the development aid that was required to put that belief into practice.

Following his service at IDRC, Ivan assumed the Chair of North–South Studies and became the first Director of the Liu Centre at the University of British Columbia. Through my own involvement with the Centre, I've witnessed the way he has challenged scholars and students alike to engage themselves in the most important issues facing our interdependent world. The result has been research and writing of the highest academic quality that has deepened our understanding of global concerns and sought to influence the international community in finding fair and enduring ways of managing them.

The title of this volume is 'Humanizing Our Global Order.' In many ways and in many places that has been Ivan Head's goal. It's a goal he has pursued with unfailing intelligence, skill, and compassion. I am pleased that the IDRC, whose Board of Governors I am privileged to chair, has contributed to the realization of this excellent collection of studies, which is being published to honour a man who has done as much as any living Canadian to advance us toward that goal.

Gordon Smith
Chair, International Development Research Centre

Preface

Ivan Leigh Head's towering stature in foreign policy and international law circles is widely acknowledged, not just in Canada but the world over as well. But so is his warm, humble, optimistic, and humane personality. Rarely in our own experience have so many positive qualities coexisted so happily in the same person. This happy coincidence testifies to the extraordinarily well-rounded character of this great scholar and diplomat.

As a tribute to the life and times of this living icon of Canadian foreign policy and international law, this book seeks to recognize and celebrate his remarkable achievements and exceptional contributions to the search, both scholarly and diplomatic, for a more humane global order.

Though at different times and in different places, both of us first met Ivan Leigh Head when we were relatively young though somewhat experienced graduate law students at the University of British Columbia in Vancouver, Canada. Before coming to UBC, each of us had spent a number of years working in academia and/or in legal practice. Both of us were immediately impressed by the brilliant and intricate mind of this great scholar and by his simple and approachable, if measured, disposition. We were to become even more impressed as we developed our separate relationships with him, partly as his doctoral students, partly as his intellectual disciples, and partly as avid students of his well-honed diplomatic craft. Both of us came to admire greatly his sharp mind, extraordinary work ethic, mellifluous prose, and consistently respectful treatment of *all* those around him. In him we saw an accomplished scholar and diplomat; we also saw a down-to-earth human being whose concern for humanity at large extended far beyond the narrow confines of his university and his country. In Ivan we saw a man who had remained as constant as any person could be to an admirable vision of a more humane global order. We have never stopped being impressed – hence this *Festschrift* in his honour.

We consider it a great honour to have had this opportunity to conceive, compile, and edit this book, which consists of scholarly essays of the highest quality, each on a topic that reflects on the current global situation, each in honour of Ivan Leigh Head – a great scholar and diplomat if ever there was one. We can only hope that brilliant as they are, the essays we have collected are worthy of his extraordinary life and work.

Obiora Chinedu Okafor   Obijiofor Aginam
Toronto, Canada   Ottawa, Canada
June 2002   June 2002

Acknowledgments

Our zeal to undertake this project was tried and tested by prior commitments to our families, to our own students, and to our employers. Nevertheless, because of the character of Ivan Leigh Head, in whose honour we were undertaking it, and because of our great admiration for his life and work, this project was always a priority for us. Needless to say, the project absorbed a fair amount of time, energy, and commitment, not only our own but also that of many other people, some of whom had never even met Professor Head, in whose honour this book is being published.

In this connection, we express our profound gratitude to our families. Obijiofor Aginam would like to thank his wife Chi-Chi, his mother Osodieme, and his father Onyekachi. Obiora Chinedu Okafor would like to thank his wife Atugonza, his son Ojiako, his mother Lechi, his father Okwuegbunam, his deceased parents-in-law Mary and Amon Bazira, his sisters Adaobi, Ojiugo, and Chibuzo, his brother Okey, his other brothers and sisters Baguma, Abi, Jeff, Dan and Solo, and his aunt-in-law Joyce Ssembajwe. In one way or the other, all of you helped make this book possible.

We are grateful to the University of Toronto Press, especially its executive editor, Virgil Duff, for agreeing in principle to publish the book at a time when we were just starting to imagine it. The publisher's early encouragement was vital to the project's success. In a similar vein, we want to express our appreciation to the president and staff of the International Development Research Centre in Ottawa. Your financial and other help was vital to the success of this book.

Osgoode Hall Law School was quite supportive of this project and deserves special mention here. Its generous provision of research monies to Obiora Chinedu Okafor enabled him to secure the research assistance that was critical to the early completion of the project. In a similar vein, Obijiofor Aginam expresses his gratitude to the Department of Law at Carleton University for its support and encouragement.

We must also acknowledge the most helpful research assistance provided to us by Bernard Assan and Tanya Cianfarani, both LLB students at Osgoode Hall Law School.

Thank you one, thank you all!

Obiora Chinedu Okafor   Obijiofor Aginam
Toronto, Canada   Ottawa, Canada

Notes on Contributors

Obijiofor Aginam is an Assistant Professor of Law at Carleton University, Ottawa, Canada, where he teaches international law, law of international organizations, and global governance. In 1999–2001 he was Global Health Leadership Officer at the World Health Organization, Geneva, Switzerland, where he worked on regulatory approaches to the global spread of infectious diseases, and WHO's Framework Convention on Tobacco Control. He holds an LLB (Hons) from the University of Nigeria; an LLM from Queen's University, Kingston, Canada, and a PhD from the University of British Columbia. He has recently published 'From the Core to the Peripheries: Multilateral Governance of Malaria in a Multicultural World' (2002) 3 *Chicago Journal of International Law* 87. His other recent publications have appeared in *Indiana Journal of Global Legal Studies*, *International Journal of Public Health*, and *Journal of Law, Social Justice and Global Development*. He has been selected as one of the 2003 SSRC–MacArthur Foundation Research Fellows on Global Security and Co-operation to study global health security. He is presently consulting for the World Health Organization on aspects of globalization, trade, and public health.

Olivier A.J. Brenninkmeijer is the Fellowship and Internship Coordinator at the United Nations Institute for Disarmament and Research (UNIDIR), Geneva, Switzerland. He is also a PhD candidate at the Graduate Institute of International Studies, Geneva, where he obtained his Diploma of Graduate Studies (DES). He holds a BA and MA in political science from the University of British Columbia, Canada, and has worked for many years in the private sector, in the social service sector, and in academia. His most recent publications include *Internal Security beyond Borders: Public Insecurity in Europe and the New Challenges to State and*

Society (Bern/Frankfurt/New York: Peter Lang Academic Publishers, 2001); and 'Conflict Prevention and the OSCE High Commissioner on National Minorities' (trans. into Russian) in *The World Economy and International Relations Journal* 3 (Summer) 2002.

Jutta Brunnée is Professor of Law and Metcalf Chair in Environmental Law at the University of Toronto. Her teaching and research interests are in the areas of Public International Law, International Environmental Law, and the intersection of international law and international relations theory. She is the author of *Acid Rain and Ozone Layer Depletion: International Law and Regulation*, and of numerous articles on topics of international environmental law and international law, both in collections of essays and in journals such as the *American Journal of International Law*, the *Columbia Journal of Transnational Law*, *Environmental Conservation*, the *Harvard International Law Journal*, and the *Leiden Journal of International Law*. She is a member of the World Conservation Union's (IUCN) Environmental Law Commission, was a member of the International Expert Group on the 'Programme for the Development and Periodic Review of Environmental Law for the First Decade of the 21st Century (Montevideo Programme III)' of the United Nations Environment Programme, and editor-in-chief of the *Yearbook of International Environmental Law* (1997–2001). In 1998–9, Professor Brunnée was the Scholar-in-Residence in the Legal Bureau of the Canadian Department of Foreign Affairs and International Trade, advising, *inter alia*, on matters under the Biodiversity and Climate Change Conventions.

Thomas M. Franck is Murray and Ida Becker Professor of Law at New York University's School of Law. One of the most respected international lawyers of our time, Professor Franck has recently published *Recourse to Force: State Action against Threats and Armed Attacks* (Cambridge: Cambridge University Press, 2002). He is a former editor-in-chief of the *American Journal of International Law* and a past President of the American Society of International Law (ASIL).

Karen Guttieri is on faculty at the Department of National Security Affairs, Naval Postgraduate School, Monterey, California. She is also an affiliate of the Center for International Security and Cooperation (CISAC), Stanford University. She was a Social Sciences and Humanities Research Council of Canada (SSHRC) Post-Doctoral Fellow at CISAC from 1999–2001, where she studied the intersection of politics and technology in the revolution in military affairs. Prior to that she had taught at the University of British Columbia and Simon Fraser University. Dr. Guttieri earned her doctoral degree in Political Science from the University of British Columbia. Her publications include articles in *Journal of Conflict*

Resolution and *International Insights.* Dr. Guttieri has also written on national security decision-making and is co-author of 'Archival Analysis of Thinking and Decision-Making: Assessing Integrative Complexity at Distance,' in *The Psychological Evaluation of Political Leaders: Method and Application* (Cornell University Press, 2001). Her primary focus is upon military operations in civilian environments. This focus includes studying the effectiveness of civil-military operations, military organizational learning from peace operations, and civil-military relations issues in peace implementation.

Karin Mickelson, A.B. (Duke) 1983, LLB (UBC) 1988, LLM (Columbia) 1991, is Associate Professor of Law at the University of British Columbia, Vancouver, Canada. She has taught in the areas of international law, international environmental law, environmental law, and legal theory. Her recent research activities have focused on the South-North dimension of international law, with an emphasis on international environmental law. She is also a contributor to leading Canadian casebooks on international law and environmental law. She is the author of 'Rhetoric and Rage: Third World Voices in International Legal Discourse' (1998) 16 *Wisconsin International Law Journal* 353.

Kirsty Middleton is a lecturer in law at the University of Strathclyde in the United Kingdom, where she specializes in European law and competition law. She holds an LLB (Hons) and a Dip LP from the University of Strathclyde. She also holds an LLM from the University of British Columbia. She has recently written a text on UK and EC competition law (Oxford University Press, 2003) with Barry Rodger and Angus MacCulloch. Other recent publications include 'European Law and the Sports Sector' in *Sport and the Law* (T&T Clark, 2000), 'The Euro-clause' in *UK Competition Law – A New Era?* (Hart, 2000), and *UK and EC Competition Law*, 3rd ed. (Oxford University Press, 2003). She is a member of the Competition Law Group, the International Law Association, and the Scottish Lawyers European Group. She is also a founding member of the Competition Law Scholars Forum, established in 2003 to promote scholarship in the field of competition law throughout the United Kingdom and the European Union.

Obiora Chinedu Okafor is an Associate Professor at Osgoode Hall Law School of York University, Toronto, Canada. He was most recently an SSRC–MacArthur Foundation Fellow on Peace and Security in a Changing World, as well as a Visiting Scholar at Harvard Law School's Human Rights Program. He has also served on the law faculties of Carleton University, Ottawa, Canada, and the University of Nigeria, Enugu Campus, Nigeria. He holds an LLB (Hons) and an LLM from the

University of Nigeria, Enugu Campus, Nigeria, and an LLM and a PhD from the University of British Columbia, Vancouver, Canada. Widely published, his most recent publications include *Re-Defining Legitimate Statehood* (The Hague: Martinus Nijhoff, 2000), *Legitimate Governance in Africa* (The Hague: Kluwer Law International, 1999) (co-edited with Kofi Quashigah), and 'After Martyrdom: International Law, Sub-State Groups, and the Construction of Legitimate Statehood in Africa' (2000) 41 *Harvard International Law Journal* 503.

Robert Shum researches and practices international trade law. He has also worked for the United Nations High Commissioner for Refugees. His research interests include the interaction of trade policy with other global issues such as human rights. He holds degrees in law and public policy from the University of British Columbia and Harvard University's Kennedy School of Government, respectively.

Ronald St John Macdonald C.C., Q.C., LL.D is the Honorary President of the Canadian Council of International Law, and a former Judge of the European Court of Human Rights. A member of *l'Institut de Droit International*, he is currently Professor Emeritus at Dalhousie Law School, Halifax, Canada. One of the most distinguished and widely acclaimed public international lawyers of our time, Judge St. J. Macdonald is very widely published. His is co-editor (with Douglas M. Johnston) of *The Strucure and Process of International Law* (The Hague: Martinus Nijhoff, 1983).

HUMANIZING OUR GLOBAL ORDER:
ESSAYS IN HONOUR OF IVAN HEAD

Chapter One

Humanizing Our Global Order:
An Introduction

OBIORA CHINEDU OKAFOR AND OBIJIOFOR AGINAM

Humankind today, for the first time in five millennia of recorded activity, faces circumstances of global dimensions: possible nuclear cataclysm, environmental degradation, economic collapse. These are dangers of a quality that may not permit recovery. The circumstances contain margins of error so narrow as to be almost meaningless. Moreover, the combination of today's technologies and yesterday's politics has produced trends that, unless altered significantly, may well become irreversible.[1]

This grave charge and the accompanying challenge appeared almost fifteen years ago in a paper that encapsulates the ethics, idioms, and visions that have characterized Ivan Head's always seminal, constantly inspiring, and strikingly well-couched contributions to the study and practice of South–North relations.[2] These prophetic words aptly summarize the diverse existential turmoils that *all* of humanity currently faces. Caught as we *all* are in a complex web of global relations that all too often produce a world order widely acknowledged as patently unfair, the tumultuous state of our globe is all the more disturbing.[3] Much as in the past, today's world – a world that some have characterized as a 'global *neighbourhood*'[4] – is characterized by profoundly disquieting turbulence and gross human suffering: by the threat of nuclear annihilation; by the continuing threat posed by chemical and biological weapons; by the rampant spread of civil conflict; by the accelerating ecological crisis; by the dangers posed by food insecurity; by the ubiquity of abject poverty in most of the world; by the severe and growing disparities in living standards, both within and among nations; and by the cross-border spread of infectious diseases. Seen as a whole, our world is a semifeudal, virtually ungovernable entity split by intrastate conflicts, largely devastated by persistent violence, and weakened by extreme poverty.[5] A tiny portion of it is prosperous, the rest is extremely poor.[6]

Disturbing as this panoramic picture of our world may be to many, the fact that our world is so tense and turbulent, and characterized by such extreme polarities between the 'resource haves' and the 'have nots,' should not surprise any keen observer. Nor should it surprise us[7] that our generation already has the human and economic resources to confront these unfortunate aspects of the current global situation. What *should* surprise and challenge us is the glaring failure of our generation to tackle effectively the causes and symptoms of the fundamental malaise we face. The question that *all of us* – policymakers, scholars, and multilateral institutions alike – must confront head on is this: How are we to foster and deploy the political will necessary to ameliorate the serious crises our world now faces? How are we to marshal the required knowledge and resources? The answer will involve nothing less than *humanizing our global order*.

As scholars like Ivan Head have long recognized, at the heart of this challenge lies the need to establish more humane forms of global relations and governance, animated by a broader-based and people-centred concept of development, one that is far more aware of and accepting of the demands emanating from the South.[8] Yet as Head himself has pointed out, if this process of humanization is to bear fruit, it cannot – as it has tended to do in the past – proceed without a solid, in-depth recognition and acceptance that the countries of the South must play a critical role in the project. If the world's forest resources, confined as they are largely to the countries of the South, are not to be completely destroyed in the understandable yet ceaseless quest for firewood and timber; if social and political instability in both South and North are not to lead to outside interventions in the South and the escalation of great power confrontations; if economic uncertainty, unsustainable debt burdens, threats of protectionism, and the ferment of widespread unemployment are to be contained, the cooperative involvement of developing countries – home as they are to the vast majority of the world's peoples – is going to be essential.[9] And just as essential to this enterprise will be the need to secure the cooperation of the developing world's scholars and intellectuals.

In this context, two crucial questions arise: How do we enhance human dignity by protecting the human family *as much as possible* from the threats of hunger, disease, wars and conflicts, environmental insecurity, illegitimate governance, and poverty? And is there a way we *all* can escape these palpable 'South–North dangers'?[10] These and similar questions express the complexity of the challenge that confronts our generation – a challenge that most serious South–North scholars agree must be met with both intellectual rigor and human vigour.

It is mainly to this end that the contributors to this book have embarked on the incredibly complex and difficult task of engaging seriously – albeit in broadly different ways – the theme of this volume: *the humanization of our global order.* With commendable intellectual rigor, each of the contributors explores an issue that relates in some significant way to our current global circumstances. With equally commendable human vigour, each contributor seeks to reassess a specific topic. Thus, this book offers innovative perspectives that cover the matrix of our current theme.

The perspectives offered by the contributors are both *critical* and *timely. Critical* in the sense that most of them seriously challenge or at least rigorously analyse the tired old ways of conducting global relations and constituting our global order. *Timely* because our current generation inhabits a season of rare opportunity, a time of ferment – a moment of transition, a moment that presents us with a unique opportunity to reflect on our common destiny and to reassess and reshape the dynamics and character of the global order.[11] Inspired to varying degrees by Head's seminal and widely acknowledged commitment to South–North scholarship and practice, and by his lifelong involvement in the drive to humanize our global order, almost all the contributors explore various dimensions of our current theme. And they have done so in ways that are likely to contribute significantly to the humanization of our common future.

Several broad subthemes are discernible in this book: the environment; sustainable development; the common heritage of humankind; the use of force; the protection of minorities; the civil dimensions of military strategy; the International Seabed Authority; the modernization of competition law; and the legitimacy of the international trading system. Let us now briefly turn to them.

The 1990s witnessed far too many acrimonious South–North debates on a plethora of environmental issues: the regulation of forest resources, the conservation of biodiversity, the depletion of the ozone layer, and climate change, to name a few. A number of multilateral negotiations relating to various environmental issues were held in the hope of establishing effective *global* governance mechanisms in the environmental field. Yet such multilateral environmental agreements (MEAs) operate in a complex milieu characterized most notably by persistent assertions of state sovereignty – assertions that all too often are not conducive to the emergence of effective international environmental regimes. Concerned about the tensions within such MEA regimes revolving around issues of sovereignty, efficiency, and legitimacy, and having assessed the role of the conferences of the parties (COPs) in the functioning of MEAs, Jutta Brunnée analyses and compares the '*standard* conception' of lawmaking in international law with the alternative '*interactional* framework' for such lawmaking.[12] In doing so, she shows that the standard and interactional approaches actually complement each other. Brunnee argues persuasively, that although the *interactional* framework challenges some of the core assumptions of standard lawmaking, its emphasis on internal rather than formal criteria of bindingness generates insights that ultimately complement traditional, formalist approaches. Brunnee concludes that timely and effective responses to new and emerging global environmental concerns will become more likely within a treaty regime that embraces genuine *interactional* lawmaking. Furthermore, as Brunnee shows, the interactional approach provides a stronger framework for fostering genuine dialogue, both within and outside environmental regimes and across the South–North divide. In this way that framework can contribute significantly to what must inevitably become a *cooperative process* of humanizing our global order.

Still on the broad issue of the legitimacy and legitimation of global environmental norms, Obijiofor Aginam investigates the legitimacy deficit of the norm in favour of sustainable development as that concept is currently understood. Focusing on the ecological devastation that multinational oil corporations have wrought in the Niger Delta and in the Amazon Basin, and on the decision of the International Court of Justice in the *Gabicikovo-Nagymaros* project, Aginam argues convincingly that global society is in dire need of a much more *cosmopolitan* understanding of the concept of sustainable development. He also argues that the conception of this new understanding must be based on a much more genuinely multicultural *dialogue* (as opposed to *monologue*) across the South–North divide. In his view, the old way of doing things must be refashioned in ways that do not marginalize the serious ecological concerns emanating from the South. He also warns that international environmental law is running a serious risk by ignoring the values and practices of sustainable development that the world's diverse cultures have created over centuries. Aginam's chapter makes a significant contribution to how we conceptualize the future of humanity, and how we can eventually create a more humane global order.

The question of the legitimacy and legitimation of global norms and institutions is also the main concern of Robert Shum's essay. Shum considers that many groups – including the vast majority in the countries of the South – are expressing profound concerns regarding 'the very legitimacy of the WTO as an appropriate institution of global governance.' Here, nothing less than the legitimacy of the international trading system is at stake. Shum concludes that the cooperation and competition that result from the overlap of the WTO's mandate with that of a number of other international institutions may pressure the WTO and the other institutions to 'widen participation and increase accountability,' thereby enhancing their legitimacy among states, especially the weaker and more troubled countries of the South. According to Shum, it is imperative that global institutions like the WTO dramatically reduce the degree to which most countries perceive them as insensitive to their concerns.

The multilateral discussions that took place beginning in the 1960s regarding the legal status of the deep seabed foreshadowed the emergence of the concept of the 'common heritage of humankind.' This concept offered the basis for a cooperative paradigm that may eventually result in fairer global resource allocation across the South–North divide. Karin Mickelson investigates the various ways the concept of common heritage has been deployed in the literature of international law and relations. She poses two critical questions. Has the concept been coopted and deployed in ways not in keeping with the objectives of its creators? And does a critical evaluation of the concept provide some opportunity to reconceptualize the very nature of South–North scholarship? Overall, Mickelson's message accords with the warning given by former ICJ President Mohammed Bedjaoui that 'modern theory about the common heritage of mankind must not lead to a new historical function that barely conceals another form of domination.'[13] In this way Mickelson's chapter, at the very least, presents a vivid idea of how *not* to go about humanizing our global order.

Ronald St J. Macdonald's discusses the challenges and opportunities that the International Sea-Bed Authority has presented to our generation. The very existence of this institution points out the importance of global cooperation in the regions of our globe that are not (and cannot be) so easily subjected to exclusive national sovereignty and occupation. It also points out the need for continued albeit much more genuine dialogue across the South–North divide. His examination of the authority's potential reminds us of the raucous debates that took place in the 1960s and 1970s regarding the need to create an authority that would harness undersea resources for the benefit of *all*, and not simply to enrich the few nations with the advanced technologies to harvest those resources in the first place. It seems that mutually beneficial cooperation across the South–North divide – which does not dispossess the have-nots simply because they lack technology – must figure centrally, in any serious reimagining of the global order.

Any endeavour that aims to humanize our global order must be firmly anchored in legal norms that prohibit or authorize the use of force. In his essay, Thomas Franck explores the tensions between 'humanity' and 'unreason' with regard to the legality of the use of force both under and outside the purview of the United Nations Charter. Franck points out that the UN Charter's regime regarding the use of force has been challenged by four new developments: the Cold War (which incapacitated the Security Council); the tactical replacement of open military aggression with surrogate warfare; the development of weapons of overwhelming and instant ('mass') destruction; and the powerful resonance of anticolonialism and antiapartheid issues in the UN General Assembly and the UN Security Council. As Franck shows, Article 51 of the UN Charter (which allows states a *limited* right of self-defence) has been relied on by certain states in very doubtful and hotly contested ways. In his view, South Korea, Hungary, the

Dominican Republic, Grenada, Panama, Pakistan (Bangladesh), Czechoslovakia, Uganda, Egypt, Lebanon, Iran, and Kuwait come to mind as situations that match this characterization. As Franck also notes, regional organizations have sometimes resorted to the use of force in situations of extreme necessity, ostensibly to prevent humanitarian disasters. The resort to the use of force by NATO in Kosovo and ECOWAS in Liberia – in both places force was used without the prior approval of the UN Security Council – are two examples Franck offers in favour of this proposition. In Franck's view, recourse to the doctrine of extreme necessity raises a conundrum: if such use of force is in conformity with UN objectives (e.g., the prevention of genocide), but in violation of the requirement that such uses of force receive the prior approval of the Security Council, should the UN Charter be interpreted creatively to accommodate the spirit of 'extreme necessity'? Franck proposes a middle course: the UN Charter must be viewed as a kind of quasi-constitution for the global system. And since no constitution ought to be allowed to become so dry that its branches snap in the winds of extreme necessity, and since no constitution can flourish if its branches can be torn off by any malevolent passer-by, some creative reinterpretation of the UN Charter is both inevitable and desirable if the ethic of humane governance is to be brought to bear on the legal use of force in our turbulent world.

The 1990s witnessed a surge in internecine conflicts around the world. Crises of legitimate governance, gross violations of human rights, and the suppression of minority rights all led in one way or another to deadly conflicts in many parts of the world. Olivier Brenninkmeijer explores the potency of the multilateral mechanisms for preventing internal conflicts in the context of severe tensions among peoples of identifiably separate ethnicity, and notes that 'in the final years of the 1990s and into the new century, approximately 25 new and ongoing conflicts were being fought around the world.' His essay focuses on the mandate and conflict prevention initiative of the Organization for Security and Co-operation in Europe (OSCE) and its High Commissioner on National Minorities (HCNM). He holds that the mandate and conflict-prevention facilities of the OSCE are innovative and effective. He supports the widely acknowledged aphorism that early prevention is the best approach to violent conflict.[14] Preventive diplomacy has been good for the member states of the OSCE; it follows that such an approach should be valuable the world over, especially in the context of past attempts by many other regional organizations to prevent deadly conflicts in their spheres of influence. Our global order can hardly be called humane as long as millions of people die annually in civil wars that could have been prevented.

Civilian populations in postconflict societies often face a range of difficult challenges. They lack basic services: a police force, a functioning legal system, good schools, basic necessities such as food, shelter, and water, and basic sanitation. Yet the relevant military forces often lack the capability and the 'mindset' to meet these onerous obligations they face in postconflict environments. In her essay Karen Guttieri explores the civil dimensions of military strategy in postconflict environments. In postconflict military operations, military forces are faced with having to provide the basic needs of civilian populations and construct the institutions of civil governance. Guttieri considers how the military forces of the United States and other countries address questions of civilian operations. She shows that prevailing political norms and evolving military doctrine affect the character of postconflict civil military operations; this being so, it should be rather obvious that the task of ensuring that the conduct of postconflict civilian-related operations by military forces is humanitarian in focus, and sensitive to the needs of the local civilian population, is key to the project of humanizing our current global circumstances.

In her essay, Kirsty Middleton discusses the modernization of the European Community competition law through the abolition of the European Commission's centralized system of control. This is giving national competition authorities and courts a greater role in enforcing EC competition rules. The modernized EC competition law recognizes that commerce is no longer purely national or European, but is increasingly global. As the recent agreements between the United States and the European Union show, global cooperation in tackling the monopolies exerted by large-scale worldwide cartels is extremely important to the work of the European Commission, a body that is ordinarily regional in its orientation. It is not unreasonable to suggest that the imperatives of *global cooperation* (because no region can isolate itself from global currents) and *decentralization* (because of the need to involve those who do not operate in the international centres of power) must figure prominently in any serious debate over how our global order can be made more humane.

The views of the contributors to this volume build on the efforts of those who in the past have worked on similar themes and subthemes.[15] As Richard Falk and other scholars have wisely noted, all such previous efforts have been critically important to the overall project of thinking through and eventually imagining and offering *alternative* global order models – models that often present a viable alternative to our current global order.[16] In Falk's own words:

> The current ideological climate, with its neo-liberal dogma of minimizing intrusions on the market and downsizing the role of government in relation to the provision of public goods that compose the social agenda, suggest that the sort of global civilization that is taking shape will be widely perceived, not as fulfilment of a vision of unity and harmony, but as a dysutopian result of globalism-from-above that is mainly constituted by economistic ideas and pressures.[17]

This volume, in honour of one of the truly great of Canada's postwar makers of foreign policy, is both explicitly (in some cases) and implicitly (in others) a modest effort to feed the ongoing, never-ending, development of more humane models of global order. Ivan Leigh Head, in whose honour we have compiled this book, presented *On a Hinge of History* not as a prophecy of doom but as a kind of 'end-of-millennium benediction.'[18] In *Humanizing Our Global Order* we present the various views of our diverse contributors as a kind of 'dawn of millennium' wake-up call.

NOTES

1 I.L. Head, 'The Contribution of International Law to Development' (1987) 25 Can. Y.B. Int'l L. at 29.
2 *Ibid.*
3 See T.M. Franck, *Fairness in International Law and Relations* (New York: Oxford University Press, 1995). See also U. Baxi, 'Voices of Suffering and the Future of Human Rights' (1998) 8 *Transnational Law and Contemporary Problems* 125 at 140–169; M. Camdessus, 'The IMF at the Beginning of the Twenty-First Century: Can We Establish a Humanized Globalization?' (2001) *Global Governance* at 363.
4 We borrowed this expression from the title of the report of the Commission on Global Governance. See *Our Global Neighbourhood: The Report of the Commission on Global Governance* (Oxford: Oxford University Press, 1995). We must note, however, that the irony of characterizing as a 'global neighbourhood' a world that is as deeply cleavaged as ours, in which the vast majority of people cannot move around freely (or at least as freely as the privileged minority), is not lost on us. For a very important study of this inherent contradiction in the theory and practice of prevailing forms of globalization, see A. Simmons, ed., *International Migration, Refugee Flows and Human Rights in North America: The Impact of Free Trade and Restructuring* (New York: Centre for Migration Studies, 1996).
5 Franck, *supra* note 3.
6 *The Challenge of the South: The Report of the South Commission* (New York: Oxford University Press, 1995) at 1.
7 Franck, *supra* note 3
8 See I.L. Head, *On a Hinge of History: The Mutual Vulnerability of South and North* (Toronto: University of Toronto Press, 1991).
9 Head, 'The Contribution,' *supra* note 1 at 29.
10 I.L Head, 'South–North Dangers' (1989) 68 *Foreign Affairs* 71.
11 *'We the Peoples': The Role of the United Nations in the 21st Century* (Millennium Report of the Secretary General of the United Nations) (New York: The United Nations, 2000).

12 Brunnee's interactional framework is an amalgam of Lon Fuller's legal theory and the constructivist theory of international relations that produces international law through mutually generative interaction between states and other international actors.

13 M. Bedjaoui, *Towards a New International Economic Order* (Paris: UNESCO, 1979) at 224.

14 B. Boutros-Ghali, *An Agenda for Peace: Preventive Diplomacy, Peacemaking and Peace-keeping* (New York: United Nations, 1992) (defining preventive diplomacy as 'action to prevent disputes from arising between parties, to prevent existing disputes from escalating into conflicts and to limit the spread of the latter when they occur').

15 An example of such earlier work can be found in the reports that have been produced by the various world commissions of past years. See *North–South: A Programme for Survival: The Report of the Independent Commission on International Development* (chaired by Willy Brandt) (London: Pan Books, 1980); *Our Global Neighbourhood: The Report of the Commission on Global Governance* (co-chaired by Ingvar Carlsson and Shridath Ramphal) (Oxford University Press, 1995); *Carnegie Commission on Preventing Deadly Conflicts* (co-chaired by David A. Hamburg and Cyrus R. Vance) (New York: Carnegie Corporation, 1997); *Our Common Future: The Report of the World Commission on Environment and Development* (chaired by Gro Harlem Brundtland) (Oxford University Press, 1987).

16 R. Falk, 'The Coming Global Civilization: Neo-Liberal or Humanist,' in A. Anghie and G. Sturgess, eds., *Legal Visions of the 21st Century: Essays in Honour of Judge Christopher Weeramantry* (The Hague: Kluwer, 1998) at 15.

17 R. Falk, *The Coming Global Civilization*. For a detailed discussion of an alternative vision of world order by Falk, see generally, R. Falk, *Law in an Emerging Global Village: A Post-Westphalian Perspective* (New York: Transnational Publishers, 1998); *On Humane Governance: Towards a New World Politics* (College Park: Pennsylvania State University Press, 1995).

18 I. Head, *On a Hinge of History, supra* note 8 at xii.

Chapter Two

Saving the Tortoise, the Turtle, and the Terrapin: The Hegemony of Global Environmentalism and the Marginalization of Third World Approaches to Sustainable Development

OBIJIOFOR AGINAM*

We are part of nature with the forests and the animals[1]

> The flames of Shell are flames of Hell,
> We bask below their light,
> Nought for us to serve the blight,
> Of cursed neglect and cursed Shell[2]

It is a great problem for the whole of mankind to strike a satisfactory balance between more or less contradictory issues of economic development on the one hand and preservation of the environment on the other, with a view to maintaining sustainable development.[3]

The Crux of the Argument: (Un)sustainable Development?

In 1987 the World Commission on Environment and Development, chaired by Dr Gro-Harlem Brundtland[4] (hereafter 'the Brundtland Commission'), defined sustainable development as 'development that meets the needs of the present without compromising the ability of future generations to meet their own needs.'[5] Since then, sustainable development has become the buzzword of contemporary global environmentalism. It is explicitly referred to in a plethora of emerging multilateral environmental conventions, bilateral treaties, and 'soft law' mechanisms.[6] Policymakers in national governments, corporate actors, civil society groups, and activists (many of them self-anointed environmentalists) have embraced this buzzword. All too often these groups claim – implicitly at least – to have mastered the problem of sustainable development, and attempt to monopolize the term in policy and academic discourses. In doing so they suggest that the term is an infallible benchmark for ecological struggles worldwide. These claims leave us with the fundamentally flawed impression that sustainable development is now firmly entrenched in the vocabulary of global environmentalism.

As a concept, sustainable development was not entirely alien to environmentalism prior to the work of the Brundtland Commission. Philippe Sands has suggested that the body of international law that catalysed Principle 27 of the Rio Declaration on Environment and Development 1992 (which commits states and people to further develop 'international law in the field of sustainable development') possibly predates the work of the Brundtland Commission.[7] This body of international law, according to Sands,

> comprises those principles and rules which are derived, principally, from the *lex specialis* of prior and emerging international law in three fields of international cooperation: economic development, the environment and human rights. Historically, these three subjects have for the most part followed independent paths, and it is only with the advent of the concept of sustainable development, endorsed by the international community ... that they will increasingly be treated in an integrated and interdependent manner.[8]

In this chapter I argue that in a multicultural world marked by South–North tensions, cultural differences, and disagreements over the *modus operandi* of sustainable conservation of floral and faunal resources, questions must be asked about the evolution and efficacy of the concept of sustainable development in the global arena. The multiculturalism of our global society presents enormous challenges for the governance of such environmental issues as biological diversity, aquatic and marine environmental protection, international trade in endangered species, and forestry and desertification, to name just a few.

From time immemorial, many societies within nation-states have followed environmentally friendly and sustainable conservation practices. To what extent are these practices part of the evolutionary process of sustainable development in a global policymaking framework? How 'sustainable' is the concept of sustainable development in a multicultural world? I argue that in a globalizing world in which multinational corporations – especially in the oil, gas, pharmaceutical, and chemical industries – can abuse the environment with impunity, the concept of sustainable development as it stands in contemporary international scholarship and policymaking smacks of hegemonic globalism. Within a broader set of phenomena, this construct functions in ways that erode the valid conservation practices of many indigenous peoples. By remaining silent on the erosion of indigenous ecological values and norms, sustainable development implicates itself as a collaborator in, and an engine of, environmental injustice. By failing to establish an effective international legal regime to mitigate the environmentally harmful operations of multinational corporations, this construct has also facilitated environmental injustice. I agree completely with Mickelson's recent indictment of international environmental law for its appalling tendency to provide an ahistorical account of the discipline and for portraying the South as a grudging participant rather than an active partner in global environmental policy formulation. In this paper I articulate sustainable indigenous ecological practices that have been relegated to the margins.[9] These practices must be taken more seriously if international environmental law is to achieve its humanist ambitions.

I propose a three-dimensional inquiry to support my thesis that environmentally sustainable practices and norms in the postcolonial societies of the global South have been relegated to the periphery of global environmentalism. I focus on indigenous conservation practices in Africa and South America as examples of the creativity and practices of most of the postcolonial societies of the South. I apply emerging international normative and adjudicative frameworks, as exemplified by the decision of the International Court of Justice in *Gabcikovo-Nagymaros*, to argue that international law's timidity in articulating normative canons of sustainable development (based on multicultural approaches to environmental protection) has dealt a further blow to the already marginalized Third World approaches to conservation. This timidity is analogous to what Koskenniemi has broadly characterized as 'apology' and 'utopia' in international legal discourse.[10] Timidity, apology, and utopia have led to a problematic dichotomy in the global environmental movement. As a result, discourses and actors in the policy and scholarly edifice of sustainable development are operating in a fuzzy environment of logical inconsistencies and policy contradictions. In this essay I explore one of these contradictions – one that in the end serves to maintain a colonial-type relationship in a supposedly postcolonial world – a relationship that Makau Mutua has recently 'satirized' as emblematic of the relationships that exist among 'savages, victims, and saviors.'[11] It is clear from the notorious Bhopal tragedy in India, and from the environmentally degrading operations of multinational oil corporations in Nigeria's oil-rich Niger Delta and the Ecuadorian Amazon, that sustainable development discourses must begin responding to environmental abuses by multinational corporations. Global environmentalism must move beyond the narrow confines of state-centric interests to holistically incorporate ecologically sound practices of indigenous societies.

Inexorably linked to this holistic and inclusive dynamic is the need to establish an effective legal regime with the tools to protect the emerging sustainable development dynamic. I argue that notwithstanding the submissions to the contrary of well-known scholars like Philippe Sands,[12] the contemporary international normative order on which the principle of sustainable development is built is substantially weak. From the start, international environmental law has failed – incidentally or by design – to take into account those practices and belief systems of the countries of the South that are relevant to sustainable development. In this sense, I am a follower of Judge C.G. Weeramantry, former Vice-President of the International Court of Justice. I agree completely with that great judge's opinion that in view of emerging ecological questions and disputes, international environmental law will have to do more than weigh the rights and obligations of parties. The global concerns of humanity as a whole – what international lawyers call *erga omnes* obligations – also need to be addressed by international environmental law.[13] Global multiculturalism thus compels us to rethink global environmentalism so that it integrates indigenous approaches from the global South into the framework of sustainable development.

My three-dimensional inquiry considers the operations of multinational oil companies in Nigeria's Niger Delta and the Ecuadorian Amazon, as well as the decision of the International Court of Justice in *Gabcikovo-Nagymaros Project (Hungary v. Slovakia)*. In the first two sections of this essay I sketch how one aspect of globalization – the erosion of national boundaries in the global South due in part to the perceived need for foreign investment by MNCs in those societies – has placed severe pressures on indigenous conservation practices. In the third section I demonstrate that the environmental abuses perpetrated by MNCs in Nigeria's Niger Delta and in the Ecuadorian Amazon offend the principles of sustainable development (this assumes that some level of agreement can be reached regarding the ramifications of that principle from an inclusive South–North perspective) and have generally not been redressed in international law. The conundrum faced by international environmental law, as a result of its non-responsiveness to the anti–sustainable development operations conducted by MNCs in the South, exposes that body of legal norms and principles as substantially weak and ineffectual. This weakness implicitly maintains the *status quo's* questionable silence with regard to the identity of the victors and victims of the current forms of globalization and corporatization. The law's silence has had a complex, two-pronged impact on the victors and victims of globalization. In the first instance, this silence approves of – or at least does not destabilize – the privileged position of the victors/saviours (generally of Northern and/or MNC extraction); in the second second, sanctions do not ameliorate the plight of the victims/savages (generally of Southern and/or indigenous extraction). Before beginning my inquiry, it would be useful to explore the nature and character of the sustainable development strategies and practices in the indigenous societies of the South.

Are We Part of Nature? Indigenous Ecological Conservation Strategies and Practices

It is now widely accepted that ecological conservation practices have existed in almost every society. What differed perhaps was how these practices were given legal protection in radically different cultures. In her seminal work, Professor Edith Brown Weiss observed that

> knowledge of natural systems is critical to managing them effectively. Before the existence of writing, profound knowledge of nature's 'secrets' was passed orally from one generation to the next. In ways that are exceedingly difficult to understand today, pre-industrial and pre-historic societies perpetuated and built upon accumulated ancestral knowledge of the natural world through folk/cultural techniques involving teachings and stories told by community elders. Today this legacy is threatened with extinction. We are witnessing large-scale destruction of tribal [sic] cultures and the global transformation of traditional societies.[14]

Weiss has identified five main ways in which indigenous knowledge is vital to modern environmentalism. One of these is that all indigenous peoples share a *holistic view* of the place of the human species in the natural environment, a view animated by a reverence for the land and its bounty and by the desire to live in harmony with it, if only from necessity.[15] Ogbu Kalu has argued persuasively that across African societies

> crucial to indigenous traditions is a religious cosmology with an awareness of the integral and whole relationship of symbolical and material life. Ritual practices of the cosmological ideas which underpin society cannot be separated from daily round of subsistence practices ... By sacralizing nature, indigenous worldviews purvey an ideology which is at once eco-sensitive, eco-musical and devoid of the harsh flutes of those who see nature as a challenge to be conquered, exploited and ruled. They see the environment not in terms of competing interests but as the playing field on which all other interests intersect.[16]

In most of the South these cosmological ideas and the intersection and conglomeration of communal interests shape humanity's relationship with the environment. This humanity environment relationship is in turn founded on indigenous approaches to conserving flora and fauna – approaches marked by the twin concepts of conservation and sustainable use. Indigenous environmental practices take various forms, including folklore, social taboos, and intergenerational communication of knowledge. Among the Maasai people of Kenya, great importance is attached to livestock. Cows are regarded as sacred. A danger to Maasai cattle is thus a danger to the entire Maasai community.[17] In a detailed study of customary environmental law in Nigeria, Adewale examined a range of ecologically sustainable practices protected by age-long customary laws and norms among the Okrika, Kajju, and Badagry communities.[18] These practices include customary laws and practices relating to forests, hunting, fishing, biological diversity, water resources (preservation of streams), and agriculture, as well as ecofeminist approaches to environmental protection in rural societies.[19] In many communities in eastern and western Nigeria, customary law prohibits the killing of certain animals and the cutting of certain trees either because they are regarded as sacred[20] or because they have been proven to have medicinal or other value. According to Adewale,

> this traditional ... belief has afforded certain species of animals some degree of protection. Some of these animals include some species of snakes, *hippopotamus amphibius* and *cercopitheans eythrotis sclaten*. Among the *Ajar* community in *Badagry*, which is a predominantly hunting community, some hunting festivals are observed. During this festival, only certain types of animals are hunted. This has some conservative effects.[21]

N.A. Ollennu has asserted that in Ghana, customary land tenure is not simply land holding; it also encompasses the social milieu – the beliefs of the people and their ways of life.[22] In Ghanaian customary land law,

> land and environmental protection was the responsibility of the entire society. The Chief assisted by the Chief Priest of the Earth Goddess (Asaase Yaa) could inflict instant punishment on those who desecrate the earth ... In Akan areas, it was the belief that if one dug a trench on the earth surface indiscriminately, the goddess would create a filter in the person's palms to drain the money that comes to her/him. It was also believed that defecating on the earth amounts to defecating into the mouth of the goddess. It was also forbidden under customary law for one to clear bushes on the banks of a river, which were considered to be the resting places of the 'river gods' and their children.[23]

It is an enormous challenge to enforce customary sustainable conservation practices. In Nigeria, native and customary courts substantially enforce native laws and customs. Prior to the advent of customary courts,

> each community had different ways of enforcing their customs and customary laws ... In the case of taboo or religious customs, the fear of the gods (impressed in the

mind of the people which is passed from generation to generation) make the members of the community comply ... In many rural settings the evening period witnesses stories and folklore about the customs and beliefs of the community. This form of indoctrination from an early age leaves a permanent mark in the heart of members of the community as time progresses. There is, therefore, a natural tendency to comply with such norms and laws.[24]

This is radically different from British concepts of law and enforcement. A synthesis of British traditions and precolonial customary law seems remotely possible, but remember here Laura Nader's warning that in the study of non-Western societies, it is unwise to adopt wholesale Western jurisprudential categories as yardsticks for analysing exotic legal traditions.[25] Furthermore, Western concepts of law, as theorized by scholars such as Max Weber, are narrowly focused and miss most of the essential ingredients of law and legal obligation in non-Western societies. So it would be out of place to apply them to the observance, obligation, and customary enforcement of indigenous environmental norms in most of the global South.[26]

Considering all this, it is pertinent to consider how the age-old environmental practices protected by the customary laws of precolonial societies have interacted with international environmental law to develop the corpus of sustainable development. Simply put, does customary environmental law constitute part of the *corpus juris* of global environmentalism? Following the Weberian tradition, is customary law to be dismissed as a primitive or uncivilized legal tradition? Has customary environmental law anything to contribute to sustainable development in the global arena? The next two sections, relating to Nigeria and Ecuador, may point to answers to these questions.

Multinational Oil Operations, Environment, and Sustainable Development in Nigeria's Niger Delta

Crude oil was discovered in Nigeria in commercial quantities in 1957 at Oloibiri, a village in the Niger Delta. Before that year, since 1914, Shell had enjoyed a monopoly in oil prospecting in the area.[27] The 1960s and 1970s marked the political decolonization of Africa. Soon enough, the newly (politically) independent states realized that political independence would mean little without economic self-determination. This led to agitation at the United Nations for a new international economic order. The era that saw the passage of resolutions on Economic Rights and Duties of States and Permanent Sovereignty over Natural Resources by the UN General Assembly was also the era that witnessed an upsurge in foreign direct investment in Nigeria's oil industry. The 1960s and 1970s witnessed the arrival of oil multinationals such as Gulf Oil (now Chevron), Mobil, and Texaco (all from the United States); Elf and Total (from France); and the Italian oil giant AGIP. These corporations joined Shell-BP, an Anglo-Dutch oil conglomerate that till that time had maintained an oil-prospecting monopoly in Nigeria.

With these new opportunities arose new challenges. That 'oil is black gold' is a truism. This truism points to the affluence that crude oil production has brought to many societies. As a major exporter of crude oil, Nigeria has experienced both the economic fortune and the environmental misfortune of oil operations. As observed by Mbanefo:

> Since the Nigerian economy is largely dependent on oil, Nigerians tend to look only to the positive side of the oil industry – its role as the baker of the national cake, which we all share and consume with great enthusiasm. The bad news is that oil is a murky substance, which has a great capacity for causing enormous damage to the environment when it escapes.[28]

At almost every stage of oil operations – prospecting, exploration, drilling, and refining – an oil operator has to grapple with various environmental hazards. The implications of these hazards for the environment and human life itself are enormous. Most of Nigeria's oil wells are in the Niger Delta, an ecologically delicate region. The delta and the Nigerian coastal wetlands are among the most sensitive and fragile ecosystems in the world. Only 30 per cent of the delta is unaffected by flooding. Most parts are densely populated, averaging 1,250 people per square kilometre.[29] The ethnic minorities inhabiting Nigeria's resource-rich Niger Delta include Ogonis, Okrikas, Ikwerre, Ijaw, Andonis, and Kalabaris; there are many others. For these communities, communal streams and rivers abound, providing water for bathing, drinking, and many other needs. From time immemorial, fishing and farming have been the main occupations of these communities. The scramble by multinationals for oil concessions has placed severe pressure on the delta's sensitive ecology and done it severe damage.

Nigeria's oil production is concentrated in the delta. Pollution takes the form of oil spills that all too often pollute drinking water, contaminate fishing grounds, and destroy fishing gear. Damage to pipelines and oil installations in turbulent waters has degraded the aquatic environment. Let us consider a few examples. In January 1980, Texaco's Funiwa 5 oil well blew up, spilling 100,000 barrels of oil in thirteen days and polluting mangrove swamps, creeks, and rivers of a number of coastal settlements in the Niger Delta – Sangama, Fishtown, Kulama 1 and 2, and Olua.[30] Other ecologically devastating spills include a Shell-BP oil well blowout in Dere village, leakage of a pipeline in Bodo West, and an oil well blowout at Bonny that contaminated streams around the island of Finima.[31] There were blowouts at Nembe 2, where Shell produces 140,000 barrels of crude oil daily,[32] and at Yorla, where the resulting spill polluted the community's only source of drinking water and affected the neighbouring communities of Buan, Lubara, Kwawa, and Luuwa.[33] At Asaramotoru, an oil spill affected twenty-four flow stations owned by Shell northeast of Bonny terminal.[34]

Regarding air quality, oil companies operating in Nigeria are notorious for gas flaring. Flaring destroys vegetation, poisons the atmosphere, and causes acid rain. The health consequences of this practice for the people of the Niger Delta are enormous. During flaring, carbon dioxide and sulphur dioxide are emitted. Hydrocarbons such as methane, ethane, and iso-buthane deprive the air of sufficient oxygen to support respiration. Carbon monoxide, a gas hazardous to human health, is also emitted. Commenting on the toxicology of organic compounds, Manahan states that hydrocarbons – alkene, alkyne, methane, ethane, and n-buthane – are readily absorbed by blood, from which they are taken up by fatty tissues. Inhalation of air containing benzene has a rapid effect on the central nervous system manifested progressively by excitation, depression, respiratory system failure, and death. Chronic benzene poisoning leads to blood abnormalities, including a lowered white cell count and an abnormal increase in blood lymphocytes. In severe cases, leukemia and cancer may also result.[35]

Regarding the land of the Niger Delta, pollution has degraded the soil of the native farming communities. Farm crops need nitrates, potassium, and phosphates. Crude oil spills transform these natural soil ingredients into compounds that are hardly supportive of farm crops. This contributes immensely to soil infertility.

The implication of all this is that as Nigeria navigates between the Scylla of oil operations and the Charybdis of environmental protection, indigenous communities in the Niger Delta have become environmental refugees. The Niger Delta is witnessing 'reckless' as opposed to 'sustainable' development. In one case brought before the courts, the plaintiffs – whose land, fish pond, and communal creek had been polluted by an oil spill – applied for an injunction. The court refused to grant one, ruling that nothing should be allowed to disturb the operations of Shell (the defendant), which was the main source of Nigeria's foreign exchange.[36]

Multinational Oil Corporations, Environment, and Sustainable Development in the Ecuadorian Amazon

The Oriente province in Ecuador is a resource-rich tropical rain forest. It is home to a vast range of plants and animals and is inhabited by eight different indigenous peoples: Quechua, Shuar, Huaorani, Secoya, Siona, Schiwiar, Cofan, and Achuar. Norman Myers observed that the region 'is surely the richest biotic zone on earth and deserves to rank as a kind of global epicentre of biodiversity.'[37] Regarding one of the groups, the Huaorani, Brady states that 'the prospect of oil development in the biologically rich but fragile tract of Amazonian rainforest that is the homeland of the *Huaorani* – a tribe[38] of semi-nomadic hunter-gatherers in the Amazonian Oriente region of eastern Ecuador – threatens the tribe's cultural and physical survival.'[39] In late 1960s a consortium of oil companies including Texaco and Gulf discovered crude oil in commercial quantities in Oriente.[40] Since then the challenge of balancing oil operations with the imperatives of environmental protection has proved to be extremely difficult. The Center for Economic and Social Rights states that

> the Oriente now houses a vast network of roads, pipelines and oil facilities. Settlers attracted by the roads and encouraged by government land policies have entered in large numbers, clearing vast regions of the rain forest and displacing indigenous inhabitants. This process has contributed to a deforestation rate of almost a million acres a year in the *Oriente*, one of the highest rates in Latin America. Experts have questioned the environmental soundness of practices and technologies used by Texaco and Petroecuador for oil exploration in the Oriente.[41]

In the Oriente, as in the Niger Delta, oil particulates have been discharged into the atmosphere from burning waste pits; these particulates contain drilling fluids with pentachlorophenols. Pollution has damaged the people's health, contaminated their water, and deprived them of fish, game, and crops.[42] Like the communities in the Niger Delta and in line with indigenous approaches to nature conservation, the indigenous peoples of the Ecuadorian Amazon follow customs and traditions that have evolved from time immemorial. These customs 'are inextricably bound to the rain forest in which they have lived for thousands of years. Their economic and spiritual existence revolves around sustainable management of forest resources.'[43] Brady states that 'as hunter-gatherers, the Huaorani have fundamental social, cultural, and spiritual ties to their lands.'[44] In Ecuador, one devastating consequence of oil operations is that the environmentally sustainable practices of the indigenous populations are being significantly eroded. Scholars who have studied this problem in considerable detail allude to the relevance of international legal principles – human rights, sustainable development, and self-determination – in arriving at solutions. In light of this possibility, the following section explores the deployment one of these suggested strategies – the principle of sustainable development.

The Poverty of Sustainable Development and of the International Order

One fairly recent case that exposes the stand-off that often arises between development and environmental protection, and by logical extension that also exposes the poverty of international jurisprudence on sustainable development, is the judgment of the International Court of Justice in Case Concerning the Gabcikovo-Nagymaros Project (Hungary v. Slovakia),[45] decided on 25 September 1997. Although admittedly there were other international legal issues involved in the case – especially the interpretation, enforcement, and repudiation of treaties – I must point out that the court missed a window of opportunity to lay a solid juridical foundation for what should constitute the *corpus juris* of sustainable development.

The case arose out of a 1977 treaty between Hungary and the former Czechoslovakia relating to the construction and operation of the Gabcikovo-Nagymaros system of locks on the Danube River. According to the preamble to the treaty, the barrage system was designed to attain 'the broad utilization of the natural resources of the Bratislava-Budapest section of the Danube River for the development of water resources, energy, transport, agriculture and other sectors of the national economy of the Contracting Parties.' The project's goals were to produce hydroelectricity, improve river navigation, and protect the adjacent banks from flooding. The parties to the treaty undertook to ensure that the river's water quality would not be impaired as a result of the project.

The Danube has always played a vital role in the commercial and economic life of the countries it runs through, and reinforced their mutual interdependence in conformity with the time-hallowed maxim of *sic utere tuo ut alienum non laedas*[46] in international river law. The 1977 treaty outlined the principal works to be constructed: one in Gabcikovo (in Czechoslovakia), the other in Nagymaros (in Hungary). In the wake of profound political and economic changes in Central Europe, the Gabcikovo-Nagymaros Project became a subject of public and scientific controversy. Uncertainties included the economic viability of the project and its environmental impact. In May 1989 the government of Hungary suspended work on the Nagymaros. To justify this, it argued 'ecological necessity' – that if the dam had been built, the bed of the Danube upstream would have silted up and that the quality of the water drawn from the bank-filtered wells would have deteriorated as a result. Slovakia argued that 'ecological necessity' or 'ecological risk' could not, in relation to the law of state responsibility, constitute a circumstance precluding the wrongfulness of an act. The court ruled that Hungary was not entitled (in 1989) to suspend and subsequently abandon the Nagymaros Project; the Treaty of 16 September 1977 and related instruments required it to finish the work.

Despite the clear environmental issues raised by the Gabcikovo-Nagymaros case, the majority of the judges of the International Court of Justice focused, unduly and narrowly, on the law of treaties and shied away from analysing the international legal implications of sustainable development. Judge C.G. Weeramantry deserves praise for reminding international lawyers, in a separate opinion, that the time had come to begin articulating enforceable canons of sustainable development. According to Weeramantry:

> Had the possibility of environmental harm been the only consideration to be taken into account in this regard, the contentions of Hungary could well have proved conclusive ... The court must hold the balance even between the environmental considerations and the developmental considerations raised by the respective Parties. The principle that enables the court to do this is the principle of sustainable development ... Since sustainable development is a principle fundamental to the determination of the competing considerations in this case, and since, although it has attracted attention only recently in the literature of international law, it is likely to play a major role in determining important environmental disputes of the future, it calls for consideration in some detail. Moreover this is the first occasion on which it has received attention in the jurisprudence of this court.[47]

Furthermore, Judge Weeramantry emphasized *the need for international law to draw on the world's 'diversity of cultures'* (an issue that is of interest in this chapter) in harmonizing development and environmental protection:

> In drawing into international law the benefits of the insights available from other cultures, and in looking to the past for inspiration, international environmental law would not be departing from the traditional methods of international law, but would, in fact, be following in the part charted by Grotius. Rather than laying down a set of principles *a priori* for the new discipline of international law, he sought them also *a posteriori* from the experience of the past, searching through the whole range of cultures available to him for this purpose ... Environmental law is now in a formative age, not unlike international law in its early years. A wealth of past experience from a variety of cultures is available to it. It would be a pity indeed if it were left untapped merely because of attitudes of formalism which see such approaches as not being entirely *de rigueur*.[48]

Weeramantry identified the following as useful principles for developing modern environmental law: continuous environmental-impact assessment, the thoughtful application of environmental norms, and the handling of *erga omnes* obligations in judicial procedure *inter partes*. On the application of *erga omnes* obligations in environmental disputes, he stated:

> We have entered an era of international law in which international law subserves not only the interests of individual states, but looks beyond them and their parochial

concerns to the greater interests of humanity and planetary welfare. In addressing such problems, which transcend the individual rights and obligations of the litigating states, international law will need to look beyond procedural rules fashioned purely for *inter partes* litigation.[49]

I totally agree with Weeramantry's judicial opinions. It is international environmental law's non-responsiveness to the world's diverse cultures that cloaks it with a hegemonic flavour – a hegemony that banishes indigenous approaches to sustainable development to the margins of global environmentalism and international environmental law. Its focus on the parochial concerns of individual states (as opposed to the greater interests of humanity) has turned it into an engine of injustice in the unabated ecological destruction of Nigeria's Niger Delta and the Ecuadorian Amazon. To paraphrase Mickelson, the standard 'accommodationist' approach of international environmental law has relegated Third World environmental concerns to the margins, rather than integrating them into the core of the discipline and its self-understanding.[50] To build on Weeramantry's three principles for developing modern environmental law, it is critically important for us to flesh out the implications to international law of transnational corporate activities in the South as exemplified by the MNCs in Nigeria's Niger Delta and the Ecuadorian Amazon. In this endeavour, it is trite to point out that the emerging canons of international environmental law have largely been confined to the edifice of 'soft law.'[51] In order to transform sustainable development into a legally binding norm of international law that can be applied effectively to redress the ecologically degrading activities of MNCs, international environmental law will have to radically move away from its obsession with soft law approaches to transnational ecological problems. Admittedly, international environmental law is generally a weak discipline that is slow to evolve. Nonetheless, the enormous influence of MNCs almost demands that sustainable development be transformed somehow into a legal principle capable of regulating the ecological activities of MNCs in the South. MNCs are transnational in character and so are the ecological consequences of their operations. International law must therefore devise effective transnational solutions to transnational problems and to the complexities of MNCs.

Epilogue: Toward a South–North Ecological Dialogue

Various societies in the South have indelible norms and multifacted ways of conserving floral and faunal resources. Clearly, the concept of sustainable development has long been embedded in the mores and practices of the world's diverse cultures. From time immemorial, societies around the world have bonded with the environment in ways that recognize the twin concepts of conservation and sustainable use. Today we are witnessing an erosion of multicultural ecological values as a result of the pressures of globalization – pressures fuelled in part by the operations of MNCs. Also, sustainable development as we understand it today smacks of hegemonic globalism built on an appalling legitimacy deficit and unequal playing field. To close this deficit, we need to remind policymakers that international environmental law – and by extension sustainable development – is not beyond its fruit-bearing age. For sustainable development to bear the expected fruit, the world's diverse ecological cultures must be harnessed in search of a holistic, inclusive, and multistakeholder environmental regime. Also, an effective framework for *erga omnes* obligation on environmental issues must evolve.[52] With respect to multicultural environmental dialogue, what is happening now is comparable to what Nicholas Hildyard characterized as 'foxes in charge of the chickens,'[53] and indigenous ecological values from the South remain mostly peripheral to global environmental regimes. The North and the MNCs are the foxes in charge of the chickens – the South and its peoples. This has turned many people in the Third World into environmental refugees.

This chapter does not provide all, or indeed any, of the answers. Its purpose is to point out the complicity of international law in impoverishing conceptions of sustainable development and in suffocating Third World contributions. The result has been a failure to address the environmental decay of societies in the Third World, where powerful MNCs operate. The South–North ecological dialogue I propose in this chapter should be sensitive to customary enforcement of ecological norms and practices, be they folklore, religious beliefs, or taboos handed down from past generations in the South.

NOTES

* An earlier version of this paper, 'Strategies for Sustainable Development and the Pressures of Globalization,' was presented at the Annual Meeting of the Academic Council on the United Nations System (ACUNS), in Puebla, Mexico, 15–17 June 2001. I would like to thank Jean Krasno, the Executive Director of ACUNS, for her support; and Professors Ivan L. Head, Karin Mickelson, and Obiora Chinedu Okafor for their inspiration over the years that I have known them. I would also like to thank my co-panellist at the ACUNS meeting in Mexico, Professor Clement Adibe, and Dr Douglas Bettcher of the World Health Organization, for urging me on. I dedicate my thoughts in this paper to the memories of Ken Saro-Wiwa and Chico Mendes, two environmental martyrs who gave their lives in the ecological struggles in Nigeria's Niger Delta and the Amazon Basin.

1 Evaristo Nugkuak, Leader of the Coalition of Indigenous peoples in the Amazon, Cordinadaro de las Organizaciones Indigenas de la Cuenca Amazonica (COICA), as quoted in Diane Dumanoski, 'Amazon Indian Lobbyists Come to the US,' *Boston Globe* (22 October 1989) 24.

2 Song of the *Ogonis*, one of the minority ethnic groups in the resource-rich Niger Delta, whose environment is being severely polluted by multinational oil companies.

3 Judge Shigeru Oda in Case Concerning the Gabcikovo-Nagymaros Project *(Hungary v. Slovakia)* (1998) 37 I.C.J. Rep. 162 [dissenting opinion].

4 Dr Gro-Harlem Brundtland, former Prime Minister of Norway, is presently the Director-General of the World Health Organization in Geneva, Switzerland.

5 See World Commission on Environment and Development, 'Our Common Future' (Oxford: Oxford University Press, 1987) at 43.

6 See for instance, Principle 4 Declaration of the UN Conference on Environment and Development, Rio de Janeiro, 3–14 June 1992; Preamble to the United Nations Convention on Biological Diversity, 1992, reproduced in (1992) 31 I.L.M. 822; and Article 3(1) of the UN Framework Convention on Climate Change, 1992, reproduced in (1992) 31 I.L.M. 849.

7 P. Sands, 'International Law in the Field of Sustainable Development: Emerging Legal Principles,' in W. Lang, ed., *Sustainable Development And International Law* (Boston: Graham & Trotman, 1995) at 53.

8 *Ibid.*

9 Karin Mickelson, 'South, North, International Environmental Law and International Environmental Lawyers,' in J. Brunnée and E. Hey, eds., Yearbook of International Environmental Law, vol. 11, 2000 (Oxford: Oxford University Press, 2001) 52.

10 M. Koskenniemi, *From Apology to Utopia: The Structure of International Legal Argument* (Helsinki: Finnish Lawyers' Publishing Group, 1989).

11 For an extensive discussion of this relationship in international human rights law and practice, see Makau Mutua, 'Savages, Victims, and Saviors: The Metaphor of Human Rights' (2001) 42 Harvard J. of Int'l Law 201.

12 Projecting sustainable development as a legal principle, Sands, *supra* note 7 at 56, argues that 'an emerging international legal principle requires states to ensure that they develop and use their natural resources in a manner that is sustainable ... The practice of states, as reflected in the adoption of early international environmental treaties, suggests that the concept of "sustainability" as used in the Brundtland Report has been a feature of international relations since at least 1893, when the United States asserted its right to ensure the legitimate and proper use of seals and to protect them, for the benefit of mankind, from wanton destruction.'

13 See *Case Concerning the Gabcikovo-Nagymaros Project (Hungary v. Slovakia)*, (1998) 37 I.C.J. Rep. 162. The dispute involved the environmental sustainability of development projects on the Danube River.

14 E.B. Weiss, *In Fairness To Future Generations: International Law, Common Patrimony And Intergenerational Equity* (New York: Transnational Publishers, 1989) at 265.

15 Weiss, *In Fairness.*

16 Ogbu U. Kalu, 'The Gods Are to Blame' (Proceedings of the 6th International Congress on Ethnobiology, Whakatana, New Zealand, 24–26 November 1998) [unpublished], quoted by M.M. Iwu in Preface to P.A.G.M. De Smet, *Herbs, Health, and Healers: Africa As Ethnopharmocological Treasury* (Netherlands: Afrika Museum, 1999). See generally J.S. Mbiti, *African Religions and Philosophy* (London: Heinemann, 1969).

17 J.K. Asiema and F.D.P. Situma, 'Indigenous Peoples and the Environment: The Case of the Pastoral Maasai' (1994) 5 Colorado J. of Int'l Env'tl. Law & Policy 149 at 158.

18 O. Adewale, 'Customary Environmental Law,' in M.A. Ajomo and O. Adewale, eds., *Environmental Law And Sustainable Development In Nigeria* (Lagos: Nigeria Institute of Advanced Legal Studies, 1994) at 158.

19 Adewale, 'Customary Environmental Law.'

20 In eastern Nigeria, the Agulu community regards the tortoise and the turtle as sacred animals. It is customarily forbidden to kill them. Also, the Agulu Lake is natural home to crocodiles that are regarded as sacred. In the Awka community, monkeys are regarded as sacred because folklore has it that in ancient times when the Awka community fought a war with a neighbouring community, monkeys in the community forest always appeared to warn them that their enemies were approaching. In many parts of eastern Nigeria, pythons are regarded as sacred; as well as a wide variety of trees and plants.

21 See O. Adewale, *supra* note 18, at 160 (also stating that in the *Badagry* community, snakes are prohibited). In the *Bolo* community in *Okrika* Local Government Council, the *odumo* (the python) is a sacred animal and must not be touched.

22 N.A. Ollennu, *Principles of Customary Land Law* (London: Sweet & Maxwell, 1962).

23 *See* M. Opoku-Agyemang, *Environmental Management in Ghana: A Proposal for Effective Control: Gold Mining as Case Study 10* (LLM Thesis, Queen's University, 1996) [unpublished].

24 O. Adewale, *supra* note 18 at 161.

25 L. Nader, 'The Anthropological Study of Law' (1965) 67 American Anthropologist 3 at 25. See also C. Geertz, 'Local Knowledge: Fact and Law in Comparative Perspective,' in C. Geertz, *Further Essays in Interpretive Anthropology* (New York: Basic Books, 1989).

26 For a useful critical perspective on the Weberian conception of the legitimacy of law and legal systems, see O.C. Okafor, 'The Concept of Legitimate Governance in the Contemporary International Legal System' (1997) 44 Netherlands International Law Review 33.

27 Nigeria being a colony of Britain, section 6(1)(a) Mineral Oils Act of 1948 provided

that grants to search for and win oil could only be made to British subjects and to those companies that had their principal place of business in Britain or in its dominions and whose chairmen or majority shareholders and directors were British subjects. See G. Etikerentse, *Nigerian Petroleum Law* (London: Macmillan, 1985).

28 L.N. Mbanefo, *Essays on Nigerian Shipping Law* (London: Professional Books, 1991) at 79.

29 D. Fubara et al., 'The Endangered Environment of the Niger Delta: Constraints and Strategies: An NGO Memorandum of the Rivers Chiefs and Peoples' (unpublished and on file with O. Aginam). See also Greenpeace International, *The Environmental and Social Costs of Living with Shell in Nigeria* (July 1994) at 5.

30 *Nigerian Chronicle* (14 August 1980).

31 *See Nigerian Daily Times* (18 June 1974) 2; *Nigerian Daily Times* (7 October 1974) 11, *Nigerian Tide* (1 May 1 1974) 1.

32 Incident occurred on 8 March 1994.

33 Incident occurred in August 1995.

34 Incident occurred in October 1997. See, generally, G.U. Ojo, *Ogoni: Trials And Travails – Report Of The Environmental Rights Action* (Lagos: Civil Liberties Organization, 1996) at 3.

35 S.E. Manahan, *Environmental Chemistry* (Chelsea, Michigan: Lewis Publishers, 1991).

36 *Allar Irou v. Shell-BP Petroleum Development Company* (unreported, Suit No. W/89/71, High Court of Warri, Nigeria)

37 N. Myers, 'The Primary Source: Tropical Forests and Our Future (1984),' cited in *Rights Violations in the Ecuadorian Amazon: The Human Consequences of Oil Development* (Center for Economic and Social Rights, 1994) Health & Human Rights 83.

38 Although the word 'tribe' appears in a quote in this context, I take it to mean an 'ethnic group'; in most of the literature it is a derogatory term for 'primitive people.'

39 J. Brady, 'The Huaorani Tribe of Ecuador: A Study in Self-determination for Indigenous Peoples' (1997) 10 Harvard Human Rights Journal 291.

40 T.S. O'Connor, '"We Are Part of Nature": Indigenous Peoples' Rights as a Basis for Environmental Protection in the Amazon Basin' (1994) 5 Colorado J. of Int'l. Env'tl. Law and Policy 193. This paper states that an initial player in the Amazon was Texaco. In 1964 a Texaco/Gulf group received oil concessions of nearly 1.5 million hectares of rain forest in the Oriente. The Texaco group struck oil there on 29 March 1967 at Lago Agrio.

41 Meyers, 'The Primary Source,' *supra* note 37.

42 *Ibid.* (citing Canadian Center of Occupational Health and Safety stating that inhalation of high levels of crude oil fumes can have adverse effects on the nervous and respiratory systems, sometimes causing life-threatening chemical pneumonitis and other systemic effects).

43 *Ibid.*

44 J. Brady, *supra* note 39 at 291.

45 See *supra* note 13.

46 'Use your property in a way not to injure another person's property.' *See* H.C. Black, *Black's Law Dictionary*, 6th ed. (St. Paul, MN: West Publishing, 1990) at 1380.

47 See *supra* note 13 at 204

48 *Ibid.*

49 *Ibid.* See also T.S. O'Connor, 'Are We Part of Nature,' stating that international environmental law is often limited by assertions of territorial sovereignty. In particular, sovereign state governments usually claim an absolute right to the ownership of natural resources within their borders.

50 See K. Mickelson, *supra* note 9.

51 Examples of soft law environmental instruments that focus on the environmental hazards of the operations of MNCs include the moribund United Nations Code of Conduct for Transnational Corporations, 1988, the OECD Guidelines for Multinational Enterprises, 1976, and Agenda 21 of the United Nations Conference on Environment and Development, 1992.

52 For a useful analysis of enforcement of international environmental law, See E. Hey, 'Reflections on an International Environmental Court' (text of a paper on accepting the Chair in International Natural Resources Law, Faculty of Law, Erasmus University, Rotterdam, 6 October 2000) [unpublished].

53 N. Hildyard, 'Foxes in Charge of the Chickens,' in W. Sachs, ed., *Global Ecology* (Halifax: Fernwood, 1993).

Chapter Three

Multilateral Prevention of Internal Conflicts in the Face of Interethnic Tensions: The Case of the OSCE and Its High Commissioner on National Minorities

OLIVIER A.J. BRENNINKMEIJER

The rise of violent conflicts in the 1990s gripped television viewers around the world and led many international observers to ask whether all these wars and massacres could have been prevented. The violent conflicts most often covered by the international media happened in Africa (Ethiopia, Eritrea, Rwanda), Western Europe (Northern Ireland, Spain) Central and Eastern Europe (Azerbaijan, Armenia, Russia, ex-Yugoslavia), the Middle East, West and South Asia (Afghanistan, Kashmir, Sri Lanka), and Southeast Asia (Indonesia, East Timor). Many of these flare-ups of violence were referred to as 'ethnic' conflicts. There have also been many less 'publicized' conflagrations between ethnically distinct communities, with countless victims – for example, in other parts of Africa, Latin America, and Central Asia.[1]

In the late 1990s and into the new century, around twenty-five major armed conflicts were being fought in the world. Only two of these could be considered international in scope – between Ethiopia and Eritrea and between India and Pakistan.[2] Roughly during the same period, some seventy low-intensity confrontations and a similar number of violent political conflicts could be counted.[3] Most of these were between government forces and armed minority groups – that is, they occurred within individual countries and were considered 'internal conflicts.' This sort of violence shows no signs of diminishing, and the dead and displaced are growing in number. The causes are complex, but generally, these conflicts are over methods of governance and/or control of territory. Modern communications, increased mobility, and asymmetric economic development have also contributed to the growing demands by communities around the world for the right to govern their own affairs.

In this essay I offer one answer to the question of how states and their international organizations can prevent violent conflicts. The study concerns those conflicts which originate within individual countries and are somehow linked to ethnic identity. Enormous human suffering has resulted from ethnic cleansing in recent years, so the question of how such disasters can be prevented is critically important. This is not only because of the human suffering that results from these conflicts and the costs associated with international humanitarian interventions. Prevention is a vital issue because in most internal conflicts, one of the parties is a state government, and such governments don't usually reach out for international help to prevent an eruption of violence. What can other concerned governments do when one of their peers is fighting a war against some of its own citizens, or cannot or will not recognize the demands made by minority groups within its territory? What can the international community do when interethnic and minority majority tensions in a country rise and the threat of violence becomes real?

This essay introduces one approach to preventing violent conflict within states. The following are discussed: states and ethnic communities; defining ethnic groups and minorities; international conflict prevention and state sovereignty; the OSCE and its High Commissioner on National Minorities; and the experiences of the first High Commissioner. Contested terms such as 'ethnicity' and 'minority' are discussed because the values attached to these are intimately tied to the causes and solutions of disputes and civil wars. On the basis of this discussion, the thorny problem of international prevention and the protection of minorities is then taken up. The approach offered here is that of the Organization for Security and Co-operation in Europe (OSCE).[4] There are two reasons why. First, the OSCE has developed normative standards for officially recognizing the existence of minorities. Second, the OSCE has established the High Commissioner on National Minorities (hereafter 'the HCNM') as one of its conflict prevention mechanisms. A brief analysis of the HCNM's mandate and of his activities follows. The essay concludes by summarizing those OSCE mechanisms for conflict prevention which can be considered innovative.

States and Ethnic Communities

Between international wars and peaceful stability there are countless degrees of tension, which may or may not escalate into violence. Most of the world's countries are home to more than one ethnic community. In the OSCE's geographic region (from Vancouver to Vladivostok), interethnic tensions and, in some countries, politically motivated violence and terrorism plague local communities and national governments. We have all become aware of intercommunal tensions and violence in the Balkans (Bosnia, Kosovo, Macedonia, Montenegro), the Caucasus (Armenia, Azerbaijan, Georgia), Western Europe (France, Northern Ireland,

Spain), Russia (Chechnya), Central Asia (Tajikistan), and Turkey (Kurd minority). Found in all these regions are minorities that perceive themselves as having a distinct ethnic identity, that complain of discrimination, and/or that are demanding greater political autonomy if not outright independence.

One of the greatest challenges facing national governments is how to manage state affairs in such a way that all distinct communities feel equally respected. In response to the violence between communities, often referred to as ethnic or intercommunal conflict, liberal democracy is hailed as the remedy. But how is democratic governance to be established? There are no simple answers to this. Every country has its own unique history, political culture, and 'facts on the ground' (i.e., demographics), and all of these influence how the local and national political elites promote democratic governance. In the West as in the East, the question of how best to develop democratic governance is highly contentious. Concepts such as decentralization, regionalism, federalism, local autonomy, and self-government or local self-determination are often little-known. Many national governments worry that calls for regional or local self-government are first steps toward territorial secession by minorities. Some countries, including Greece, France, and Turkey, even avoid recognizing minorities within their borders.

One place where decentralization is being seriously attempted is Russia, with regard to Tatarstan.[5] Another is France, where the debate is about whether – and if so, how – Corsica could be given a special form of self-administrative status. This is in response to the demands for self-determination by local groups such as the Corsican National Liberation Front. Politicians in Paris are now debating how the French constitution, which states that the French nation is indivisible, should be (re)interpreted.

Often, the more centralized a government is – democratic or not – the less possible it is for minority or non-dominant groups to rule their own affairs. Admittedly, it is natural for a distinct population group to want to control its political agenda; no community wants to be ruled by those with whom they share no identity or affinity. Many countries with more or less centralized rule – the former communist regimes as well as some traditionally democratic ones – experience a constant tension in their political discourse between devolving power from the centre to the periphery and centralizing power to prevent a break-up of the country. When it comes to preventing violent conflicts between communities within a country, the greatest difficulty lies in the character of the relationship between the state and its 'nations' – or, to put it differently, between the government and the various ethnic communities that share its national territory.

The question of prevention is crucial where it addresses that critical relationship. The HCNM does just that by striving to diffuse tensions between governments and ethnic or minority communities. Before I present the normative initiatives of the OSCE and the work of the HCNM, however, it would be useful to discuss two important concepts: 'ethnicity' and 'minority.'

The Ethnic Group

The terms 'ethnic' and 'minority' are used so often that one can easily forget to ask what they actually mean and why considering them is important. To begin, 'ethnic group' implies the existence of some natural and chosen group attributes that are maintained and reinforced through the members' conviction that they are different from all other human communities. 'Ethnicity' and 'ethnic' can be understood as combining three principle characteristics of identity: (1) natural, (2) belief, and (3) acquired.

'Natural' characteristics include ancestral ties that can be traced genealogically (i.e., that are genetically verifiable). 'Belief' characteristics imply that the community believes its ancestral ties are real and natural and that they bind an entire population group or nation (which may not in fact be the case). These are fused with various 'acquired' elements of identity, which are added over time.

This third point requires elaboration: acquired characteristics are non-biological elements of identity that communities rely on to distinguish themselves from others. They include language, religion, culture, material resources, territory and goods, and sociopolitical organization. Furthermore, many communities make great efforts to physically alter or mark their bodies so as to permanently link each individual to the group. Underlying these acquired characteristics, and linked to beliefs and/or convictions, are a shared history and shared community ideals (nationhood, cultural emancipation, religious calling, etc.). The ethnic group maintains its cohesiveness by perpetuating the conviction that its shared characteristics are real and render it permanently distinct from all other communities.[6] One might say, then, that the ethnic group is a 'named collectivity' that shares 'a common myth of origin and descent,' which may be reinforced by natural characteristics and/or physical attributes on the body, a common history, and a territorial association.[7]

An understanding of what 'makes' ethnicity is important for conflict prevention because the more firmly members of a community believe their acquired characteristics of identity are permanent, the more strongly a party to a dispute will link its political demands to its ethnicity. This implies that demands – even political or economic ones – become non-negotiable in the same way that identity cannot be negotiated. In an interethnic dispute, mediators who are attempting to prevent an escalation of tensions and of violence must find solutions that do not challenge the identity of the communities or parties involved.

The Minority and the Problem of Protection

Liberal democratic principles suggest that all of a country's citizens, regardless of their identity, should receive equal treatment and respect from their government and from other citizens. Equality among all population groups is rare, especially in countries with little or no tradition of democracy. When, in the early 1990s, socialist regimes in Central and Eastern Europe ceased to be, there was 'no workable concept for integrating minorities and distinct ethnic groups into the state in a manner consistent with the notion of participatory government.'[8] Communications technology became much more available around the same time the communist world was disintegrating. As a result minorities everywhere could learn much more easily about the possibilities for their own emancipation, and called for more representative political participation and greater autonomy. This has become more and more common around the world.

To avoid an overly complex definition of minorities, it may be useful to reduce the concept to its distinguishing elements. Most important is the element of individual choice. Members of minorities can be seen as individuals who *choose* to be part of a particular religious, linguistical, or socially distinguishable community. However, individuals are not permanently tied to their community. They can leave, settle elsewhere, and identify themselves with other populations. Thousands of migrants do so every year.

The existence of biological features – one of the characteristics of identity mentioned earlier – cannot be denied. That being said, people make choices, even if the choice is to stay in a 'home' community. In the present context, a minority group is a group of individuals associating freely for an established purpose, whose shared interest differs from that expressed by the majority or by other population groups in the country.[9] This is important for conflict prevention, just as 'belief' and 'acquired' characteristics are important. Membership in a minority, like ethnic identity, must not be put into question in dispute negotiations.

As noted earlier, protection for minorities at the international level is problematic, because by definition, minorities are within a single, sovereign country. In simple terms, a minority problem exists when a population group in a country cannot come to terms with the politically dominant group, which most often also comprises the majority in the country concerned. The problem can manifest itself in two ways: first, the minority may claim it is being subjected to consistent prejudice or discrimination at the hands of the politically dominant group, and second, the government may be unable or unwilling to respond to demands made by the minority, or may disagree with its leaders on policy changes in central and regional public affairs. Typical examples of the first scenario are when members of a minority group are not given the same opportunity to enter the civil service, enjoy freedom of association, or join higher levels of authority. Other examples are when language laws make it more difficult (or impossible) for the children of a linguistic minority to receive official education in their own mother tongue and when religious or political leaders of the minority are 'silenced' in ways that clearly indicate blatant discrimination, intimidation or violations of fundamental human rights.

Human rights abuses, discrimination and general public prejudice are the minority problems most often discussed, but such issues can also arise in an opposite manner. This refers to the second point mentioned earlier. Demands made by a minority may be too high for a government to satisfy either by decree or through democratic processes. For example, minorities may ask for special recognition of their distinctness in the letter of the law, or insist on receiving national funds to support the development of their identity (minority language, religion, etc.). In most countries, even in Western democracies, special policy packages to support minorities generate heated debate. However, as long as debates are carried out in democratic institutional settings and without violence, they can constitute a healthy search for solutions. Unfortunately, frustrations about inequality are especially felt when minority leaders cannot participate in such debates nor in national or local decision-making that concerns their community's affairs. This can be particularly distressing when differential treatment or consistent discrimination is analogous to frontiers separating ethnic, linguistic, or religious communities. An example is where interethnic tensions result from long-term uneven investment in the minority's local economy, and when this is not corrected through a decentralization of economic policymaking.

From an international relations perspective, the essence of the minority problem rests in the difficulty of securing international support and protection when a minority within a country is subjected to consistent discrimination or human rights abuses. Because policies of accommodation toward minorities fall within the purview of states' internal affairs, communities that suffer and complain of discrimination at the hands of a national government cannot usually have their problems addressed outside their country's polity.[10] At best, the minority remains dependent for its welfare on the degree of democratic decentralization 'offered' to them by the dominant majority; at worst, it is subject to the good will of the majority population's ruling elite.[11]

Because they cannot count on international assistance, minorities often try to internationalize their struggle against the state. They do this by trying to influence the foreign policies of other states in which their kin group lives. In this manner, one country's internal affairs may become an international concern. Two often-cited examples: Hungary has expressed concern over the treatment of Hungarian minorities in Romania, the Slovak Republic, and the Federal Republic of

Yugoslavia; and during the Cold War and in its aftermath, Germany expressed concern about the treatment of ethnic Germans in other countries in Central and Eastern Europe.[12]

Over the years, international organizations and some supporting governments have tried to develop an international protection mechanism for minorities similar to the mechanisms for protecting human rights.[13] However, it has turned out to be impossible to define in internationally acceptable terms what a minority is. Many governments would hesitate to accord population groups a legal existence equal to that of individual persons and states. Definitions of minorities have been suggested many times to the UN General Assembly, the UN Human Rights Committee, and the Sub-Commission on Prevention of Discrimination and Protection of Minorities.[14] Also, the European Union and the OSCE have struggled to define minorities and arrive at means of protecting them. No legally acceptable definition is available, so the UN, the Council of Europe, and the OSCE generally speak of persons belonging to minorities.[15]

At the practical level of third-party conflict prevention – where the OSCE High Commissioner on National Minorities works – the existence of a minority is never questioned.[16] The OSCE's member states have gone so far as to accept that 'to belong to a national minority is a matter of a person's individual choice and no disadvantage may arise from the exercise of such choice.'[17]

The choice an individual makes to belong to a minority or an ethnic group is never negotiable. Choice in this sense equates with identity, and this is something that no amount of political argument can do away with. Since identity and choice are never questioned, the protection of individual members of a minority is promoted mainly through existing human rights provisions and standards. The CSCE made this clear in its 1991 Geneva meeting when it affirmed that 'human rights and fundamental freedoms are the basis for the protection and promotion of rights of persons belonging to national minorities.'[18] This has been reaffirmed many times by the CSCE, and later by OSCE member states. The most recent statement on this issue was released at the organization's 1999 Istanbul Summit. It was stated at that meeting that 'the protection and promotion of the right of persons belonging to national minorities are essential factors for democracy, peace, justice and stability within, and between participating States.'[19]

State Sovereignty and International Conflict Prevention

Great strides have been made in elaborating human rights; that being said, the question of how people can be protected when their fundamental rights are being abused within a single country continues to plague international observers.[20] The United Nations and other international bodies have struggled to come to terms with this problem. A catalyst in international discussions on preventing violent conflicts was former UN Secretary-General Boutros-Ghali's *Agenda for Peace*. In it, he suggested that greater international efforts to prevent violence and war are indispensable if peace among countries is to be fostered.[21] On a purely practical level, however, the problem of *how* to initiate and manage international preventive efforts has so far been insurmountable. This is because so many violent conflicts originate in the domestic affairs of sovereign states; in a given dispute or conflict, state governments themselves are often considered by minorities or other states to be a party.

Boutros-Ghali in the *Agenda for Peace* provided the now widely accepted definition of preventive diplomacy: 'action to prevent disputes from arising between parties, to prevent existing disputes from escalating into conflicts and to limit the spread of the latter when they occur.'[22] However, conflict prevention, preventive diplomacy, and dispute settlement should not be confused with peace-building activities such as peace enforcement, peace making, conflict settlement, and conflict management; such activities are carried out after violence polarizes the opposing parties.[23]

While conflict prevention may incorporate some peace-building activities, it is taken here to mean the prevention of violent conflict *before* it occurs. More specifically, conflict prevention is a short-term activity that usually attempts to facilitate communication among the parties in a dispute and to promote their cooperation in areas about which they presently do not agree. It may address both structural and proximate causes of tensions. Ideally, conflict prevention should initiate or contribute to the establishment of national or local mechanisms (democratic institutions) that the parties concerned can apply in order to prevent a deterioration in their relations. In this way, conflict prevention can help establish a viable multiethnic method of governance; but this is not the same as government building or nation building.

Given the localized and often ethnically based nature of so many conflicts, attempts to prevent violence require that the causes of underlying tensions be addressed at a level independent of the parties directly involved. This implies the engagement of a third party. Depending on how critical the tensions among communities in a country are, the third party must consider two broad categories of causal factors. On the one hand, there are the 'structural underlying causes' of conflict. These may include factors related to state weakness, poverty, political injustice, and economic deprivation. When tensions among parties are not yet high or critical, but still require attention to rectify governance problems vis-à-vis distinct population groups, structural causes of the tensions can be rectified. This can be done through various forms of democratic representation, decentralization, federalism, or sectoral autonomy. On the other hand, when tensions are critically high in a dispute situation, a third party must look at the 'proximate causes' of conflict. These may be the result of 'deliberate decisions by determined leaders or political demagogues to make violent responses to contentious issues' and exploit a political vacuum or a strong grievance.[24]

When tensions and the risk of violence are high, conflict prevention efforts must aim to reduce the vulnerability of certain groups in order to protect them from exploitation or persecution (ethnic cleansing, genocide). This can be and sometimes is done through the interposition of neutral armed forces or peace-keepers. At the same time, stronger efforts at mediation among all the parties to a dispute are necessary to prevent leaders from exploiting weaknesses or uneven political representation and thereby 'engineering' conflict.

Many non-governmental organizations (NGOs) are working today around the world to alleviate interethnic or communal tensions.[25] Depending on local circumstances and the ability of NGOs to work freely, they may address both types of causal factors – that is, the structural ones relating to governance problems as well as the proximate ones, which may reflect highly politicized and emotionally charged grievances. The aim of much conflict prevention by NGOs 'in the field' is to analyse community-level frustrations and grievances and report these to governments and international observers. Some NGOs act as third-party negotiators to prevent violence or to provide an outlet through which local communities can call for wider awareness of their cause.

Where state governments themselves are a party to a dispute or a conflict, international help to prevent violence involves getting governments to accept a neutral third party as a facilitator or negotiator. Some efforts are underway to promote prevention that includes state governments. Some of these efforts are multilateral prevention efforts initiated by the UN or by regional organizations and contact groups. As the largest multilateral organization, the UN works in many parts of the world to prevent conflicts.[26] However, it has found it difficult to get its member states to agree to multilateral intrusions with respect to problems within their own borders. Until it can resolve this issue, the UN's use of international observers as third parties will be highly problematic.

The Search for Solutions

Attempts at prevention that do get off the ground often amount to mere 'looking' and 'commenting' by observers. Multilateral organizations such as the UN, the Council of Europe, the OSCE, the Organization of American States, and the Organization of African Unity initiate observer, monitoring, and fact-finding missions to try to alert the international community to dangerous interethnic and communal tensions or to violations of human rights. However, mere warnings of rising tensions and risks of violence do not constitute prevention. Something else is needed. The OSCE has been trying to do more than look, comment, and warn. Since the early 1990s it has developed operational capacities in the field based on and supported by new normative standards to which all its member countries have agreed.

One of the OSCE's normative standards requires that member states accept that to effectively prevent conflicts, the organization must be able to address matters that traditionally have been considered the internal affairs of member states. To accepting that the OSCE should have the capacity to overstep state sovereignty, so to speak, the organization's members not only agreed that the international protection of human rights is fundamental; they also agreed that full respect for the rights of persons belonging to ethnic or minority groups within a State is vital to security among themselves. In other words, if there is conflict within one member state, it may affect neighbouring countries where ethnic groups live. Local security is thus indivisible from international security.

The first time that representatives of the CSCE (the former name of the OSCE) put this concern for the welfare of people in member states in writing was at a conference in Geneva. In doing so, they introduced a new dimension to the concept of state sovereignty by declaring that 'issues concerning national minorities, as well as compliance with international obligations and commitments concerning the rights of persons belonging to them, *are matters of legitimate international concern and consequently do not constitute exclusively an internal affair of the respective State.*'[27]

This was restated in stronger language at the CSCE Conference on the Human Dimension in Moscow later the same year.[28] In the preamble to that document the CSCE members stated:

> The participating States emphasize that issues relating to human rights, fundamental freedoms, democracy and the rule of law are of international concern, as respect for these rights and freedoms constitutes one of the foundations of the international order. They categorically and irrevocably declare that the commitments undertaken in the field of the human dimension of the CSCE are *matters of direct and legitimate concern to all participating States and do not belong exclusively to the internal affairs of the State concerned.*[29]

This step away from absolute sovereignty and in favour of human rights does not constitute a change in the legal status of states, but it does establish a normative standard for the international protection of human rights – albeit only within the geographic region covered by the OSCE's member countries. This was possible because earlier in 1990, CSCE members had affirmed that human rights apply equally to all people and that members of minority and ethnic communities have an equal right to enjoy their human rights. The member states agreed that 'persons belonging to national minorities have the right to exercise fully and effectively their human rights and fundamental freedoms without any discrimination and in full equality before the law.'[30] This principle was reaffirmed at the CSCE conference in Geneva in 1991 in the statement that 'human rights and fundamental freedoms are the basis for the protection and promotion of rights of persons belonging to national minorities.'[31]

Because they have established standards in support of the equality of all people regardless of their ethnic characteristics, these documents are a remarkable achievement. They were possible because at the time, wars and ethnic cleansing threatened to engulf not only the Balkans but also large swaths of the many multination or multiethnic states of the former communist East. A crucial element in the search for solutions to the minority problem, then, related to promoting methods of governance that would not challenge or question the concept of ethnicity or the existence of minorities. Conflict prevention should favour a democratic process that enables distinct communities in a national population to participate in decision making and so feel included and recognized.

The search for a solution by the CSCE countries included efforts to develop practical and operational conflict-prevention mechanisms. The member states embarked on this effort by, on the one hand, reaffirming the normative standards that make up the framework of political commitments of the CSCE (later OSCE), and, on the other hand, developing institutional mechanisms, including the Conflict Prevention Centre (CPC) in Vienna, an Office for Democratic Institutions and Human Rights (ODIHR) in Warsaw, and the High Commissioner on National Minorities (HCNM) in The Hague.[32] The CPC took over the task of managing long-term missions in various member countries, while the HCNM was developed as an instrument of conflict prevention at the earliest possible stages. As such, it links multilateral conflict prevention with the root causes of interethnic or majority–minority conflicts, and with the search for solutions through good governance by democratic means.

The OSCE High Commissioner on National Minorities

After the end of the Cold War, the OSCE developed for itself the role of promoting norms of good governance, respect for human rights, and the prevention of conflicts. During the Cold War, the former CSCE's success lay in developing confidence-building measures (CBMs) between the military institutions of the two superpowers and their allies. At its first post–Cold War summit meeting in Paris in 1990, the CSCE heads of state mandated the organization to look for ways to prevent violent conflicts through political and diplomatic means.[33] In the years that followed, the CSCE and later OSCE developed several operational instruments and normative standards that provide for a 'soft' approach to security. These promote constitutional democratization. For example, they support and monitor human rights such as the freedom of expression and journalism (overseen by the OSCE Representative on Freedom of the Media). Through various organs in Vienna, including the Secretariat, the Permanent Council, and the rotating chairmanship (held by the foreign minister of one of the member states), all member countries have an equal voice in all decision making.

The OSCE promotes comprehensive security. This is reflected in its three dimensions of concern: international peace, economic development within and among member countries, and respect for human rights. Together, these represent the OSCE's 'community of values' and suggest methods of good governance.[34] The OSCE adheres to the principle that comprehensive security is best achieved and maintained by embracing the following: democratic governance, an independent judiciary, transparency in military affairs, a free market economy, and full respect for human rights (including the rights of those belonging to national minorities).

The organization's mechanisms and policies are intended to support democratization in all member countries, with a special focus on states that previously were governed by authoritarian regimes. The OSCE's standards and mechanisms are not legally binding; rather, they are put into practice through activities such as the following: peace-building missions, educational seminars, election monitoring, interstate discussions, and round table and conflict prevention meetings. Most of these are initiated and carried out by the organization's offices in Vienna and Warsaw, and by long-term missions in countries where democratization and peace-building processes are presently under way.[35]

The High Commissioner on National Minorities (HCNM) is an integral part of the OSCE's security and democratization efforts. This position was created in response to growing security threats in the early 1990s and outbreaks of violence in the Balkans and the Caucasus. At the 1992 Helsinki conference, after lengthy negotiations initiated mainly by the Netherlands, all CSCE countries adopted a mandate for the HCNM.[36] The first high commissioner, Ambassador Max van der Stoel, carried out his duties from January 1993 to June 2001. He was chosen for his personal qualifications and for his reputation as a respected and experienced diplomat.[37]

The HCNM and his staff seek ways to reduce tensions that threaten peace and security among the member states of the OSCE.[38] One thing that distinguishes the high commissioner's approach to conflict prevention from other diplomatic conflict-settlement and peace-building activities is the element of time: the HCNM involves himself well before a dispute threatens to become violent. However, since the 'best' time to become involved in dispute situations can hardly be known in advance – given that it depends on local capacities and on the willingness of the disputing parties – the high commissioner's mandate deliberately leaves the time of involvement vague. It provides only general guidelines for determining 'early action at the earliest possible stage in regard to tensions [which] in the judgement of the High Commissioner, have the potential to develop into a conflict within the CSCE area.'[39]

Because of its vagueness, the mandate places a heavy responsibility on the high commissioner to be aware of, and concern himself with, all dispute situations that affect minority communities and where a potential for violent conflict exists. Ideally, early conflict prevention is carried out when there is no perceptible risk of violence but the parties in a dispute are aware that 'something' must be done to avoid a worsening of relations. The sooner conflict prevention is initiated, the greater the likelihood that the dispute will not reach a critical level where the parties cannot or will not accommodate each other's demands.

The high commissioner is expected to 'take fully into account the availability of democratic means and international instruments' to respond to minority or interethnic disputes. He is instructed to 'promote dialogue, confidence and cooperation' between the parties and to offer a 'view to possible solutions.'[40] This he does mainly by establishing communication channels – something often missing in national and regional political arenas. After the HCNM has contacted all the parties directly involved in a minority dispute, he can suggest methods for regularizing their contacts; eventually he can recommend institutional, political, legal, educational, and/or economic reforms. The point is always to find ways to begin redressing specific grievances and improving the general condition of a country's minorities.[41]

The high commissioner's mandate provides two principal instruments: 'early warning' and 'early action.' The first allows him to warn the OSCE in Vienna of a risk of impending violence in situations where he lacks the capacity to prevent its outbreak. Once he issues an early warning, the OSCE chairman-in-office (the presiding foreign minister) presents the case to the Permanent and Senior Councils; the ambassadors of all member countries can then take up the issue with the state concerned through their home governments. In this manner, political attention and international pressure from the highest levels can be directed at the parties in a dispute. The aim of this is to promote dialogue among the parties in a dispute, and more intensive consultations with the OSCE, and to encourage the disputing parties to abide by the international human rights values and commitments to which all member countries subscribe.

The high commissioner has issued one early warning so far. In May 1999 he addressed the OSCE Permanent Council regarding the situation in the Former

Yugoslav Republic of Macedonia. It concerned the delicate ethnic balance of the republic and the massive influx of refugees from Kosovo. He warned that greater international effort was required to help that country deal not only with the refugee crisis and the migration of ethnic Albanians, but also with the economic crisis that the conflict in southeast Europe had created.[42] In most situations the HCNM tries to engage in early conflict prevention so as to render warnings of impending violence unnecessary. Mr van der Stoel has carefully avoided issuing many early warnings because such warnings may hurt rather than help the chances for the parties in a dispute to compromise on their positions. In other words, a public early warning can foster the perception that the parties in the dispute are being 'pushed,' either to back down from their demands in humiliation or to escalate the tensions toward conflict.[43]

It is important for the HCNM to be sensitive to political interests and the public image of minority community leaders and government representatives. The HCNM has stated that the mere fact of his involvement in a dispute situation has been enough to alert the OSCE community of the existence of a minority issue requiring-third party involvement. In addition, to obtain greater support for his engagements, Mr van der Stoel has expressed his concerns about interethnic tensions publicly. While never blaming or accusing any specific government or minority community, he has discussed issues and problems in public talks and interviews.[44]

Regarding the second instrument provided by the mandate, 'early action,' the high commissioner can collect information, conduct on-site fact finding, and issue recommendations. Most importantly, the mandate offers the HCNM the prior consent of all OSCE member states for him to move freely in all member countries to do his work. State governments are not permitted to restrict his travels. This is the first time that a third-party officer from a multilateral organization has had such freedom.

The CSCE members have agreed to this almost revolutionary freedom of movement because they recognize that blatant discrimination against minority populations poses a real threat to international security. This realization developed out of several CSCE negotiations and declarations in the early 1990s. At that time, violence was ravaging the Balkans and spreading interethnic conflicts were causing many member governments to fear regional instability. However, permission for the high commissioner to travel freely in all CSCE member countries was extended *in return* for acknowledging that states had the right to fully and autonomously control their own national security. In particular, member countries insisted on sovereign control over terrorist crises within their borders.

Terrorism was an especially sensitive issue. During the negotiations for the high commissioner's mandate in 1992, many countries in the West and in the former

Communist Bloc were facing terrorist insurgencies. These were (and still are) often carried out in the name of freedom and independence for particular ethnic communities. Many countries, including Great Britain, France, the United States, and Turkey, refused to let third parties – such as the high commissioner – involve themselves in their violent internal conflicts. These CSCE countries did not want to suggest to terrorists and other organized non-state actors that engage in violence that, through the HCNM, they could count on international support for their calls for secession, for a change in state borders, or for changes in government policy.

Furthermore, at the time the HCNM's mandate was being negotiated, the CSCE member states did not want to look as if they were conferring international rights on population groups. By conferring an international status to minorities as groups, they would have been opening a debate about their position vis-à-vis states. This is why the high commissioner is bound by all CSCE/OSCE normative standards and other international agreements regarding state sovereignty and territorial integrity, and why his mandate forbids him to address groups that condone and/or support terrorism or violence of any kind.[45] In sum, the high commissioner's mandate restricts him to minority disputes in which terrorism and political violence are absent.

Despite these restrictions, the high commissioner has considerable freedom to define and engage in 'early action.' He can obtain information on dispute situations from just about any official or unofficial source. Considering the often sensitive nature of information on government minority and/or interethnic relations, this is a bold departure from past multilateral thinking. The mandate stipulates the types of groups the HCNM can address or receive reports from. These are first, the governments of the OSCE's participating states; second, regional and local authorities in areas in which national minorities live; and third, 'representatives of associations, non-governmental organisations, religious and other groups' that represent the interests of national minorities.[46] Finally, he can consider reports on dispute situations provided from the media and other independent non-governmental organizations. Thus, the high commissioner enjoys a wide variety of possible contacts and almost unlimited sources of information, investigation, and analysis.[47]

However, there are some important limitations on his contacts. The high commissioner cannot consider violations of OSCE commitments by individuals, nor can he address specific violations of human rights – that is, he is not to act as a human rights observer or as an ombudsman for minorities. This limitation, and the ones regarding terrorism, restrict the high commissioner's activities, but they also release him from involvement in situations that are beyond the early preventive stages. They allow him to focus on minority issues without becoming embroiled in individual grievances and in the demands made by groups that condone or engage in terrorism.

As a third party, the HCNM must not be asked to take a stand – his mandate expressly requires him to remain impartial. The disputing parties would lose confidence in him if they could not see him as neutral. The high commissioner often has to address politically sensitive issues, so he cannot afford to be identified with one party or another. This explains why paragraph 4 of his mandate stipulates that 'based on CSCE principles and commitments, the High Commissioner will work in confidence and will act independently of all parties directly involved in the tensions.'

This emphasis on confidentiality and a low profile helps cultivate trust in the high commissioner's office; it also helps avoid any escalation of interethnic tensions *as a result* of his involvement. Governments and minority representatives 'often feel they can be more co-operative and forthcoming if they know that the content of their discussions will not be revealed to the outside world.'[48]

For conflict prevention to be successful, support – especially political support from the OSCE and from its individual members – is vital. The HCNM's independence must not result in him being ignored by the OSCE countries; his independence must be balanced with a measure of accountability to the OSCE. Thus, the mandate insists on a close link between the HCNM and the presiding OSCE chairman-in-office (CiO). The latter confers official OSCE approval and support for the high commissioner's work. Accountability here means that before, during, and after each engagement in a country, the HCNM must maintain confidential contact with the CiO to inform him or her of all activities in minority situations. The CiO serves as an outside supporter and advisor and can also consult independently with the states in which the HCNM is involved. Furthermore, this close contact between the high commissioner and the CiO provides a minimum amount of assurance for all other OSCE member states that the HCNM is following his mandate.

The high commissioner can travel to any country to carry out his work. In advance of each visit, he notifies the government of the country concerned so as to give it time to respond. While engaged in a particular dispute situation and at the end of it, he allows that government and the CiO time to respond to his recommendations before presenting these to the OSCE in Vienna (i.e., to the public). If a state government refuses entry to the high commissioner or prevents him from meeting certain individuals on its territory (which it has the legal right to do), the HCNM can inform the OSCE in Vienna about this obstructionism. This is equivalent to an 'early warning,' at which point the entire OSCE can then concern itself with the government in question. This provision in the high commissioner's mandate is revolutionary in that it reaffirms the priority given to human rights and the OSCE's human dimension principles and the importance these now enjoy in terms of the international protection of minorities.

Experiences and Recommendations of the HCNM

In his work, the HCNM adopts a dual approach. First, when recommending specific solutions, policy reforms, and/or legal measures to difuse tensions in a dispute, he refers to the agreements to which the member countries of the CSCE
(later the OSCE) have committed themselves to uphold. Second, he initiates practical, 'in the field' conflict preventive measures. The latter mainly involve meetings with government and minority representatives, but they also include local
development projects aimed at reducing specific problems that negatively affect
interethnic or majorityminority relations. The high commissioner also strives to
raise awareness of, and garner support for, specific conflict-prevention initiatives.
These may be local development projects, such as printing schoolbooks in the language of the minority, or they may involve lobbying for political support among
OSCE members or European Union officials for specific policy recommendations. His recommendations often include specific legislation to accommodate the
linguistic, educational, or cultural needs of different communities within a country. To promote initiatives, the HCNM uses his personal influence by speaking to
specific problems in countries where interethnic tensions risk becoming violent.

Mr van der Stoel has made three observations. First, resolving a dispute
between a government and a national minority, or between two state governments and a specific community is primarily in the long-term interest of the gov-
ernment(s) concerned. If politicians from the dominant majority are willing to
consider the needs of people belonging to a national minority, they can expect
loyalty in return. Second, when two states are engaged in a dispute concerning a
minority community, it has been useful for the high commissioner to support the
creation of bilateral treaties. These can guarantee that borders will remain as they
are and that the minorities concerned will be protected and their needs given due
attention. 'Good neighbour' treaties have been negotiated in the past decade, and
the HCNM has helped greatly in developing them. The main purpose of such
treaties is to foster trust between governments and minorities.[49]

Third, solutions to disputes should be developed as much as possible within
the framework of government institutions in the country concerned. Democratization reforms must never be pushed to the extent that existing institutional
capacities are overwhelmed. Rather, to avoid confusion and administrative collapse, legal reforms and democratization must be developed within existing structures. Solutions that accommodate national security needs with the demands
made by minority communities are not easily found in situations where a central
government is incapable of managing internal change or economic transition.[50]

Democratic reforms are often necessary to settle a dispute, yet an external
third-party mediator, such as the high commissioner, can never build such insti-

tutions within a country. The citizens themselves must do this. The point of recommending specific democratic reforms – which the HCNM does – is to offer *all* communities, be they minorities or majorities, the opportunity to assess and try more satisfactory methods of participation in local and national government. According to the HCNM, minority self-determination can be accomplished through legislation that facilitates the development and maintenance of the minority's identity. The high commissioner has sometimes gone so far as to explore the possibilities for local or regional autonomy, as was the case with Crimea in the Ukraine.[51] With regard to promoting democratic means, the high commissioner's central task 'is to address the political relationship between minorities and majorities, i.e. the democratic process in the largest sense.'[52]

In interethnic or minoritygovernment disputes, some form of autonomy for minority populations may provide a solution. However, all parties to the dispute or conflict must agree on the needed political and institutional changes. Models of decentralized democratic decision making can be developed that correspond to the needs and expectations of the parties. Some forms of decentralization allow for self-determination or self-administration in public affairs that can be managed at lower levels.[53] The UN and other international organizations have begun interpreting self-determination not as a call for independence (as was the case during colonialism), but more loosely as the right of population groups to govern their own local affairs within multination states.[54]

The standards and political commitments adopted by the OSCE states to which the high commissioner can refer can be summarized as follows: (1) the existence of minorities cannot be denied; (2) individual people have the right to choose their affiliation to a minority community or ethnic group; (3) they are not to be discriminated against because of their affiliation to that group; (4) the protection of minorities and the prevention of internal conflicts is best ensured by (a) guaranteeing fundamental human rights and (b) promoting democratic decentralization. The OSCE members have agreed that '*questions relating to national minorities can only be satisfactorily resolved in a democratic political framework* based on the rule of law, with a functioning independent judiciary.'[55] They have further pledged to 'respect the right of persons belonging to national minorities to effective participation in public affairs, including participation in the affairs relating to the protection and promotion of the identity of such minorities.'[56]

Similar statements are made in various other CSCE (later OSCE) documents. At the Istanbul Summit in 1999, member states made perhaps the clearest statement yet in support of democratic decentralization. They acknowledged that 'one way to preserve and promote the ethnic, cultural, linguistic and religious identity of national minorities within an existing state is to provide them with a degree of autonomy.'[57]

In essence, the decentralization of national politics and decision making involves developing democratic decision making in all national and local public affairs that link an ethnic or minority problem to methods of governance and for which national uniformity of laws or policies is not required.

Another standard to which the high commissioner can refer is an important OSCE document that sought to allay the fears of the leaders of some countries that democratic decentralization might lead to a breakup of existing states. The organization's members accepted that protecting minorities would improve the security of states when they declared in 1990 that 'respect for the rights of persons belonging to national minorities as part of universally recognized human rights is an essential factor for peace, justice, stability and democracy in the participating States.'[58]

The OSCE states restated the same principle in stronger language at the Istanbul Summit: 'Full respect for human rights, including the rights of persons belonging to national minorities, besides being an end in itself, may not undermine, but strengthen territorial integrity and sovereignty.'[59]

On the basis of these important OSCE commitments and standards, the high commissioner can issue recommendations to the governments of the countries in which he is involved. Questions regarding what kinds of concessions a state government ought to make to minority demands and how a dispute can be addressed so that no emotive link is forged between ethnic identity and territorial sovereignty can present great obstacles to diplomatic meditation. Mr van der Stoel has many times stated:

> I do not advocate autonomy as a panacea for minority problems, and I am opposed to secession as the solution to inter-ethnic tensions. Secession is usually based on the myth that the ethnically 'pure' nation needs its own State. Attempts to carve mono-ethnic States out of multi-ethnic environments almost invariably leads to violent conflict [...] There are ways of finding a synthesis between the claims for self-determination on the one hand and the interest in preserving the territorial integrity of States on the other. In my opinion, a good place to start is to focus more attention on so-called 'internal' self-determination whereby self-government is arranged in such a way as to respond to the desire by a significant minority group to have a considerable amount of control over its own administration without challenging the sovereignty and integrity of the State.[60]

On the basis of the standards developed by the OSCE member states and by the forums of other international organizations, the high commissioner looks for practical approaches to accommodating self-determination with state sovereignty. While not strictly provided for in his mandate, the high commissioner's recommendations are today recognized as the official 'product' of his work.[61] They are the result of findings and analyses of the underlying causes of disputes, and they usually include suggestions for political or legislative reform. At the same time, the recommendations mobilize political support for compliance on the part of state government(s) and the national minorities concerned to the aims of the OSCE.

The high commissioner's recommendations 'have generally focussed on two broad areas for improvement: (a) changes in the substance of government policy vis-a-vis minorities in order to address pressing concerns, and (b) measures to establish or strengthen institutional capacity for government-minority dialogue and communication.'[62] Mr van der Stoel strongly emphasizes the need for constant communication between governments and national minorities. To encourage this he has organized many round table meetings and supported the establishment of structures for fostering continuous dialogue within local and national democratic institutions.

While the high commissioner's recommendations are addressed to state governments, they may also include advice for minorities. Recommendations are always non-binding; however, since the HCNM requires a response from the state in question, and because the HCNM presents his recommendations to the OSCE's Permanent Council in Vienna (which generally expresses its support), there is always some pressure for the affected state to respond. None of this is found in the HCNM's mandate; this process emerged in practice as a means for informing the OSCE member states of the recommendations and for encouraging practical improvements in interethnic or minority majority relations. The result is that at the diplomatic level the high commissioner contributes to the development of institutionalized dialogue for confidence building, to greater democratic representation of minorities, and to better understanding between minorities and national governments.

For the most part, the high commissioner recommends small, realistic steps toward reconciliation. He avoids 'idealistic' statements, which could leave disgruntled minority groups impatient for results. The parties in a dispute always have their own political and social agendas, with which the HCNM must reckon. Small, negotiated steps are especially important when the parties are trying to strengthen their bargaining positions by making their interests publicly known. Especially when using emotional language to raise sympathy for their position or enmity toward adversaries, political leaders can dramatically heighten tensions between them and other parties or ethnic groups. In times of tension, if interested parties are more inclined to emphasize differences instead of considering conciliation, issues in a dispute can become intractable.

This is why the practical policy options that are often proposed by the HCNM are discussed and negotiated. The hope is to reduce tensions and prevent conflict.[63] Ethnic differences and cultural identity are not treated as causes of inter-ethnic or minority/majority tensions. Rather, discriminatory laws, weak regional or local autonomy, and ill-considered policies and their outcomes are seen as the sources of tension. When disputes are highly politicized, they always present special difficulties for the high commissioner. Here, quiet preventive diplomacy is crucial. The HCNM has learned through experience that when tensions are high, the parties in a dispute often make far stronger statements in public than they do in confidential mediation sessions. Government and minority representatives are often electioneering to maintain personal positions or power. This reality must not be ignored. Parties strive to look steadfast in public even when they are preparing to compromise at the negotiating table.

To encourage compromise, Mr van der Stoel takes a soft approach and expressly avoids interfering at sensitive times – for example, when the parties are engaged in election campaigns. He talks to the parties in confidential meetings and presents the issues in a dispute as independent elements that can be settled separately and in small steps. Most important, the emotions the parties to a dispute feel, and the grievances they have, are not left to develop into fear, anger, prejudice, and intolerance.[64] If this should happen, opportunities for conflict engineering by political demagogues can take the upper hand and make conflict prevention almost impossible. So it is vital that all efforts at preventing violent conflicts be initiated as early as possible. This is one of the key characteristics of prevention – to be proactive well before anyone dares justify the use of violence as 'politics by other means.'

Recurrent Challenges to the HCNM's Work

The main issues Mr van der Stoel had to address during his years as HCNM were (1) territorial disputes, (2) the use of the minority languages, (3) education, (4) citizenship, and (5) local self-government or 'internal' self-determination for minorities. The examples below discuss these issues and offer a quick overview of his work and the challenges that confronted him.[65]

(1) With regard to territorial disputes between sovereign states, treaties of friendship are a proven way to reduce tensions. In September 1996, the HCNM was instrumental in the writing and signing of the Treaty between the Republic of Hungary and the Republic of Romania on Understanding, Co-operation and Good Neighbourliness.[66] This treaty laid to rest accusations of extra-territorial ambitions and discriminatory policies. Both state governments recognized that national minorities form an integral part of their societies and agreed that relations between minority communities and their ethnic kin across their shared national border would not be interpreted as attempts to challenge the sovereignty of either country.

(2) Language is always a defining element of any minority or ethnic group's

identity. Most language issues that the high commissioner had to deal with concerned the demands by minorities for the right to use their mother tongue in the public sphere, in education, in the media, or in public-sector employment. One citation where Mr van der Stoel's recommendations were considered in the writing of national laws arose in the Czech Republic after the fall of the nationalist Meciar government in 1998. Past legislation had made it more and more difficult for the Hungarian minority in the southern parts of the Czech Republic to study and work in its mother tongue. With the support of the Council of Europe and the European Commission, Mr van der Stoel made several recommendations in favour of developing laws that would allow the minority to use its language in the public sphere (e.g., using Hungarian place and street names, passing university entry exams in Hungarian, and doing away with other limitations on the use of Hungarian). The high commissioner also initiated two lengthy studies, one on the use of language by minorities and the other on language rights that state governments should observe. The first study resulted in a standard-setting report titled: *The Oslo Recommendations Regarding the Linguistic Rights of National Minorities.*[67] The second was a comparative study of linguistic rights in all OSCE member states. The conclusions of these two studies were published in 1999 by the HCNM's office under the title *Report on the Linguistic Rights of Persons Belonging to National Minorities in the OSCE Area.*[68]

(3) Mr van der Stoel initiated several education-related projects during his years as high commissioner. Some were in the form of seminars, workshops, and negotiation meetings, which were organized with the support of local government institutions to promote equal opportunities for education for members of minorities. A small but interesting project was based on the HCNM's suggestion that ways be found to publish schoolbooks in the minority language where the national government did not have the means to do so. This was done, for example, for the Uzbek minority in Kyrgyzstan in 1997. A major and very impressive initiative of Mr van der Stoel was to promote Albanian university in the former Yugoslav Republic of Macedonia. The point of this project was to offer the country's largest minority a school of higher education in the Albanian language. It was one of the most ambitious 'tension-reduction projects' that Max van der Stoel ever initiated. It took him a long time to garner support for the project in the OSCE capitals, but finally, on 20 November 2001, in Tetovo, the South East European University opened its doors. The university offers badly needed higher education; with regard to conflict prevention, it also is helping settle some of the most important underlying causes of friction between the majority Macedonian population and the Albanian minority.

(4) Issues of citizenship and minority integration have often been important for Mr van der Stoel. The most prominent example relates to the Baltic states,

where he promoted the integration of Russian minorities, especially in Estonia and Latvia. Both countries are between 35 and 40 per cent Russian.

After the Soviet Union disintegrated and the Baltic states achieved independence in 1991, the vast majority of Russian speakers were treated as illegal immigrants holding only Russian citizenship. Up to 95 per cent of them had lived in the Baltic States since the 1950s and 1960s, or they had been born there and had no desire to resettle in Russia. The Estonian and Latvian governments began developing strongly ethno-nationalist policies in the early 1990s, and these raised fears among the local Russian speakers and brought strong pressure from Moscow in favour of all Russian speakers in the Baltic states. In 1993 the Estonian government confidentially asked the OSCE for help. The HCNM became involved at that point, at first to express his opinion on the legal status of aliens. Mr van der Stoel was able to prevent the enactment of legislation that would have marginalized the Russian-speaking minority. Had they become law, these policies would have brought about long-term resentments; they might also have fed Russian nationalist and expansionist voices in Moscow. In the Baltic states, Mr van der Stoel was able to bring the political leaders of the three countries as well as Moscow to agree on citizenship and language legislation. He suggested ways to integrate the members of the Russian minority into the societies of the Baltic states through citizenship law amendments; he also emphasized the need for the Russian-speaking minorities to learn the local language and thereby show their intention to integrate into the society of these countries.[69]

(5) Regarding self-administration, the high commissioner did much to develop a new constitution for the Autonomous Republic of Crimea. In March 1996 he invited representatives of the Ukrainian and Crimean governments, including Crimean Tatar leaders, to meet with internationally respected authorities in international law in the Netherlands. A month later, the Ukrainian Parliament adopted a new constitution for the Autonomous Republic of Crimea in which the majority Russian population and the minority Tatars and Ukrainians agreed on a method of governance within the national sovereign framework of the Ukrainian state.

Self-administration or self-determination for minorities or for specific ethnic communities is perhaps the most sensitive issue that the HCNM must confront. State governments jealously guard their sovereignty in matters of political reform and the centralization or decentralization of power this implies. Still, the high commissioner has suggested with increased frequency that democratic measures be developed to help resolve problems between central governments and regions or minority populations. In his many public speeches and published articles, Mr van der Stoel has not hesitated to suggest ideas for political participation, for regional autonomy, and for what he calls 'internal self-determination.' To give greater weight to his suggestions, the high commissioner brought together a group of internationally recognized experts to outline alternative methods of governance to improve the political participation of minorities. This study came to be known as the *Lund Recommendations on the Effective Participation of National Minorities in Public life.*[70]

The above examples provide a highly simplified glance at some of the work of the HCNM. His activities have not escaped criticism. Many minority leaders and OSCE member governments have expressed doubts about the HCNM's work. For example, he has been criticized many times for his refusal to become involved in Chechnya, Corsica, Northern Ireland, the Basque homeland, and in the United States; in all these places minorities have been calling for secession, greater autonomy, or special rights. Some critics have pointed to the HCNM's absence in these countries or regions as proof that he obeys the dictates of the powerful members of the OSCE (Russia, France, Great Britain, Spain, and the United States). However, the mandate of the HCNM, as it was negotiated and agreed to by all the parties in 1992, does not permit the HCNM to become involved in situations where systemic violence or terrorism already exists. Regarding minorities in the United States and in other countries where similar communities demand various self-administrative powers, the high commissioner has responded that he does not have sufficient confidence that the governments will deal with their minority issues in a democratic manner and thus resolve internal tensions without the HCNM's involvement. Similar questions have been posed with regard to Canada and its province of Quebec, Belgium with its two linguistic groups, and Scotland and Wales in Great Britain. The HCNM can become involved in any countries he chooses as long as he stays within his mandate. This mandate states that the high commissioner must use his judgment to discern minority issues that have the potential to develop into conflicts within the CSCE area that could affect peace, stability, or relations between participating states. If the potential for such instability between states is not visible, the HCNM cannot become involved.

A problem that has become a concern for the high commissioner, however, relates not so much to which minority issues has chosen to become involved in, or not, but rather to those issues which may generate problems among OSCE member states. The most notable among these relate to the minorities in Greece and Turkey. Neither country officially recognizes the existence of minorities in its territory and neither sees the needs of specific ethnic groups as being any different from those of all citizens. Both argue essentially that all their citizens are equal before the law and therefore do not need special attention.

With regard to Greece, the high commissioner was able to visit the country, discuss minority concerns with members of Greek political parties, and issue a statement on national minorities in Greece on 23 August 1999. However, the Turkish government categorically refused to meet Mr van der Stoel, continuing to maintain that there was no need for Turkey to consider special policies for its Armenian, Kurdish, Greek, and Jewish minority communities. According to Mr van der Stoel, this is a very serious development that could set a precedent for other countries that want to avoid involvement by the HCNM or that want to discredit expressions of concern by other OSCE member states.[71]

Given the challenges facing the high commissioner's work, it is clear that conflict prevention – even under the favourable conditions of the OSCE – remains politically sensitive and difficult to appraise or evaluate. This is for several reasons. First, governments rarely ask for help, and often go to great lengths to cover up internal interethnic tensions until (as so often has happens) a violent confrontation or terrorist acts reveal the issue to the international community. Second, without a clear indication that prevention will succeed, few politicians are willing to support it. Finally, success in conflict prevention is mostly invisible to the international community, since it involves mainly an *absence* of violence. What *is* visible are legislative changes, political reforms, or election results that favour greater participation by minorities – developments that are rarely explained in the media. This implies that preventive work by the HCNM or by anyone else will always face two major challenges: one that is political (state sovereignty, governance, and human rights), and one that is practical (the mitigation of tensions so as to reduce the potential for violent conflict).

Conclusion

The main question discussed in this essay was how states can attempt to provide international protection to ethnic or minority populations in situations where tensions between the latter and national governments risk developing into violent conflicts. For the international community, the greatest difficulty in preventing violent conflicts within individual states relates to how multilateral measures may positively influence the relationship between national governments and distinct ethnic or minority communities within a country. Four broad issues were presented: ethnic identity, the right of persons to choose to belong to a minority, multilateral conflict prevention, and the work of the OSCE and its High Commissioner on National Minorities. The novel elements in this multilateral attempt can be summarized as follows:

- The OSCE's development of a body of normative standards in the 1990s that recognize the right of minorities to exist. Every human being has the right by virtue of her his or fundamental human rights to belong to an ethnic or minority group. Such belonging is non-negotiable, and this must be accepted by all governments.

- The prior consent of state parties to the involvement of the HCNM in the internal affairs of member countries, where tensions between ethnic groups or minority and majority communities may lead to violent conflict.
- The OSCE's development, through the HCNM's capacity to engage in 'early action,' of a practical diplomatic approach to multilateral conflict prevention that allows the organization to promote security in a more pragmatic way.

The OSCE is not known for creating media headlines, but it deserves to become better known as an institution that has tried hard to overcome a crucial dilemma in international relations – the tensions between state sovereignty and the international protection of human rights. This is exemplified by the capacity of the high commissioner to investigate internal minority issues within OSCE member countries – something that during the Cold War would have been considered as an inadmissible interference in the internal affairs of sovereign states. In this way, the OSCE high commissioner links high-level diplomatic efforts for international security directly with the causes of interethnic disputes, and to reforms in favour of democratic governance. He thereby embodies an approach to security that is notable for its comprehensiveness.

NOTES

1 The word 'conflict' is used here for both, violent and non-violent confrontations. In the text the term 'dispute' implies a non-violent confrontation or struggle in which tensions are lower than in situations where violence has erupted.
2 In part from *SIPRI Yearbook 2000: Armaments, Disarmament and International Security* (Oxford: Oxford University Press, 2000) at 15. 'Major armed conflicts' and 'high-intensity conflicts' are defined as organized military violence where the battle-related deaths amount to at least 1,000 people per year. See also http://projects.sipri.se/conflictstudy/MajorArmedConflicts.html.
3 Low-intensity conflicts can be understood as those which cause between 1,000 and 100 deaths directly from the fighting. Violent political conflicts are those which cause fewer than 25 deaths per year; these may include acts of terrorism. Most of these conflicts are explained as the result of long-lasting and unresolved disputes among distinct ethnic communities or minorities and majorities within countries. See *Prevention and Management of Violent Conflict: An International Directory,* 1998 ed. (European Platform for Conflict Prevention and Transformation, 1998), pp. 41–45.

4 Until 1 January 1995 the OSCE was known as the Conference on Security and Co-operation in Europe (CSCE).

5 R.S. Khakimov, 'Prospects of Federalism in Russia: A View from Tatarstan' (1996) 27 *Security Dialogue* 1 at 69.

6 The term 'permanently distinct' is taken from D. Horowitz, *Ethnic Groups in Conflict* (Berkeley: University of California Press, 1985) at 51.

7 Taken in part from A.D. Smith, 'Ethnic and Nation in the Modern World' (1985) 14 *Millenium* 2

8 S.R. Ratner, 'Does International Law Matter in Preventing Ethnic Conflict?' (2000) 32 N.Y.U. J. Int'l L. & Pol. 598

9 This definition is borrowed from J. Packer, 'On the Definition of Minorities,' in K. Myntti and J. Packer, eds., *The Protection of Ethnic and Linguistic Minorities in Europe* (Turku and London: Abo Akademi University Institute for Human Rights, 1993), p. 45.

10 For a discussion of problems associated with human rights law and the existing mechanisms for the protection (or lack thereof) of minorities, see J. Symonides, 'The Legal Nature of Commitments Related to the Question of Minorities' (1996) 3 *Int'l J. on Group Rights* 4 at 301–23.

11 Adapted from: V.Y. Ghébali, 'La CSCE et la question de la protection des minorités,' in A. Liebich and A. Reszler, eds., *L'Europe centrale et ses minorités: vers une solution européenne?* (Paris: Presse Universitaire de France, 1993) at 72.

12 P. Dunay, 'Concerns and Opportunities: The Development of Romanian-Hungarian Relations and National Minorities,' in G. Bichler, ed., *Federalism against Ethnicity?* (Chur, Zürich: Verlag Ruegger AG, 1997) at 215; Hans-Joachim Heintze, 'The International Law Dimension of the German Minorities Policy' (1999) 68 Nordic J. Int'l L. at 117.

13 An excellent guide to international standards that develop the rights of persons belonging to minorities can be found in G. Alfredsson and M.G. Goran, 'A Compilation of Minority Rights Standards' (1997) 24 Raoul Wallenberg Inst. H.R. & Hum. L.R. For an analyses of the minority question, see A. Phillips and A. Rosas, eds., *Universal Minority Rights* (Turku and London: Abo Akademi University Institute for Human Rights, 1995); A. Fenet et al., eds., *Le droit et les minorités: analyses et textes* (Bruxelles: Etablissements Emile Bruylant, 1995); J. Raikka, ed., *Do We Need Minority Rights?* (The Hague: Kluwer Law International, 1996); I. Shapiro and W. Kymlicka, eds., *Ethnicity and Group Rights* (New York: New York University Press, 1997); and G. Bichler, ed., *Federalism against Ethnicity?* (Chur, Zürich: Verlag Ruegger AG, 1997).

14 See for example *Report of the UN Commission on Human Rights, Sub-Commission on Prevention of Discrimination and Protection of Minorities,* 45th sess., E/CN.4/Sub.2/1993/34/add.4 (1992). See also F. Capotorti, *Study on the Rights of Persons Belonging to Ethnic, Religious and Linguistic Minorities* (UN Sales No. E.91.XIV.2, 1991).

15 For a discussion of the Council of Europe's work and its Framework Convention, see *The Protection of Minorities* (Strasbourg: Council of Europe Publishing, 1994); and M.A. Estébanez and G.L. Kinga, *Implementing the Framework Convention for the Protection of National Minorities* (Flensburg: European Centre for Minority Issues, 1999). Concerning the CSCE/OSCE, see: V.Y. Ghébali, *L'OSCE dans l'Europe post-communiste, 1990-1996: Vers une identité paneuropéenne de securité* (Bruxelles: Etablissement Emile Bruylant, 1996) at 492.

16 Accepting this, however, is not equally simple for all OSCE members. France, for example, admits that minorities do exist in other countries, but is not (yet?) willing to recognize that ethnic minorities on its soil deserve greater local self-governance. The situation regarding Corsica is the most telling as an analysis shows in E. Sipry, *Pratique francaise du droit international des droits de l'homme – le cas des minorités* (University of Geneva, Graduate Institute of International Studies, 1998) [unpublished PhD thesis].

17 CSCE, Copenhagen Conference, *Document on the Human Dimension of the CSCE,* c. IV, para. 32 (1990) [hereinafter 'Copenhagen Document'].

18 CSCE, Geneva Meeting, *Report of the Meeting of Experts on National Minorities,* c. II (1991) [hereinafter 'Report on National Minorities'].

19 OSCE, Istanbul Summit, *Charter for European Security,* c. 3, para. 19 (1999).

20 A short historical overview of the minority question is provided in F. Rousso-Lenoir, *Minorités et droits de l'homme: l'Europe et son double* (Bruxelles: Etablissement Emile Bruylant, S.A., 1994).

21 B. Boutros-Ghali, *An Agenda for Peace: Preventive Diplomacy, Peacemaking and Peacekeeping.* 47th Sess., UN Doc. A/47/277/ S/24111 (1992) [hereinafter 'Agenda for Peace']

22 B. Boutros-Ghali, 'Agenda for Peace,' *supra.*

23 Boutros-Ghali differentiates preventive diplomacy from peace building by saying that it 'seeks to resolve disputes before violence breaks out,' whereas peace building is 'action to identify and support structures which will tend to strengthen and solidify peace in order to avoid a relapse into conflict' (taken from *Agenda for Peace*). Furthermore, preventive diplomacy is not peacemaking or peace keeping. The latter two activities are intended to bring the hostile parties to agree to halt their conflict and then to maintain peace.

24 Quoted passages in this paragraph are taken from F. Tanner, 'Conflict Prevention and Conflict Resolution: Limits of Multilateralism' (September 2000) 82 *International Review of the Red Cross* 839 at 544.

25 For an excellent overview of conflict prevention organizations and NGOs, see *Prevention and Management of Violent Conflicts: An International Directory,* 1998 ed. (Utrecht: European Platform for Conflict Prevention and Transformation, 1998). See also the publisher's web page: www.euconflict.org.

26 The United Nations initiates prevention and peace-building efforts through the Secre-

tary-General's office, special representatives, and the UN Secretariat as well as through several of its specialized agencies and regional offices. See also C. Peck, *Sustainable Peace: The Role of the UN and Regional Organizations in Preventing Conflict* (Lanham: Rowman & Littlefield, 1998).

27 CSCE, 'Report on National Minorities,' *supra* at note 18. [emphasis in original]. This was restated in the *CSCE Helsinki Document of 1991 – The Challenge of Change* ('The Helsinki Summit Declaration,' para. 8, 1991), in which the HCNM's mandate is also stated.

28 The term 'human dimension' refers to the principles concerning human rights, fundamental freedoms, and self-determination; these are seen by the OSCE as the basis for democratic reform and the peaceful prevention of conflicts.

29 The quote (emphasis in original) is from the Preamble of the Moscow Document – Conference on the Human Dimension of the CSCE, 3rd Meeting of the Conference on the Human Dimension of the CSCE, 4 October 1991.

30 CSCE, 'Copenhagen Document,' *supra* note 17 at c. IV, para. 31

31 CSCE, 'Report on National Minorities,' *supra* note 18

32 In this text the High Commissioner on National Minorities is also referred to as the 'HCNM' or simply as the 'High Commissioner.'

33 CSCE, *Charter of Paris for a New Europe* (Paris, 21 November 1990).

34 These values developed through various CSCE and OSCE declarations and agreements can be summarized as comprising ten principles, which were first enumerated in the CSCE's founding document, the 1975 *Helsinki Final Act*. These represent the outer limits of consensus on the fundamentals of security such as state sovereignty, refraining from the use of force, and the peaceful settlement of disputes. The principles that concern human rights, fundamental freedoms, and self-determination are known as the Human Dimension and are seen as the basis for democratic reform. Many official documents and commitments of the CSCE and OSCE can be found in A. Bloed, ed., *The Conference on Security and Co-operation in Europe: Analysis and Basic Documents, 1972–1993* (Dordrecht: Kluwer Academic Publishers, 1993). See also A. Bloed, ed., *The Challenge of Change: The Helsinki Summit of the CSCE and its Aftermath* (Dordrecht: Martinus Nijhoff Publishers, 1994); and J. Cohen, *Conflict Prevention in the OSCE* (The Hague: Netherlands Institute of International Relations, 1999).

35 The OSCE has field missions in Albania, Azerbaijan, Belarus, Bosnia and Herzegovina, Croatia, Estonia, Georgia, Kosovo (Federal Republic of Yugoslavia), Latvia, Skopje (the former Yugoslav Republic of Macedonia), Moldova, Tajikistan, and Ukraine, and in Belgrade, Federal Republic of Yugoslavia. Additional centres oversee activities in Kazakhstan, Kyrgyzstan, Turkmenistan, and Uzbekistan.

36 The mandate is part of the *CSCE Helsinki Document of 1992 – The Challenge of Change* ('The Helsinki Summit Declaration,' c. II (1991) [hereinafter 'Helsinki Document'].

37 The mandate stipulates that the High Commissioner must be 'an eminent international personality with long-standing relevant experience from whom an impartial performance ... may be expected.' Mr van der Stoel fits this description. He brought into the position as HCNM almost fifty years of experience in Netherlands Parliamentary and political offices. He was a Dutch parliamentarian, a member of the Parliamentary Assembly of the Council of Europe, Netherlands Minister for Foreign Affairs, Permanent Representative to the United Nations in New York, a human rights advocate, and head of the Dutch delegation to numerous CSCE conferences. The second High Commissioner is Swedish Ambassador Rolf Ekeus who took up his post in July 2001.

38 The HCNM has been involved in the following countries (in alphabetical order): Albania, Croatia, Estonia, Greece, Georgia, Hungary, Kazakhstan, Kyrgyzstan, Latvia, Lithuania, Former Yugoslav Republic of Macedonia, Moldova, Romania, Slovakia, Tajikistan, Turkey, Ukraine, Uzbekistan, and the Federal Republic of Yugoslavia. The HCNM also reported on the Roma (Gypsy) populations in 1993, 1999, and 2000. (See www.osce.org/hcnm/recommendations/).

39 CSCE, 'Helsinki Summit Declaration,' *supra* note 36 at c. II, para. 3.

40 *Ibid.* at c. II, paras. 6, 12 and 16 respectively.

41 Many of the ideas underpinning Ambassador Max van der Stoel's official recommendations as well as his thoughts on his work can be found in his own articles. A now well-known article is M. van der Stoel, 'The Heart of the Matter: The Human Dimension of the OSCE' *Helsinki Monitor* 6:3 (1995) at 23. His public speeches and recommendations are on the OSCE's website: www.osce.org

42 OSCE, Press Release 99/05, 'OSCE High Commissioner on National Minorities addresses Permanent Council on situation in the Former Yugoslav Republic of Macedonia' (12 May 1999).

43 Interview with Mr van der Stoel (July 1998) (hereinafter 'author's interview').

44 See the web page: www.osce.org. See also 'Van der Stoel warnt vor Fundamentalismus,' *Frankfurter Allgemeine Zeitung* (23 November 1999) 2; 'Max van der Stoel, Minority Man' *The Economist* (11 September 1999) 36; 'OSCE Minorities Chief Aims for Early Action' *Financial Times* (19 May 2000) 3; and 'The Multiethnic State,' Letter to the Editor, *International Herald Tribune* (2 February 2000). A comprehensive overview of the HCNM's work can be found in W. Kemp, ed., *Quiet Diplomacy in Action: The OSCE High Commissioner on National Minorities* (The Hague: Kluwer Law International, 2001).

45 Paragraphs 5(a), 23(a), and 25 of the HCNM's mandate. This means that the High Commissioner cannot become involved in conflict situations such as in Spain, Northern Ireland, Chechnya, or Turkey.

46 Paragraphs 23(a) and (b), 26(a) and (b), and 29 in the HCNM's mandate stipulate the persons which whom the HCNM can be in contact.

47 At the start of his mandate in 1993, the first High Commissioner, Mr van der Stoel,

made immediate use of this freedom to find information by affiliating his office with an NGO specially created for the purpose. It was called the Foundation on Inter-ethnic Relations, and it supplied the HCNM with in-depth field studies that the OSCE could not provide at the time.

48 *The Role of the High Commissioner on National Minorities in OSCE Conflict Prevention: An Introduction* (The Hague: The Foundation on Inter-Ethnic Relations, 1997) at 22.

49 For more information on such treaties on good neighbourliness and co-operation, see K. Gál, 'Bilateral Agreements in Central and Eastern Europe: A New Inter-State Framework for Minority Protection?' (Flensburg: European Centre for Minority Issues, 1999).

50 'Author's interview,' *supra* at note 43. An elaboration of this point is offered in M. van der Stoel, 'The Role and Importance of Integrating Diversity' (Conference on Governance and Participation: Integrating Diversity, Locarno, 18 October 1998), available on the OSCE web page: http://www.osce.org/hcnm/documents/speeches/.

51 J. Packer, 'Autonomy within the OSCE: The Case of Crimea,' in M. Suksi, ed., *Autonomy: Applications and Implications* (The Hague: Kluwer Law International, 1998) at 295 [hereinafter 'The Case of Crimea'].

52 J. Packer, 'The OSCE and International Guarantees of Local Self-Government,' in *Local Self-Government, Territorial Integrity and Protection of Minorities* (Strasbourg: Council of Europe Publishing, 1996) at 265.

53 W. Danspeckgruber, 'Self-determination, Self-governance and Security,' *International Relations* 15 (April 2000) 1 at 11.

54 See A. Eide, 'Territorial Integrity of States, Minority Protection, and Guarantees for Autonomy Arrangements: Approaches and Roles of the United Nations,' in *Local Self-Government, Territorial Integrity and Protection of Minorities* (Strasbourg: Council of Europe Publishing, 1996).

55 'Copenhagen Document,' *supra* note 17 (emphasis in original). Notably, the accord of the CSCE heads of state to this phrase was reaffirmed in the *Charter of Paris for a New Europe* at the CSCE's summit meeting in November 1990.

56 *Ibid.* at c. IV, para. 35

57 V.Y. Ghébali, 'The OSCE's Istanbul Charter for European Security' (Spring/Summer 2000) 48 *NATO Review* at 23. Passage paraphrased from OSCE, Istanbul Summit, *Charter for European Security*, c. 3, para. 19 (1999) (hereafter 'Charter for European Security').

58 'Copenhagen Document,' *supra* note 17 at c. IV, para. 30

59 'Charter for European Security,' *supra* note 57

60 M. van der Stoel, 'Minority Rights, Participation and Bilateral Agreements' (International Seminar on Legal Aspects of Minority Rights: Participation in Decision-Making Processes and Bilateral Agreements on Minority Rights, Zagreb, 4 December 2000) [unpublished].

61 Recommendations of the High Commissioner are all made publicly available at the OSCE's Prague office and can be found on the web page www.osce.org/hcnm/.

62 *The Role of the High Commissioner on National Minorities in OSCE Conflict Prevention: An Introduction* (The Hague: The Foundation on Inter-Ethnic Relations, 1997) at 31–2.

63 An example of the HCNM's work can be found in J. Cohen, *Conflict Prevention in the OSCE: An Assessment of Capacities* (The Hague: Netherlands Institute of International Relations, Clingendael, 1999) at 58; V.Y. Ghébali, *L'OSCE dans l'Europe post-communiste, 1990–1996: Vers une une identité paneuropéenne de securité* (Bruxelles: Etablissement Emile Bruylant, 1996) at 533–547; 'The Case of Crimea,' *supra* note 51.

64 'Author's interview,' *supra* at note 43.

65 For an overview of the HCNM's involvement in national minority situations, see W. Kemp, ed., *Quiet Diplomacy in Action: The OSCE High Commissioner on National Minorities* (The Hague: Kluwer Law International, 2001).

66 M. Van der Stoel, 'The role of the OSCE High Commissioner in Conflict Prevention,' in C.A. Crocker, F.O. Hampson, and P. Aall, eds., *Herding Cats: Multiparty Mediation in a Complex World* (Washington, D.C.: United States Institute of Peace Press, 1999), p. 76.

67 Copies of this set of recommendations can be obtained from the HCNM's office or from the OSCE itself. For further information see the web page www.osce.org For a discussion of these recommendations see J. Packer, 'The Protection of Minority Language Rights through the Work of OSCE Institutions,' in S. Trifunovska and F. de Varennes, eds., *Minority Rights in Europe: European Minorities and Languages* (The Hague: T.M.C. Asser Press, 2001).

68 See also 'Part Three – National Activities and Documents,' which follows up on the above-mentioned Report by the High Commissioner in S. Trifunovska and F. de Varennes, eds., *Minority Rights in Europe: European Minorities and Languages* (The Hague: T.M.C. Asser Press, 2001).

69 With regard to Estonia, see R. Zaagman, *Conflict Prevention in the Baltic States: The OSCE High Commissioner on National Minorities in Estonia, Latvia and Lithuania* (Flensburg: European Centre for Minority Issues Monograph, 1999) at 27, 28, and 32.

70 This text can be obtained directly from the HCNM's office or from the OSCE's website.

71 This is taken from the Notes for a talk given by Mr van der Stoel at the Annual Meeting of the OSCE Cluster of Competence, Graduate Institute of International Studies, Geneva, 21 September 2001.

Chapter Four

Between Sovereignty, Efficiency, and Legitimacy: Lawmaking under Multilateral Environmental Agreements*

JUTTA BRUNNÉE[†]

> Humankind today, for the first time in five millennia of recorded activity, faces cir-
> cumstances of global dimensions: possible nuclear cataclysm, environmental degra-
> dation, economic collapse ... The combination of today's technologies and
> yesterday's policies has produced trends which, unless altered significantly, may well
> become irreversible.[1]

Ivan Head, keen observer of international law and politics, has long urged us to
focus our attention and efforts on the growing number of 'global issues.' He
made the above remarks in an address to the annual conference of the Canadian
Council on International Law in 1986. His particular concern in that address, as
in much of his work, was to highlight the extent to which 'South-North' issues
are interwoven with global issues, demanding the cooperative involvement of
developing countries in efforts to address them. Ivan Head's remarks are as pertinent today as they were fifteen years ago. International environmental law, for
example, continues to wrestle with the challenges of South-North interaction
around global environmental concerns.[2] At the same time, it must grapple with a
host of other symptoms of the 'combination of today's technologies and yesterday's policies.' This essay explores one cluster of such 'symptoms' – the tensions
between the increasing urgency of coordinated action to counter global environmental decline and the constraints inherent in a legal system the task of which it
is to structure the interaction of sovereign states. Needless to say, the 'South-
North' dimension is very much intertwined with this particular cluster of issues.

In the efforts to address global environmental concerns, it has become common
for international environmental law to be 'made' pursuant to multilateral environmental agreements (MEAs).[3] In this treaty-based lawmaking arena, state consent
remains central to the creation of legal commitments[4] and is seen as an important

protection for states' sovereignty. Yet the consent requirement is also widely perceived as undercutting the dynamic forces that can unfold within a regime and pull participants toward collective action.[5] As a result there have been various calls for new approaches to international environmental lawmaking, including approaches that could help temper the constraints of the consent requirement.[6]

In this context, attention has recently focused on the role of Conferences of the Parties (COPs), the plenary bodies that have emerged as the key forums for lawmaking under MEAs.[7] Yet, while some would very much welcome more influential or even autonomous COPs and a relaxation of consent requirements, and even call for 'global environmental legislatures,'[8] such developments have also begun to prompt questions regarding the legitimacy of international environmental governance.[9] Thus, lawmaking under MEAs occurs in the context of three types of considerations, which can pull in opposite directions: concerns over loss of sovereign control, the need for efficient lawmaking processes,[10] and questions regarding the legitimacy of increasingly influential international environmental institutions.

In this essay, against the backdrop of the apparent tensions between sovereignty, efficiency, and legitimacy considerations, I want to examine more closely the role of COPs in MEA-based lawmaking. To this end, I juxtapose the standard conception of international law and an alternative, interactional framework. In the standard framework, the focus is on decision-making procedures and, as already implied, on state consent as pivotal in bringing legal norms into existence.[11] Thus, COPs can be considered to 'make' law only to the extent that their decisions produce rules that are directly binding on states.[12] In assessing their role within the standard framework, I offer examples of COPs' involvement in lawmaking under different environmental agreements,[13] ranging from the adoption of texts that are subsequently ratified by the parties to what, indeed, appear to be more autonomous forms of lawmaking. I then explore COPs activities' in light of an alternative conception, which sees lawmaking not simply as crystallized in formal approval procedures but as a continuous interactional process. In this interactional framework, law exists not by virtue of formal state consent, but rather when norms meet certain internal legitimacy criteria, which are closely related to lawmaking and application processes.[14] I suggest that from this standpoint the range of genuine lawmaking by COPs can be considerably broader than the formal account would allow. At the same time, however, the interactional account actually places greater demands on lawmaking activity than a purely formal perspective.

My goals in this essay are twofold. The first is to highlight the points at which the two conceptions lead to different conclusions regarding the nature of the COPs' activities. The second is to illustrate that while the standard and the interactional views may seem to point to different approaches to resolving the sovereignty efficiency legitimacy tensions under MEAs, their insights are actually complementary. I argue that the interactional account can provide important guidance to lawmakers even as they operate within a formal, consent-based framework.

The Role of COPs in the Standard Conception of Lawmaking

It is probably fair to say that the emergence of MEAs – notably in the increasingly common 'framework–protocol' form – is largely due to efforts to overcome the sovereignty–efficiency tension that has vexed international environmental law-making. The framework–protocol model is designed to foster conditions under which common understandings regarding the problem at hand, and legal commitments, can develop.[15] Typically, an initial framework agreement contains general commitments of the parties to address the problem, provides for information gathering, establishes a COP or other plenary body for regular exchange among the parties, and creates basic decision-making procedures. In subsequent protocols, parties can develop specific commitments dealing with all or part of the underlying concern.[16] A further hallmark of the framework–protocol approach is that it allows the regime to adapt to changing circumstances and changing knowledge.[17] Indeed, the bulk of lawmaking activity often takes place not with respect to an MEA's initial adoption, but in the subsequent process of expansion and adaptation, of which the original treaty is only the starting point. It is through this continuous process of treaty expansion and adaptation that COPs have come to be the main forums for lawmaking activities and, therefore, the focus of the recent interest in shifting patterns in international environmental lawmaking.[18]

While firmly anchored in the requirement of state consent to legal commitments, the law of treaties does offer some flexibility regarding the method of consent. Beyond the formal methods that are normally required, such as ratification, the Vienna Convention on the Law of Treaties (VCLT) provides that a state can express its consent by 'any other means if so agreed.'[19] Thus, to determine the nature of COPs' involvement in the further development of MEAs, a standard analysis must clarify whether and to what extent any of the lawmaking methods under MEAs are truly shifts away from consent-based lawmaking, or whether they consist merely of simplified forms of consent-based decision-making. Three broad types of approaches are now commonly employed to expand or modify parties' obligations under MEAs. First, as already noted, parties can adopt a new protocol,[20] or they can opt for an amendment to the original treaty or to an existing protocol.[21] Secondly, parties can adopt or amend annexes that provide operational detail to flesh out the terms of the treaty.[22] Finally, a treaty or protocol may also provide that additional rules are to be elaborated by the COP and adopted by its decision.[23] Each of these three methods of treaty adaptation entails different approaches to consent, with varying implications for the role of the COP in the lawmaking process.

Lawmaking Involving Formal Consent

The adoption of a new protocol to an MEA, or the amendment of the treaty itself or an existing protocol, in keeping with the standard process set out in the VCLT,[24] usually requires the adoption of the text by the parties (by consensus or, as a last resort, by majority vote) and the subsequent formal approval by the parties. Thus, the protocol or amendment will not enter into force unless ratified (or accepted) by a specified number of parties, and enters into force only for those parties that so approve it.[25] As a result, while individual states cannot be compelled to bind themselves to new treaty terms, neither can they prevent the adoption of a protocol or an amendment. In adhering to the standard treaty law model of formal consent, the protocol or amendment approach maximizes sovereign control. The COP merely facilitates the elaboration of relevant texts. Although it is usually the COP that adopts the new treaty terms by decision,[26] states' subsequent consent is required to give them formal legal force.

Lawmaking through 'Other Means' to Express Consent

The most common context in which formal consent requirements are being relaxed involves the adoption or amendment of annexes to a framework agreement or protocol. Such annexes tend to provide technical detail that fleshes out treaty terms (such as generic references to 'regulated substances'), rather than create independent substantive commitments.[27] The content of annexes, as a result, tends to be less controversial than that of provisions in the treaty itself. Like amendments to the treaty itself, annexes (or amendments to annexes) are adopted at a session of the COP, if possible by consensus. Annexes and amendments to annexes, however, do not require the deposit of instruments of acceptance by a majority of parties to enter into force. Rather, it is common for annexes to enter into force for all parties except those who notify, within a specified period of time, that they do not accept.[28] Thus, again, although the COP adopts the relevant text, state consent remains decisive and parties can avoid being bound. It is merely the method of consent that has been simplified – consent is presumed unless parties explicitly opt out.

Lawmaking through Binding COP Decisions

Some COP decisions do not fit neatly into the standard framework. The most frequently cited example is that of Article 2.9 of the Montreal Protocol on Substances that Deplete the Ozone Layer. It allows for changes to the ozone-depleting potential of substances that are already subject to the protocol, or their phase-out schedules. These 'adjustments' can be adopted, as a last resort, by a two-thirds majority decision.[29] Unlike ordinary amendments, adjustments are binding on all parties.[30] Article 2.9 of the Montreal Protocol, therefore, stipulates two deviations from the normal consent requirements and process of treaty law. First, parties are bound directly by the decision adopted by the Meeting of the Parties (MOP) to the protocol – there is no further consent step, whether actual or presumed, to be taken by parties.[31] Second, if it comes to a majority decision, parties may be bound without consenting at all, and even against their will. Of course, Article 2.9 can be construed as remaining within the consent-based framework and as expressing the general consent of parties to the adjustment of the control measures as needed in light of new information.[32] Nonetheless, Article 2.9 is remarkable in that it allows for formally binding lawmaking by the MOP in relation to alterations of the treaty's substance, indeed, of its central commitments.

The Montreal Protocol furnishes a further example of decisions with some legal, or at least *de facto* effect. According to Article 14 of the protocol,[33] amendments to the scope of control measures require ratification by a two-thirds majority of states to enter into force. Yet in 1990, the MOP decided to adopt an amendment with an entry into force requirement of only twenty ratifications.[34] The relevant stipulation amounts to an amendment, by simple MOP decision, to the amendment rules in the protocol. In adopting that decision, the MOP thus went beyond the powers allocated to it in the protocol. The Montreal Protocol's terms were effectively modified in this regard.[35]

Other examples of COP decisions with direct, or *de facto*, legal effects include the many cases where COPs, under various MEAs, have adopted interpretations of the underlying treaty.[36] To the extent they can be seen as the parties' 'subsequent agreement ... regarding the interpretation of the treaty or the application of its provisions,'[37] or as constituting their 'subsequent practice in the application of the treaty' in a way that establishes agreement 'regarding its interpretation,'[38] the decisions would merely clarify what was originally intended. However, the boundaries are fluid, and it will often be difficult to distinguish interpretation from modifications to the terms of the treaty, which would normally require an amendment.

The ongoing work under the Kyoto Protocol to the UN Framework Convention on Climate Change (UNFCCC) points to another, potentially far-reaching area of direct lawmaking by a COP. The Kyoto Protocol asks the UNFCCC COP and its counterpart, the 'Conference of the Parties serving as the Meeting of the Parties' to the protocol (COP/MOP), to elaborate and adopt the guidelines, rules, and procedures that are needed to flesh out several of the protocol's key provisions.[39] Much of what the Kyoto Protocol delegates to COP decisions pertains to the kinds of terms that have tended to be added to a treaty through protocols, amendments, or annexes – and thus through the requisite formal or simplified consent procedures. Deviations from this approach, notably if they involve binding decision-making powers for a COP, are normally explicitly provided for, such as in the case of Article 2.9 of the Montreal Protocol. None of the above-mentioned Kyoto Protocol provisions, however, explicitly authorizes binding decision making by the COP or COP/MOP. In fact, most of the provisions use terms that have no connotation of bindingness at all,[40] or no necessary connotation of bindingness.[41]

Whatever the correct interpretation of these Kyoto Protocol provisions with respect to the COP's or COP/MOP's lawmaking powers, the draft decisions that emerged from the resumed sixth meeting of the COP in July 2001 use language that is normally reserved for legally binding commitments ('shall'). For example, under the draft umbrella decision on the Kyoto Mechanisms,[42] industrialized parties' access to the trading of emission rights or credits is made contingent upon their compliance with certain of their protocol commitments, as well on several other access requirements established in the decisions on the individual mechanisms.[43] Thus, whether or not the mechanism's rules are binding in a legal sense, they will significantly affect the legal position of a party under the agreement. In this regard, the relevant COP decisions under the Kyoto Protocol resemble the examples of interpretative decisions, or of the *de facto* amendment to the Montreal Protocol's amendment rules.

COPs as Lawmakers?

In most of the preceding examples of MEA-based lawmaking, states are bound not by the decision of a COP, but only through their consent, be it explicit (e.g., protocols and amendments), presumed (e.g., opt-out procedures for annexes and their amendments), or 'general' (e.g., adjustments). From the standpoint of a formal analysis, COPs can be said to be lawmaking only in the latter, rather limited range of cases, in which they adopt decisions that are directly binding on states. In the case of interpretative decisions or the decisions under the Kyoto Protocol that were discussed above, the legal status of the decisions is more ambiguous. It seems that in these cases, COPs are at the least emerging as de facto lawmakers.

While this trend may help expedite decision-making, it has also focused attention on questions of legitimacy. It has been observed that, to date, the firm grounding of international environmental law in consensual processes has helped shield it from concerns about lack of legitimacy and 'democracy deficit' that have plagued other areas of international law,[44] notably trade law.[45] To the extent that relevant domestic processes are triggered before international obligations are incurred, consent can afford international environmental law at least a degree of legitimization.[46] Thus, the more that the consent requirements are loosened and the more that MEA-based lawmaking is perceived as gravitating away from domestic control, the more acute concerns regarding legitimacy appear to become.

The conundrum is that when consent is given a crucial role in grounding both international rules and their legitimacy, it is difficult to fashion a coherent alternative source of legitimacy. As has been suggested by many observers,[47] increased involvement of civil society could certainly enhance the transparency of international lawmaking processes. Yet, however desirable in principle, in practice, such civil society participation is unlikely to overcome the perceived democracy deficit of international law.[48] In any case, to the degree that international law continues to operate mainly as law governing the relations of states, greater civil society involvement arguably will not remedy the gaps in the consensual basis of international rules that are of concern to the standard framework.

In sum, in the standard, formal conception of international lawmaking, an increasingly influential role for COPs is at once desirable and problematic. It is desirable because it can help overcome the constraints of international law's consent requirements and thereby improve the efficiency of MEA-based lawmaking processes. It is problematic because it entails ambiguities regarding the legal nature of COP decisions that run counter to the very premise of the formal perspective and its quest for clear indicators of binding commitments. More fundamentally, it is problematic because it exposes global environmental governance to challenges on the grounds of legitimacy. Thus, in seeking to resolve the sovereignty/efficiency/legitimacy tensions noted at the beginning of this essay, the standard conception of international lawmaking may well be caught in a vicious circle of sorts.

The Role of COPs in an Interactional Conception of Lawmaking

In previous work, undertaken jointly with Stephen Toope, I have argued for an alternative, interactional conception of international law.[49] This conception, informed by the legal theory of Lon Fuller read with constructivist international relations theory, understands international law as produced through a mutually generative process. Through their interaction, states (and other international actors) influence the scope and content of international norms and institutions. In turn, these norms and institutions provide the context within which interaction takes place and shape the identities of the actors themselves. In this continuous and mutual process, actors come to understand themselves and their interests in light of their interactions with others and in light of the norms that frame those interactions. International law is produced as patterns of social practice emerge and as increasingly influential mutual expectations and shared understandings of actors evolve. Norms and rules are not static but may be recast as shared understandings evolve and actor identities shift.[50]

This account of lawmaking processes acknowledges that all norms can shape the identities of states and that both legal and non-legal norms can be influential. It acknowledges that the boundaries between legal norms and other social norms are fluid. Indeed, rather than rely on formal indicators of bindingness, the interactional conception focuses on internal characteristics, which entail distinctive legal legitimacy and persuasiveness, to distinguish legal norms from non-legal norms.[51] These internal characteristics can be summarized as requiring that rules be compatible with one another, that they ask reasonable things, that known rules actually guide the discretion of officials, and that rules be transparent and relatively predictable.[52] While these characteristics posit modest substantive requirements,[53] they are most closely connected to processes of lawmaking and to processes of application, such as interpretation and implementation. In an interactional framework, lawmaking and application are not strictly separate – they are all part of the continuous process described above. Through interpretative processes, and processes designed to promote compliance, the scope or content of norms can shift and thus give rise to new normative understandings.

Inherent in an interactional conception of lawmaking is that all relevant actors must participate in the construction and reconstruction of norms and rules. Actors must be exposed to the normative processes that may shape their identities as participants in the regime and may promote the formation of collective identities around certain issues.[54] Only through inclusive processes can actors become engaged in the shared understandings that ground the emergence of legal norms, and that reinforce their normative commitments. Through participation in the construction and reconstruction of norms, actors learn to apply rules against the background of shared understandings. Legal arguments are legitimate and persuasive to the extent that they are broadly congruent with existing norms and practices.[55]

In sum, in an interactional framework, the bindingness of law – its ability to influence conduct and promote compliance – is 'self-bindingness.' It is not determined by formal criteria or contingent on enforceability. Rather, it flows from processes of mutual construction, legitimacy derived from adherence to internal criteria, and congruence with existing norms and practices.[56]

COPs as Lawmakers – Revisited

It should be apparent from this brief summary that the interactional framework has significant implications for understanding the role of COPs in MEA-based lawmaking. For the purposes of this essay, I focus on two central issues: the scope of COPs' lawmaking role, and its legitimacy.

An interactional framework, first, helps us appreciate COPs' lawmaking role as considerably broader than the formal perspective allows. Lawmaking, in this view, occurs along a continuum of (formally) binding and non-binding outputs that accommodates, for example, the ambiguities regarding the legal nature of the COP decisions under the Kyoto Protocol that was described earlier. Since 'bindingness' rests on internal features of norms and processes, COPs may be engaged in lawmaking whether or not their decisions are binding in a formal sense. Conversely, not all formally binding enactments are law in the interactional sense. Only if formal rules also meet the requirements sketched out above will they produce the distinctive influence of interactional law. Therefore, the interactional framework actually leads to a more demanding conception of law than the one posited by the standard account.

A further implication of the interactional conception is that formal state consent – be it in the context of COP decisions or elsewhere – plays a secondary role in the creation of law. That said, given current international legal practice, it is difficult to deny that state consent makes rules 'legal' in a technical sense and, in principle, enforceable.[57] I accept that state consent does retain significance as a trigger for a parallel, formal conception of bindingness.[58] However, I question the explanatory power of such a purely formal account, focused as it is on the notional enforceability of law. After all, few adherents to the standard conception of international law would deny that even rules that are enforceable in principle are rarely enforced (or even enforceable) in practice. The point that I am making, then, is not that state consent is irrelevant. Rather, I am suggesting that the interactional framework can provide us with a more satisfactory account of the bindingness of law and its ability to influence state conduct.[59] For the purposes of this essay, it can thus lead us to a more nuanced understanding of how law is generated within MEAs. It challenges some of the key assumptions of the formal perspective. Yet it can also help inform formal lawmaking efforts, highlighting the conditions under which consent may be most likely to have more than formal significance, and the circumstances under which states may be most likely to relinquish formal consent requirements.[60]

This leads us to the perhaps most significant element of the interactional framework – the conception of legitimacy on which it is premised. For the interactional account, legitimacy is not a yardstick against which law may or may not be measured once it is found to exist in a formal sense. Nor is it a concern that gains in importance only when lawmaking gravitates into international forums such as COPs. Rather, legitimacy is central to the very existence of law.[61] Therefore, the international lawmakers' primary concern should not be the loosening of international environmental law's consent basis. The interactional perspective points to more challenging requirements: international lawmaking must constantly refer to law's internal legitimacy and strive for rules that ask reasonable things, that actually guide the application of norms in the MEA regime (e.g., in interpretative decisions, or the work of compliance bodies) and the development of new norms (e.g., in protocols, amendments, or COP decisions), and that are transparent and relatively predictable. Furthermore, lawmakers must ensure that relevant processes are inclusive, so as to expose all relevant actors to the mutual construction of norms and identities. Inclusiveness, in turn, demands that actors be included – or excluded – on principled grounds. In the case of COPs, this means that lawmaking processes, as a general matter, have to be open to all parties to the agreement. To the extent possible, parties must also be enabled to participate on a level playing field. For example, in the case of some developing countries, genuine participation may be contingent on financial and legal capacity.[62] Interactional law, then, also speaks to the 'South–North' dimension of international environmental governance that was flagged at the beginning of this essay, and underscores the crucial importance of the full involvement of developing countries in lawmaking processes.

Reference was made also to the role of civil society involvement in enhancing the legitimacy of international lawmaking. Civil society participation too should be limited or facilitated, respectively, on principled grounds. To the extent that MEAs create commitments and entitlements for state parties, existing COPs provide appropriate lawmaking forums. Non-state actors' access to most parts of the lawmaking process, and their ability to make interventions, seem adequate within the current context.[63] Through these forms of participation, and various opportunities to engage with delegations in corridor discussions and other informal settings, non-state actors do find various ways to influence the construction of shared understandings.[64] This does not mean, however, that greater participation by non-state actors may not be needed over time. The more that MEAs have direct implications for segments of civil society, the more legitimate international lawmaking may presuppose participation of certain non-state actors. Indeed, the very concept of interactional law implies that the circle of participants in the lawmaking process may need to expand or contract depending on the context.[65]

Conclusion

The formal and interactional conceptions of lawmaking have parallel significance. I have sought to illustrate, however, that the interactional framework leads to a more nuanced understanding of how law is generated within MEAs. While the standard conception identifies formally binding and enforceable rules, an interactional understanding reveals that the lawmaking role of COPs is not limited to instances of formally binding decision-making. Furthermore, it suggests that the prerequisites for 'efficient' lawmaking are considerably more complex

than relaxing consent requirements or empowering COPs to adopt decisions that
are formally binding. In this context, the conception of legitimacy that underpins
the interactional account is highly relevant to the evolving role of COPs. Arguably, a treaty regime will be best equipped to provide timely and meaningful
responses to new concerns or knowledge if it has cultivated a practice of genuinely interactional lawmaking. By the same token, concerns regarding the loss of
sovereign control may be less acute if attention is paid to the prerequisites for
interactional lawmaking.

In short, in its emphasis on internal rather than formal criteria for bindingness,
the interactional framework challenges some of the core assumptions of the standard account. Yet its insights are ultimately complementary. Even from the standpoint of the standard framework, the interactional perspective offers important
guidance. Attention to inclusiveness and to internal legality criteria can help create the conditions under which the constraints of the consent requirement can be
overcome, and can help provide the foundations for efficient and legitimate international environmental lawmaking.

NOTES

* This essay draws on Jutta Brunnée, 'COPing with Consent: Lawmaking under Multilateral Environmental Agreements' (2002) 15 Leiden J. Int'l Law 1.

† I thank Asher Alkoby for his excellent research assistance in the preparation of this
article, and I gratefully acknowledge the support of the Connaught Fund of the University of Toronto.

1 I.L. Head, 'Contribution of International Law to Development,' in *Selected Papers on
International Law: Contribution of the Canadian Council on International Law* 59, at
59–60 (Yves Le Bouthillier et al., eds., 1999).

2 For a perceptive and challenging critique of the current state of international environ-
mental law, see K. Mickelson, 'South, North, International Environmental Law and
International Environmental Lawyers,' 11 Yearbook Int'l Env. L. 52 (2000). See also D.
French, 'Developing States and International Environmental Law: The Importance of
Differentiated Responsibilities' (2000) 49 Int'l & Comp. L.Q. 35.

3 See J. Werksman, 'The Conference of Parties to Environmental Treaties,' in *Greening
International Institutions* 55 (Jacob Werksman, ed., 1996); U. Beyerlin and T.
Marauhn, *Law-Making and Law-Enforcement in International Environmental Law after
the 1992 Rio Conference* (Berlin: E. Schmidt, 1997) at 4–5.

4 See, R. Lefeber, 'Creative Legal Engineering' (2000) 13 Leiden J. Int'l L. 1, at 2.

5 *See* Werksman, *supra* note 3 at 58.

6 For surveys in the literature, see, R. Churchill and G. Ulfstein, 'Autonomous Institutional Arrangements in Multilateral Environmental Agreements: A Little-Noticed Phenomenon in International Law' (2000) 94 Am. J. Int'l L. 623; Lefeber, *supra*, note 4; Werksman, *supra*, note 3; P. Széll, 'Decision Making under Multilateral Environmental Agreements' (1996) 26 Envt'l. Pl. & L. 210. For examples in international policy and diplomacy, *see German Advisory Council on Global Change (WGBU), World in Transition: New Structures for Global Environmental Policy – Summary for Policymakers*, at 9 (2000), online: <http://www.wbgu_jg2000_engl.html> (accessed 31 May 2001) (urging 'that an effort be made in the direction of softening the consensus principle' and suggesting that the 'principle of "tacit acceptance" ... should be used more frequently'); *Hague Declaration on the Environment*, reprinted in (1989) 28 I.L.M. 1308 (calling for 'such decision-making procedures as may be effective even if, on occasion, unanimous agreement has not been achieved'); Rt Hon. Geoffrey Palmer, *General Debate Statement of New Zealand Government*, UN Doc. A/44/PV.15, at 61, 76–7 (observing that 'the traditional response of international law, developing international legal standards in small incremental steps, each of which must be subsequently ratified by all countries, is no longer appropriate' and calling for 'the equivalent of a legislature [that] would be empowered to take binding decisions'). Reproduced in G. Palmer, 'New Ways to Make International Environmental Law' (1992) 86 Am. J. Int'l L. 259 at 279.

7 See Churchill and Ulfstein, *ibid.*, at 626, 636–42; T. Gehring, 'International Environmental Regimes: Dynamic Sectoral Legal Systems' in 1 Yearbook Int'l Envtl L. 35, at 47–50; Lefeber, *supra* note 4; G. Ulfstein, *The Proposed GEO and its Relationship to Existing MEAs*, online: <http://geic.or.jp/interlinkages/docs/online-docs.html> (accessed 31 May 2001); Werksman, *supra* note 3.

8 See Palmer, *supra*, note 6, at 279.

9 See D. Bodansky, 'The Legitimacy of International Governance: A Coming Challenge for International Environmental Law?' (1999) 93 Am. J. Int'l L. 596, at 597, 607–10.

10 That is, processes that allow an MEA to provide timely and meaningful responses to new concerns or knowledge.

11 See Article 11, Vienna Convention on the Law of Treaties, reprinted in (1969) 8 I.L.M. 679 [hereinafter VCLT]. For a comprehensive critical analysis of the preoccupation with consent, see D.M. Johnston, *Consent and Commitment in the World Community: The Classification and Analysis of International Instruments* (Irvington-on-Hudson: Transnational Publishers, 1997) at 62–3 (observing that the 'conceptual apparatus brought by the traditionalist to most treaty-related questions is dominated by the core concept of *consent*. In the positivist branch of traditional theory, it has been accepted, more or less uncritically, that international law is essentially a set of rules for sovereign states that cannot be bound except by their consent' [emphasis in the original]).

12 See, J. Sommer, 'Environmental Law-Making by International Organizations' (1996)

56 Zeitschrift Für Ausländisches Offentliches Recht und Völkerrecht 628, at 634–5 (distinguishing between three types of lawmaking: treaty-making, which requires ratification or other formal modes of consent; quasi-legislation, which is not subject to formal consent but allows states to opt out; and legislation, which is not subject to formal consent and, if adopted by majority, binds all parties).

13 Examples will be drawn primarily from the ozone layer and climate change regimes, with some references to other MEAs.

14 The interactional conception of international law outlined in this article was developed in a project undertaken jointly with Stephen J. Toope, which is funded by the Social Sciences and Humanities Research Council of Canada. See J. Brunnée and S.J. Toope, 'International Law and Constructivism: Elements of an Interactional Theory of International Law' (2000) 39 Col. J. Trans. L. 19 [hereinafter *Elements*]. For a brief overview, see J. Brunnée and S.J. Toope, 'Interactional International Law' (2001) 3 Int'l L. Forum 186 [hereinafter *Interactional Law*]; J. Brunnée and S.J. Toope, 'The Changing Nile Basin Regime: Does Law Matter?' Harv. J. Int'l L. (2002) 43.

15 See Beyerlin and Marauhn, *supra* note 3, at 28–33; J. Brunnée, 'Toward Effective International Environmental Law – Trends and Developments,' in S.A. Kennett, ed., *Law and Process in Environmental Management* (Calgary: Canadian Institute of Resources Law, 1993) 217 at 222–9; Gehring, *supra* note 7. For a critical perspective on the framework-protocol model, see, G.W. Downs, K.W. Danish, and P.N. Barsoom, 'The Transformational Model of International Regime Design: Triumph of Hope or Experience?' (2000) 38 Col. J. Transnat'l L. 465 at 471–88 (offering a survey of the arguments that have been made to suggest that regimes can be designed so as to induce 'a mutually reinforcing series of normative and cognitive shifts among member states because states in effect are socialized by the regime').

16 For an overview, see Brunnée, *id.*

17 See, M.J. Bowman, 'The Multilateral-Treaty Amendment Process – A Case Study' (1995) 44 Int'l & Comp. L. Q. 540, at 542; Lefeber, *supra* note 4; Werksman, *supra* note 3, at 58–64.

18 Of course, not all activities related to COPs' lawmaking role occur in the plenary. Indeed, the very fact that COPs are typically assisted by various subsidiary bodies, and interact with relevant bodies outside of the MEA, strengthens their ability to provide dynamic forums for dialogue in important ways.

19 VCLT, *supra* note 11, Article 11.

20 See Article 8, *Vienna Convention for the Protection of the Ozone Layer*, reprinted in (1987) 26 I.L.M. 1529 [hereinafter *Vienna Convention*]; Article 17, *United Nations Framework Convention on Climate Change*, reprinted in (1992) 31 I.L.M. 849 [hereafter UNFCCC].

21 See *Vienna Convention, id.*, Article 9; Article 14, *Montreal Protocol on Substances that Deplete the Ozone Layer* (1987) 26 I.L.M. 1550; adjusted and amended 29 June 1990, (1990) 30 I.L.M. 539 (prescribing reductions and phase-outs in the production and

consumption of various ozone depleting substances); adjusted and amended Nov. 25, 1992, (1993) 32 I.L.M. 875 [hereinafter the *Montreal Protocol*]; UNFCCC, *id.*, Article 15; Article 20, *Kyoto Protocol to the UNFCCC*, reprinted in (1998) 37 I.L.M. 22 [hereafter the *Kyoto Protocol*] (not yet in force).

22 See *Vienna Convention, id.*, Article 10; *Montreal Protocol, id.*, Article 14; UNFCCC, *id.*, Article 16; *Kyoto Protocol, id.*, Article 21.

23 See *Montreal Protocol, id.* Article 2.9; *Kyoto Protocol, id.*, Articles 3.4, 5.1, 6.2, 7.4, 8.4, 12.7, 16, 17, and 18.

24 VCLT, *supra* note 11, Articles 9–18, and 24.

25 See UNFCCC, *supra* note 20, Article 17.3 (entry into force of protocols), and Article 15.4 & 5 (entry into force of amendment). And see *Kyoto Protocol, supra* note 21, Articles 24–25 (entry into force of the protocol), and Article 20.4 & 5 (entry into force of amendments). Similar provisions can be found in *Vienna Convention, supra* note 20, Article 9.5 & 6 (entry into force of amendments to convention and protocol); and *Montreal Protocol, supra*, note 21, Article 16 (entry into force of protocol), and Article 14 (application of Vienna Convention's amendment provisions to protocol).

26 See UNFCCC, *id.*, Article 17 (adoption of protocols), and Article 15.5 (adoption of amendments); *Vienna Convention*, Article 8.1 (adoption of protocols), and Article 9.2 (adoption of amendments).

27 See UNFCCC, *id.*, Article 21.1 (providing that annexes are 'restricted to lists, forms and any other material of a descriptive nature that is of scientific, technical, procedural or administrative character'). But note that in the case of some annexes, the line between 'technical' and 'substantive' content is thin. For example, in the case of the Montreal Protocol, *supra* note 21, annexes contain lists of regulated substances or their 'ozone depleting potentials.' Thus, amendments to an annex can significantly increase the scope of parties' obligations under the protocol. See *infra* notes 29–32 and accompanying text (regarding 'adjustments' to annexes to the Montreal Protocol). In yet other cases, individual annexes are explicitly designated as 'mandatory' or 'recommendatory.' See, e.g., Article 12, *Protocol to the 1979 Convention on Long-Range Transboundary Air Pollution on Heavy Metals*, UN Doc. E/ECE/EB.AIR/66/1999, online: <http://www.unece.org/env/lrtap/welcome.html>; Article 10, *Protocol to the 1979 Convention on Long-Range Transboundary Air Pollution on Further Reduction of Sulphur Emissions*, reprinted in (1994) 33 I.L.M. 1540 (not yet in force). See, generally, Széll, *supra* note 6, at 210.

28 See *Vienna Convention, supra*, note 20, Article 10.2; UNFCCC, *supra*, note 20, Article 16.3. See also Article 30.2, *Convention on Biological Diversity*, reprinted in (1992) 31 I.L.M. 818; Article 18.2, *Basel Convention on the Control of Transboundary Movements of Hazardous Wastes and Their Disposal*, reprinted in (1989) 28 I.L.M. 675.

29 The requisite majority is 'double-weighted;' it must include a majority of both industrialized and developing countries present and voting. See *Montreal Protocol, supra* note 21, Article 2.9(c).

30 *Id.*, Article 2.9(d).

31 After six months from the communication of the decision to the parties. *See id.*

32 See Bodansky, *supra* note 9 at 609. Article 2.9(a) requires that adjustments be 'based upon' assessments pursuant to Article 6 of the protocol, which requires periodic reviews of the control measures in light of 'available scientific, environmental, and economic information.'

33 In conjunction with Article 9.5 of the *Vienna Convention, supra* note 20.

34 *See* London Amendment, *Report of the Second Meeting of the Parties to Montreal Protocol on Substances that Deplete the Ozone Layer,* UN Doc. UNEP/OzL.Pro.2/3 (1990), Decision II/2 and Annex II, Article 2, online: <http://www.unep.org/ozone/2mlonfin.shtml> (accessed 19 July 2001).

35 See also Gehring, *supra* note 7, at 48.

36 See examples cited in Churchill & Ulfstein, *supra* note 6, at 641.

37 VCLT, *supra* note 11, Article 31 (3)(a).

38 *Id.*, Article 31 (3)(b).

39 See *Kyoto Protocol, supra,* note 21, Articles 3.4, 5.1, 6.2, 7.4, 8.4, 12.7, 16, 17, and 18.

40 Articles 5.1, 6.2, 7.4, 8.4 of the *Kyoto Protocol, supra,* note 21, ask the COP or COP/MOP to adopt 'guidelines.'

41 Articles 12.7 and 18 of the *Kyoto Protocol, id.*, call for the elaboration of 'procedures;' Articles 3.4 and 17 for the adoption of 'rules.' Procedures and rules *can*, but need not, be binding. Given the exceptional nature of binding COP decisions, stronger language would arguably be required to so authorize the COP or COP/MOP. This is so, in particular, in view of the fact that Article 18 explicitly subjects non-compliance procedures and mechanisms 'entailing binding consequences' to an amendment requirement.

42 The 'Kyoto Mechanisms' are intended to give parties flexibility in meeting their emission reduction commitments under the Kyoto Protocol by allowing them to acquire emission rights or reduction credits from other parties. See *Kyoto Protocol, id.*, Article 6 (joint implementation), Article 12 (clean development mechanism), and Article 17 (international emissions trading). For a brief overview *see* J. Brunnée, 'A Fine Balance: Facilitation and Enforcement in the Design of a Compliance Regime for the Kyoto Protocol' (2000) 13 Tulane Envtl. L. J. 223, at 232–6.

43 See draft Decision -/CMP.1 (Mechanisms), para. 5; *and* draft Decision -/CMP.1 (Article 6), Annex, paras. 17–26; draft Decision -/CMP.1 (Article 12), Annex, paras. 26–32; draft Decision -/CMP.1 (Article 17), Annex, paras. 2–3; all in *Preparations for the First Session of the Conference of the Parties Serving as the Meeting of the Parties to the Kyoto Protocol (Decision 8/CP.4) – Work Programme on Mechanisms (Decisions 7/CP.4 and 14/CP.4)*, UN Doc. FCCC/CP/2001/CRP.11, online: <http://www.unfccc.int/resource/docs/cop6secpart/crp12r01.pdf> (accessed 29 July 2001).

44 Bodansky, *supra* note 9 at 597.

45 *See* G.C. Shaffer, 'The World Trade Organization under Challenge: Democracy and

the Law and Politics of the WTO's Treatment of Trade and Environment Matters' (2001) 25 Harv. Env'tl L.R. 1.

46 See R. Keohane and J.S. Nye Jr., *Between Centralization and Fragmentation: The Club Model of Multilateral Cooperation and Problems of Democratic Legitimacy*, John F. Kennedy School of Government Faculty Research Working Papers Series, (Kennedy School of Government Working Paper No. 01-004, February 2001), online: <http://papers.ssrn.com/paper.taf?abstract_id=262175> (accessed: 29 March 2001) (discussing options for ensuring a degree of 'electoral accountability,' for example, by devising clear and transparent chains of delegation for government representatives operating in an international institution).

47 See S. Charnovitz, 'Two Centuries of Participation: NGOs and International Governance' (1997) 18 Mich. J. Int'l L. 183; P.J. Spiro, 'New Global Communities: Nongovernmental Organizations in International Decision-Making Institutions' (1995) 18 Washington Q. 45; M.E. Keck and K. Sikkink, *Activists Beyond Borders: Advocacy Networks in International Politics* (New York: Cornell University Press, 1998).

48 Various proposals have been made in this regard. For a brief survey, see J. Crawford and S. Marks, 'The Global Democracy Deficit: An Essay in International Law and Its Limits,' in D. Archibugi et al., eds., *Re-imagining Political Community Studies in Cosmopolitan Democracy* (California: Stanford University Press, 1998) 72, at 82–5. For proposals pertaining specifically to international decision-making, see R. Falk and A. Strauss, 'On the Creation of a Global Peoples' Assembly: Legitimacy and the Power of Popular Sovereignty' (2000) 36 Stan. J. Int'l L. 191 at 208 (proposing an elected 'Global Peoples' Assembly'); T.M. Franck, *Fairness in International Law and Institutions*, at 483 (New York: Oxford University Press, 1995) (suggesting a two-chamber system for the UN General Assembly, with one chamber being 'directly elected in accordance with universal suffrage' and giving a voice to people rather than governments).

49 See *supra* note 14.

50 See Brunnée and Toope, *Elements, supra* note 14, at 43–64; Brunnée and Toope, *Interactional Law, supra*, note 14, at 187–8.

51 See Brunnée and Toope, *Elements, id.*, at 52–7, 70–1.

52 See *id.*, at 54 (discussing Lon Fuller's tests of the 'internal morality' of law). Fuller posited eight internal criteria of legality: generality of rules; promulgation; limiting cases of retroactivity; clarity; avoidance of contradiction; not asking the impossible; consistency over time; and congruence of official action with the underlying rules. See L.L. Fuller, *The Morality of Law* (New Haven: Yale University Press, 1969) at Chapters II and IV.

53 Fuller argued that to the extent that legal systems meet the internal requirements, they will also be likely to meet external standards of legitimacy, such as fairness or equality. See Brunnée and Toope, *Elements, supra* note 14 at 56–57. For Fuller, then, 'means'

(process) and 'ends' (substance) were not radically distinct – process is part of the ends that law serves.

54   See A. Wendt, 'Collective Identity Formation and the International State' (1994) 88 Am. Pol. Sci. Rev. 384 at 390.

55   See G.J. Postema, 'Implicit Law,' in W.J. Witteveen and W. van der Burg, eds., *Rediscovering Fuller: Essays on Implicit Law and Institutional Design* (Amsterdam: Amsterdam University Press, 1999) 255 at 265–70.

56   Brunnée and Toope, *Elements, supra* note 14 at 51–3, 72.

57   See also Johnston, *supra* note 11 at 62 (noting that the '[r]estriction to formal, legally binding instruments has limited the traditional scholar's interest to those instruments that are accepted as creating obligations enforceable by an international tribunal, as if the amenability of international disputes to settlement were the only concern for international lawyers.').

58   In part, in such a formal conception of international law, consent may serve a certain signalling function, communicating to the world and to domestic constituencies that certain rules are now 'enforceable.' On the 'signalling function' of consent and formal bindingness. See B. Simmons, 'Money and the Law: Why Comply with the Public International Law of Money?' (2000) 25 Yale J. Int'l L. 323 at 324–5, 327.

59   It may well be that consent will tend to be given when interactional processes have succeeded so that, often, formal bindingness will coincide with internal bindingness. In other words, states may be most likely to agree to make law 'enforceable' when it has become binding in the interactional sense. Alternatively, states may be most likely to insist on formal consent where there is an insufficient foundation of shared understandings (such as when a protocol or an amendment on new substances or control measures has to be negotiated).

60   In this context it is important to recall the features of the framework-protocol approach. They allow interactive processes to take shape gradually, procedural and substantive expectations to develop, and factual as well as normative understandings to grow. For example, under the *Montreal Protocol, supra* note 21, shared understandings developed regarding the concern of ozone depletion, the need to phase out certain substances, and the importance of adapting control measures in light of scientific findings. This permitted the addition to the protocol of Article 2.9, which allows for adjustments that are congruent with that framework. See *supra* notes 29–32 and accompanying text.

61   This distinguishes the role of legitimacy in the interactional legal framework presented here from the conception of legitimacy developed by T.M. Franck, 'Legitimacy in the International System' (1988) 82 Am. J. Int'l L., 705. Franck argues that there are four variables affecting legitimacy: determinacy, symbolic validation, coherence and adherence. However, Franck's variables are elements of 'process fairness,' which is distinct, in

his view, from substantive fairness, or distributive justice. See Franck, *supra* note 48, at 22.

62 Aside from financial constraints, human resource constraints can be a significant factor. For example, small developing country delegations may comprise negotiators with only limited experience or legal knowledge. See J. Gupta, 'North-South Aspects of the Climate Change Issue: Towards a Negotiating Theory and Strategy for Developing Countries' (2000) 3/2 Int'l J. Sustainable Development, 115. Lack of understanding of procedural or substantive issues can prompt obstructionist attitudes, or can lead to the adoption of rules on the basis of misunderstandings. In either case, outcomes are likely to be persuasive. Many negotiation processes seek to alleviate such difficulties by relying on workshops or informal discussions to enhance the understanding of key issues by all involved.

63 UN practice has been to admit non-governmental organizations that are qualified in relation to the matters governed by a given agreement. For detailed discussions see, e.g., Charnovitz, *supra* note 47 at 250–6.

64 See, S.D. Murphy, 'Biotechnology and International Law' (2001) 42 Harv. Int'l L. J. 47, at 104–39 (on the growing role of non-state actors in the formation of treaties in the biotechnology area).

65 See also H.H. Koh, 'Why Do Nations Obey International Law?' (1997) 106 Yale L.J. 2599 at 2656, which (highlighting the linkages between compliance and inclusive interactional processes and observes that 'if transnational actors obey international law as a result of repeated *interaction* with other actors in the transnational legal process, a first step is to empower more actors to participate. Is it here that expanding the role of intergovernmental organizations, nongovernmental organizations, private business entities, and 'transnational moral entrepreneurs' deserves careful study') (emphasis in original).

Chapter Five

The Use of Force in the Struggle between Humanity and Unreason

THOMAS M. FRANCK

An Examination of the Legality of the Use of Force Under, and Outside, the UN Charter System

On its face, the UN Charter, a treaty to which virtually every state adheres, has ushered in a new era in which aggression is prohibited and an effective international policing system has been instituted.

Even in 1945, however, there were doubts about the imminence of this new era. Thus, provision was made in Article 51 to preserve 'the inherent right of individual or collective self-defence *if an armed attack occurs.*' This provision was inserted at San Francisco to satisfy those members of the Inter-American Regional System who were concerned about subordinating their newly minted Chapultepec system of regional collective security to an unproven Security Council.

The American states, however, were forced to compromise. While Chapter VIII of the Charter does recognize the role of 'regional arrangements,' it adds the important caveat in Article 53(1) that 'no enforcement action shall be taken under regional arrangements ... *without the authorization of the Security Council.*' This attests to the concern of many states that the UN enterprise could only succeed if regional organizations as well as states were prohibited from using force at their own option except in self-defence.

Unfortunately, this idealized regime initiated by the Charter almost at once ran into four new developments in international relations that challenged it and could have made it unworkable.

One was the Cold War, which significantly incapacitated the veto-bound Security Council's ability to implement police enforcement actions under Chapter VII.

Another was the tactical replacement of military aggression with surrogate warfare waged indirectly though subversion and covert intervention in civil wars. This was not so evidently the kind of traditional 'armed attack' against which Article 51 of the Charter endorsed states' 'inherent right of individual or collective self-defence.'

A third development was the development of weapons of overwhelming and instant destruction. These made questionable Article 51's requirement that forcible measures of self-defence be employed only after an armed attack had occurred. Inevitably, this new circumstance begat a doctrine of 'anticipatory self-defence,' for which the Charter had made no provision.

The fourth new development is the hardest to assess. Undoubtedly, however, a new ethos of human rights and humanitarian protection began to develop that soon challenged traditional Westphalian notions of sovereignty. Calls to end colonialism and apartheid resonated strongly in the General Assembly and eventually in the Security Council. Article 2(7)'s promise that the UN would not intervene in matters 'essentially within the domestic jurisdiction of any state' began to be challenged by changing perceptions of sovereignty and its immunities, especially as new concepts of human rights began to be interposed between rulers and their subjects in the colonies, in South Africa, and, eventually, everywhere.

None of these developments can be considered fruitfully from outside the perspective of interpretive and other kinds of disagreements that have characterized our global order – disagreements that have divided the geopolitical North and South since the dawn of the UN era, and even before. How do we resolve the tensions that characterize efforts to relate these developments to the quest to interpret important aspects of the UN charter concerning the use of force? The answer is strongly influenced by South–North considerations, and by other kinds.

Adaption of the Charter in Practice

In the face of the four tectonic shifts in international relations discussed in the preceding section, the UN and its individual members have had to make some hard choices between letting the organization lapse into early obsolescence and promoting its rapid evolution and adaptation. Adaptation tends to be an option of constitutive instruments such as the U.S. and Canadian Constitutions. In this essay I argue that the UN Charter is a quasi-constitution capable of adaptation through the processes of its actual implementation. I seek to begin the researcher's task of measuring and mapping this adaptation in practice and examining its legal effects on the Charter regime. I hypothesize that institutional practice has affected the Charter rules applicable to the use of collective, regional, and individual state force. I hypothesize that a subtle evolution has occurred that has kept the Charter relevant to an interstate system in which values and interests have undergone momentous change.

Some of this evolution has undoubtedly been transformative. For example, although Article 27(3) provides that 'decisions of the Security Council ... shall be made by an affirmative vote of nine members including the concurring votes of the permanent members,' in practice an abstention by a permanent member is now invariably recognized as *not* constituting a veto. In some circumstances this has affected the ability of the Security Council to deploy force. It has also enabled the Big Powers – the council's permanent members – to disagree with decisions supported by the majority without blocking their implementation: a useful option often used by China.[1]

This essay examines the adaptation of the Charter in two situations involving the use of force:

1 In response to threats to a state's national security, where the threatened state uses force to resist indirect aggression or anticipated aggression.
2 In response to threats to people, where the UN or one or more of its member states deploy force to prevent a human catastrophe such as genocide or the disastrous collapse of civil society.

These two circumstances have become far more common than traditional interstate warfare. This has led to changes in the practices pertaining to the use of force by the United Nations and – with the active or passive consent of the UN system – by individual states, groups of states, and regional organizations.

Adaption of the UN's Authority to use of Force

The second half of the twentieth century saw few traditional acts of military aggression by one state against another. Still, the UN did have to deal with North Korea's invasion of South Korea in 1950, the Israeli, British, and French invasion of the Sinai in 1956, the Belgian invasion of the Congo in 1960, Iraq's invasion of Kuwait in 1990, and the Federal Republic of Yugoslavia's aggression in Bosnia in 1992.

The responses of the UN system to these instances have fallen into several categories: (1) where the Security Council has authorized the deployment of UN military forces under the Charter's Chapter VII; (2) where the Security Council has deployed peace-keeping forces authorized not under Chapter VII but rather under an *imagined* 'Chapter 6 1/2'; (3) where the Security Council has authorized a state, group of states or regional organization to deploy forces; (4) where the Security Council has made a decision without explicitly providing for its enforcement, but the decision has been enforced by states or regional organizations with the tacit acquiescence of the UN; and (5) where, the Security Council being blocked by the veto, the General Assembly has invoked its 'secondary' authority to 'recommend' military action by states under 'Chapter 6 1/2.'

In each of these categories the UN has organized, authorized, recommended, or tacitly acquiesced in the use of force in a manner not foreseen by the strict text of the Charter. In other words, the Charter has been adapted through consensual practice. The most striking instance is the evolution of what is widely known as Chapter 6 1/2, the 'Blue Helmet Peacekeeping Operation,' which became an important part of the system's response to conflict resolution in the context of the Cold War. Another is the 'Uniting for Peace' resolution, by recourse to which the General Assembly has expanded its role in authorizing the use of force in the face of Security Council paralysis.

Perhaps even more significant is the growing willingness of the Security Council to define, under Article 39, the range of circumstances that constitute a 'threat to the peace, breach of the peace, or act of aggression' and against which the systemic police power may be used. The Security Council's authorization of forceful measures against Rhodesia, South Africa, and the Haitian junta are just a few examples of this sort of adaptation in practice to treat gross violations of human rights and democracy as appropriate situations for collective measures.

A further example of adaptation pertains to the military forces available for UN deployment. Article 43 of the Charter envisaged that member states would 'undertake to make available to the Security Council on its call and in accordance with a special agreement' the armed forces needed to police the peace. However, no such agreements were forthcoming. Instead, institutional innovation has substituted a new idea – 'coalitions of the willing' – to fill the void. In practice, the council (sometimes along with the assembly) has authorized the Secretary-General to use military contingents volunteered *ad hoc* by their governments. The UN forces (UNPROFOR) deployed to Bosnian 'safe areas' under UN command are in this mode.[2] At other times the council has 'franchised' a state or states to deploy its forces on behalf of objectives defined by the council. An example is the authorization by the council of UNITAF, consisting of U.S. forces, to intervene in Somalia in 1992.[3]

Adaption of States and Regional Organizations to Use of Force

The preceding was an account of some of the ways the UN has deployed, or authorized the deployment of, force in order to prevent or mitigate a disaster using creative alternatives to Article 43, which may suffer lapse through desuetude. It is notable that these various pragmatic alternative modalities appear to have secured over time the acquiescence of the international system.

In the fifty-five years since the Charter's adoption, there have also been many times when individual members, alliances, and regional organizations have used force without the prior authorization of the Security Council.

Article 51 of the Charter retains states' 'inherent right of self-defence.' This reserved power has been exercised frequently, often in very doubtful situations but sometimes in ways that have been justified through acquiescence and practice.

In the first category are the instances of the aggressive use of force against South Korea, Hungary, the Dominican Republic, Czechoslovakia, Pakistan (Bangladesh), Uganda, Egypt, Lebanon, Iran, Grenada, Panama, and Kuwait. In each instance the use of force was justified by the state engaging in it, usually by reference to its 'right' of 'self-defence.' In almost every instance the claim to be acting in self-defence was hotly contested; in most but not all instances it was specifically rejected by the UN system.

In still other instances, states and regional organizations have resorted to force in situations of extreme necessity, to prevent a humanitarian disaster. In some cases the intervenors have not had the prior approval of the Security Council; either they applied and it was not forthcoming, or they did not apply because it might have been blocked by a veto. The actions of ECOWAS in Liberia and of NATO in Kosovo are two such instances. These 'regional' actions were sometimes justified on the grounds that a humanitarian disaster, although it was occurring within only one state, nevertheless required an international response because of its spillover effects, such as the generating of massive outflows of refugees.

Such recourse to a doctrine of 'extreme necessity' to justify actions by states – actions in conformity with UN objectives (e.g., the prevention of genocide) but in violation of the procedural requisites of prior Security Council approval – creates a conundrum. Should the Charter be interpreted creatively to accommodate departures from its text in cases of extreme necessity? Secretary-General Kofi Annan captured the essence of the matter when, in his address to the General Assembly on 20 September 1999, he asked 'in the context of Rwanda, if, in those dark days and hours leading up to the genocide, a coalition of States had been prepared to act in defence of the Tutsi population, but did not receive prompt Council authorization, should such a coalition have stood aside and allowed the horror to unfold?'[4]

The same sort of conundrum arises when a state claims to be engaging in 'anticipatory self-defence.' Israel's attack on Egypt in 1956 is an example. Neither Articles 2(4) nor Article 51 of the Charter, read literally, seem to authorize a state to use force before it has actually been attacked. But as U.S. Supreme Court Justice Arthur Goldberg has observed in reference to his country's constitution, one should infer that the Charter 'is not a suicide pact.'[5]

It cannot yet be determined to what extent these and other instances of the use of force have (or have not) affected the structure and political principles of the UN system. Obviously, not every breach of a rule creates a new rule. Nevertheless, legal rules do adapt in the face of their interpretation by courts, institutions, and governments.[6] To address this paradox would require a careful examination of the range of responses of the system to each instance of the 'off the Charter' use of force for what has been claimed to be valid and overriding humanitarian or security reasons.

There is abundant evidence that UN organs have not always insisted on a literal interpretation of the Charter's text. Debates and resolutions in UN organs (or sometimes the eloquent absence of debate) reveal a continuum of responses from *post hoc* endorsement (ECOMOG in Liberia), adoption (NATO in Kosovo), and silent approval (France's forceful removal of Emperor Bokassa, Tanzania's ouster of Idi Amin), through mild disapprobation (India's intervention in Bangladesh, Israel's 1976 incursion at Entebbe in Uganda), to outright condemnation (Russia's invasion of Hungary, the United States' invasion of Grenada, Iraq's invasion of Kuwait). A careful, multidimensional examination of how the system has responded to these various text-challenging instances of the use of force could reveal a calibrated range of tolerance depending on ascertainable and perhaps definable contextual variables. It might also demonstrate the evolution of some new principles governing the use of force.

The Role of Facts in Adapting Charter Norms

The conundrums to which I have made reference are not too difficult to resolve in the abstract. To take the example cited by Secretary-General Kofi Annan (above): if the Organization of African Unity had had ten thousand troops ready and able to save a million Tutsis in Rwanda, a one-country veto of Security Council authorization should not have prevented it from acting. A legal system can recover from a violation but not from a *reductio ad absurdum*.

But crises rarely make their appearance in such starkly clear configurations. The facts are often fuzzy, and when they are the conundrum becomes much deeper. What if the Tutsis are not really in danger, or only a few are at risk? What if, in an effort to save the Tutsis, more people are likely to be killed than are spared? What if the humanitarian rescue of the Tutsis is really a cover for some less high-minded intervention by other states?

A recent 'comprehensive review of the whole question of peacekeeping operations in all their aspects' authorized by the UN Secretary-General and chaired by Lakhdar Brahimi, the former foreign minister of Algeria, has recognized the overriding importance of reliable, current and impartial data in resolving, crisis by crisis, whether the Charter should be interpreted flexibly or strictly. The Brahimi panel of experts urged 'the Secretary-General's more frequent use of fact-finding missions to areas of tension' and stressed members 'obligations ... to give "every assistance to such activities of the United Nations."[7]

It is almost self-evident that the choice between implementing the letter of the law, and bending it, cannot sensibly be made without precise information specific to a particular set of circumstances. That the Charter is capable of flexibility has been established, precedent by precedent. Indeed, the right of the Secretary-General to engage in fact-finding *in situ* is itself a very attenuated reinterpretation of the Charter's Article 99. That provision, while it specifies no such thing, has been interpreted in many instances to authorize fact-finding missions even when undertaken at the sole discretion of the Secretary-General.[8]

It comes to this: the Charter is a quasi-constitution for the global system. No constitution should be allowed to become so dry that its branches tend to snap in the winds of extreme necessity. On the other hand, no constitution can flourish if its branches can be torn off by any malevolent passer-by. Flexibility in fundamental law needs to be supported by the inflexible probity of the factual and contextual evidence to which that law is applied.

NOTES

1 A good example is China's abstention on the resolution in effect ending the 'Kosovo war.' See UN Doc. S/RES/1244, 10 June 1999.
2 UN Doc. S/RES/836, 4 June 1993.
3 UN Doc. S/RES/794 3 December 1992.
4 UN GAOR, 54th Sess., 4th Plen. Mtg.,UN Doc. A/54/PV.420 (1999) at 2.
5 *Kennedy v. Mendoza-Martinez*, 372 U.S. 144 (1963) at 159–60
6 An oft-cited instance is the effect on customary law of the sea of the 'Truman Continental Shelf Proclamation,' 10 Fed. Reg. 12303 (1945). The International Court of Justice has acknowledged that this unilateral action was 'the starting point of the [development] of the positive law on the subject [of the continental shelf].' See *The Cases Concerning North Sea Continental Shelf (Federal Republic of Germany v. Denmark and v. Netherlands)*, [1969] I.C.J. Rep. 3 at 32–3.
7 UN Doc. A/55/305-S/2000/809, 21 August 2000, Annex III, Rec. 1(b) at 54.
8 See T.M. Franck and G. Nolte, 'The Good Offices Function of the UN Secretary-General,' in A. Roberts and B. Kingsbury, *United Nations, Divided World*, 2nd ed. (New York: Clarendon Press, 1993) at 143.

Chapter Six

The Civil Dimension of Strategy*

KAREN GUTTIERI

'This hinge of history on which we endeavor to maintain our balance has posed the clearest of questions: Is the normative model of national conduct and international behaviour to be militaristic?'[1]

A realist view of international relations accepts that self-interested state concerns for security may lead to foreign policy behaviour that violates national values such as liberty (as when a powerful democracy supports a friendly tyrant) and humanitarian values, such as life itself (as when a nation goes to war). At the close of the last century, an alternative and increasingly prominent framework for conduct emphasized humanitarian motivations for the use of force, as well as humane conduct by military forces. Leaders justified military interventions in Haiti and Kosovo as being in defence of civilians harmed by their regimes; this suggested a new framework for thinking about justice *of war*.[2] Meanwhile, prevention and mitigation of civilian harm during any type of operation has been an emphasis of some – but obviously not all – military forces *in war*.[3] These trends together in the last decade or so have meant that the powerful U.S. military has often been called into operation, but increasingly constrained during operations. U.S. military leaders, reflecting on increasing calls for them to participate in 'humanitarian interventions' and their obligations to civilians during operations, might well wonder: Is military conduct to be 'humanistic'?

One imagines that in a humanized global order there would be no need or place for the use of force. Until that goal is achieved, the process of humanizing the global order will involve accommodating the use of force – a state-centric Realpolitik domain – within a global humanist framework. Military sensitivity to civilian direction and civilian conceptions seems a basic requirement for progress in humanizing the global order. Thomas Franck, in the previous essay, proposed a framework for managing the policy problem of how to go about 'war' in humanitarian interventions.[4] My essay instead maps military adaptations to civilian concerns *within* war.

How do military commanders manage problems in the civilian realm? In the first section of this essay I introduce the concept of a *civil dimension* of strategy – that is, a rational basis for strategy to interest itself in the civil realm in the long term. As I demonstrate in the second section of this essay, traditional paradigms of political science are not well suited to the problems of military operations in civilian environments. I depict the strategic rationale for civil–military operations as deriving from a general conceptual relationship between policy and force. This relationship moves through time – that is, one finds that civilians are increasingly privileged in efforts to humanize the global order and that civilian concerns are privileged as the conception of war itself changes. The third section introduces considerations of change into the relationship between policy and force, and examples of change over time. The power and values of the United States make American leadership in the civil dimension especially salient. Finally, I discuss the institutional practices of American civil affairs designed to manage the relationship between realms both civil and military, of policy and force.

My examples are drawn primarily from the American experience. I am especially interested in the U.S. military because it has been employed explicitly to defend and even to impose democracy abroad. Civil–military operations, also known as civil affairs, have vexed U.S. military commanders throughout American history, most recently in peace-keeping and humanitarian missions, which are variously called 'operations other than war,' 'complex contingency operations,' and now 'stability operations.' The Americans have developed a fully articulated doctrine, derived from doctrine on military government, that now serves as a template for other nations and multilateral organizations. U.S. military doctrine on civil affairs is the best-articulated embodiment of the U.S. military response to the civil dimension. I argue that the civil dimension of strategy has been relevant to U.S. military planners since long before the emergence of a discourse on humanitarian intervention; it is also being transformed alongside conceptions of sovereignty and militarism itself.

Strategy and Civilians

The art of strategy is generally conceived as the art of selecting the best course of action to realize goals. Strategy also implies interaction – that one attempts to choose the best course of action in light of the moves or potential moves of others.[5]

The main concern of traditional military strategy is the threat or application of military force to counter the moves or potential moves of an opposing army. An opposing army is the focus, the centre of gravity, of traditional military strategy.[6] That said, one should understand also that *civilians are often a factor in war*. Commanders have historically relied on local civilians to supply goods, labour, and information. Military procedures are established to hold civilian populations in place, and to remove civilians from the path of military operations when necessary. Once military commanders have achieved control of foreign territory, they become increasingly concerned with issues arising in the civilian rather than the military realm.

Post-conflict military operations in particular tend to involve military forces in the realm of civilian populations and civil institutions of governance. Civilian concerns arise after victory in an interstate war and during the implementation of negotiated peace agreements to settle internal war. War creates sufferings that must be addressed: hunger, illness, injury, and dislocation. The civilian population must be persuaded to stop supporting political–military factions that would return to war. Many soldiers are made civilians in the wake of a peace agreement or defeat as they are disarmed, demobilized, and reintegrated into civilian society. Many civilians require food, medical care, and shelter in the aftermath of a conflict. Displaced populations need attention before they destabilize the fragile new governance regime or spill over into neighbouring states, thus creating a regional crisis. Civilians in a post-conflict environment often lack basic services: a police force, a functioning legal system, schools, and basic necessities such as water and sanitation.

Post-conflict obligations are so onerous that satisfying them is often beyond the ability, the mandate, or the will of the military. In the period before the foreign army withdraws, military commanders rely on civilians representing various agencies – governmental, non-governmental and intergovernmental – to carry out many of the tasks necessary for rebuilding and governing war-torn societies. In postconflict operations the centre of gravity becomes civilian rather than military.

We can think of civilian-centred concerns, such as those which military commanders encounter after conflict, as part of a *civil dimension* of strategy. The civil dimension of strategy can factor into military calculus in at least three ways:

1 Military calculations must consider civilians present in the operational environment.
2 A military force relies on its own country's civilian population to support its operations. Commanders must consider how activities abroad will be perceived at home.
3 Civilian command authorities in liberal democracies create policy for military implementers.

The types of civilians in the operational environment are many. However, two of the three civilian considerations are home-grown. Military forces in liberal democracies need the support of their own civilian populations and direction from political leaders. Together, civilian leaders and publics conceive of peace and security; in other words, the civil realm sets the criteria for victory. In this respect, theories of international relations are of minimal use for policy guidance.

Theory and Policy

The disciplinary paradigms of political science are suited to looking at relations between states or within states, but rarely the two together. The zone between war and peace is also a grey area: some specialists are concerned about the use of force; and others are more interested in economic development or foreign policy over time; but few consider these facets jointly and carefully.[7] In consequence, policy movements toward the use of force are better understood than military movements *back* toward the mode of policy.

International relations scholars tend to concern themselves with interstate relations, not domestic governance. State-centric theories of international relations seem to be of little utility within the ambiguous zone where foreign military forces control territory.[8] When the use of force brings about foreign military control of territory, issues of domestic governance emerge. The suggestion that the United States create police-like expeditionary military forces for operations other than war provides an example.[9] This idea evokes the concept of policing, which belongs to the domestic realm, and transposes it to an international context.

Of the existing theoretical frameworks in international relations, liberal international theory seems promising because it attempts to bridge the divide between domestic and foreign policy. Unfortunately, as I will show, this approach offers a glib rationale for U.S. military interventions but little direction for policy implementers.

At the heart of liberal theory are values, 'a search for principles of political justice that will command rational assent among persons with different conceptions of the good life and different views of the world.'[10] According to liberal theory, civil society and institutions will rein in the proclivity to use force. One variant of the liberal school emphasizes the potential for international organizations to fill a vacuum of authority at the international level.[11] Another variant proposes a 'democratic peace' that relies on the character of states themselves, and claims that liberal states are more stable and peaceful.[12] An article published by Francis Fukuyama in 1989 fits this second stream.[13]

Fukuyama's article seemed prescient about the end of the Cold War, but it also had political consequences. It seemed to legitimize the American model of governance and the drive to export democracy.[14] American makers of foreign policy in the 1990s evidently shared the optimism inherent in liberal theory. The Clinton administration's strategic manifesto, *A National Security Strategy of Engagement and Enlargement* (1994–5), presented a shift in emphasis away from countering the communist threat toward promoting democracy and economic opportunity.[15] The document echoes the democratic peace thesis:

> While democracy will not soon take hold everywhere, we know that the larger the pool of democracies, the better off we, and the entire community of nations, will be. Democracies create free markets that offer economic opportunity, make for more reliable trading partners, and are far less likely to wage war on one another.[16]

The democratic peace thesis rehashes a familiar ideological argument in American foreign policy. Americans are predisposed to be sympathetic with a framework in which, as Laurence Whitehead describes it, 'all good things' go together, including liberalization abroad and American influence and security.[17] Certainly the Americans, in their ideological battle with communism during the Cold War, saw a liberal peace as their desired outcome. To be more precise, the United States (especially in Latin America) attempted to install and/or promote liberal democratic regimes and advocated civilian control over the military in allied states. It often came up short or compromised in this effort; even so, it was fundamental to American strategy, which was to stabilize foreign governments vulnerable to communist insurgents.

A familiar analogy employed in the last decade or so – and one evoked recently by President George W. Bush in a speech on American action in Afghanistan – is the successful post–Second World War reconstruction of Germany and Japan.[18] It seems a contradiction in terms to impose democracy, yet the United States apparently did so successfully in Europe and Japan after the Second World War. Since then, U.S. military interventions have often been presented as actions that will promote democracy or liberalization. After intervention, Americans encourage host-country nationals to organize free and fair elections, subordinate military to civilian institutions, and adopt practices consistent with principles of human rights.[19] U.S. military operations have been given monikers such as 'Restore Democracy' and 'Promote Liberty.'[20] The labels attached suggest these troops are stewards of a liberal democratic project rather than an occupation army. These labels also generate expectations, both at home and abroad, that reality will follow American rhetoric.

In light of American rhetoric, it is not unreasonable to expect that the intervention recipients will in some measure be better off as a result of the intervention. Unfortunately, the record of the United States in this respect is mixed. Mark

Peceny has concluded that the American invasion of Panama in 1989 was a successful liberalization; in contrast, Frederick Kempe has lamented that in the wake of that invasion, the Americans failed in their obligations as 'the invader – to rebuild what it has torn down and to help establish a real democracy.'[21] Even the degree to which the United States can take credit for German and Japanese transformations has been subject to dispute. It was obviously necessary to defeat the regimes in place during the Second World War so that transformation could occur. That said, Marshall Plan reconstruction was facilitated by increased American expenditures as the Cold War built up and by economic progress stemming from the Treaty of Rome.

One critique suggests that American foreign policy's emphasis on liberalization is little more than rhetoric. According to this view, the Americans failed to try.[22] Alternatively, if one believes the Americans are sincere, perhaps they have tried and failed. Mark Peceny's investigation of American interventions, proliberalization policies, and democracies found that in most interventions, the United States has not pursued proliberalization policies. Moreover, military practices tend to support local military forces in a manner that ultimately works against proliberalization efforts.[23] By Peceny's count, American proliberalization policies deserve more credit for successful democracy promotion abroad than U.S. military intervention per se.

As an early analyst of military occupation observed in 1903, 'a military government is by no means a short cut to the millennium.'[24] Although opportunities for deeper, necessary institutional change can be created by inserting a foreign military force, foreign military presence also has its costs.[25] Given questions about the sincerity or efficacy of post-conflict liberalization, it is remarkable that the activities of U.S. forces in the reconstruction phase following military intervention have been given so little attention. The international relations literature, when it concerns itself with the realm of domestic politics, suggests that certain forms of government are more prone to peace and better suited to generate prosperity. However, the role of military force in the creation of systems of peace and prosperity is underspecified. So we must examine the dimensions of conflict in each case, and identify the variables affecting military operations.

Reciprocity of Policy and Force

The decision to use military force seems to mark a transition in mode – that is, a mode of policy gives way to a mode of force. Policy implies a general direction for state action. In war the state takes up arms and military rather than civilian instruments are the locus of movement.[26] Post-conflict military operations are concerned with a *return* transition whereby the mode of force gives way to a

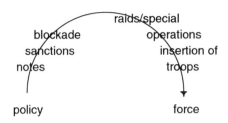

Figure 6.1   A policy–force continuum

mode of policy. The transition from force to policy can be understood in this light as the natural reciprocal of the transition from policy to force. In this respect, military operations must fit foreign policy goals.

The Prussian strategist Carl von Clausewitz defined war as an inherently political act. This enables us to understand this reciprocal relationship between policy and force. When a nation uses military force – whether in war or in operations other than war – its leaders do so to promote the national interest. War is thus the continuation of politics by other means: 'We see, therefore, that war is not merely an act of policy,' wrote Clausewitz, 'but a true political instrument, a continuation of political intercourse, carried on with other means.'[27] This definition is sometimes evoked to remind leaders that force is not an end in itself.

The formulaic conceptualization of war and politics generates many corresponding conceptual relations, implying also, for example, a clear relation between military and civil realms, and between force and policy instruments. The relationship between policy and force is more commonly conceived as a continuum from diplomacy (or policy) to war (or force) (see Figure 6.1). The progression from a mode of policy to a mode of force begins with less coercive expressions of foreign policy such as the transmission of a diplomatic note. It escalates with suspension of trade or aid; general sanctions may be organized. It goes further when the use of force is threatened or employed. Its ultimate form is interstate war that engulfs entire societies mobilized for its ends. It is also conceivable that a foreign power might attempt to push backward along the continuum, using instruments short of war to change conditions so that the use of force is not required to achieve policy goals.[28] Figure 6.1 depicts a progression from policy to force from the perspective of an intervening state.

Military force is typically associated with territory; success in war is defined as the taking or restoring of territory. However, when a nation's armed forces successfully take territory, they are not simply grabbing real estate; in one way or another, they are *holding* it. Even amid a political settlement such as a negotiated truce or peace agreement, troops are present in foreign theatres until they are

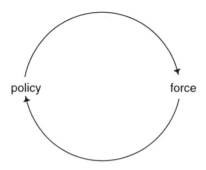

Figure 6.2   Policy–force reciprocity loop

withdrawn. The effective control of territory by these military forces constitutes a form of rule, however benign or temporary. Unless the territory is uninhabited or the force applied was so destructive as to create a wasteland, local populations remain a factor in both the taking and holding of territory.

Foreign troops that control territory assume a quasi-political role with regard to the civilian population. At this time, under the international law of occupation as expressed in The Hague and Geneva Conventions, military personnel are obligated to protect civilians. Unless military forces seek to annex or indefinitely administer this territory, their next concern is for an exit strategy. Intervening military forces that had perhaps sought to displace a foreign regime may now switch tasks to ensure the safety of a new one. The transition to local self-rule involves a transition from a mode of destruction to one of restoration. This return transition transforms the policy-to-force continuum depicted earlier. As shown in Figure 6.2, the return transition implies a circular relationship in the Clausewitzian formulation of war as a continuation of policy by other means – a circular relationship between policy and force.[29] This transition is not only one of rule; it is also a transition from war back to other modes of politics.

As the loop is completed, policy instruments are changed in such a way that the job of the military is done and local nationals again govern the site. Two transitions are thus involved in a successful military intervention:

1 The insertion of troops in foreign territory marks a transition from policy to force.
2 Post-conflict military operations mark a transition from force to policy.

In the first transition the initiator of armed intervention shifts from a non-military foreign policy mode to a war-fighting mode. The target of armed inter-

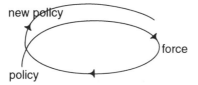

Figure 6.3   Helix configuration of policy and force

vention shifts from a mode of self-rule to a mode of subordination to foreign control.

In the second transition the intervening power shifts from a war-fighting mode to a stabilization mode that involves troop exit and the normalization of diplomatic relations. Construction or reconstruction of a functioning society becomes a concern for military leaders seeking to consolidate military operations and depart. The 'host nation' that was the target of armed intervention must shift from a mode of subordination to foreign control to one in which self-rule has been restored. The intervening force hopes to establish a friendly regime that can defend itself, but the new regime may have to rely for some time on the intervening military forces to create public order and provide services.

However, the new mode of policy is not the same as the one that preceded military intervention. Figure 6.3, illustrates the process.

The helix configuration illustrates the ultimate predominance of policy and the complex challenges facing military commanders who must implement policies. As an intervention progresses, military forces shape and also must adapt to new conditions in the policy environment. To succeed, military intervention to create or support a friendly regime requires non-military processes. Intervening troops seek to win local or host-country civilian cooperation, the point being to establish order and then depart as soon as possible. In sum, the cyclical nature of war and peace sets the context for a civil dimension to military operations.

Transformations

Because it is a social construct and because societies change over time, the civil dimension of strategy is not static. Differentiations between the terms 'civil' or 'political' and 'military' have varied over time. Furthermore, these constructs carry out designated roles in conflict, which is also a site of transformation over time. In this section I briefly review these transformations as well as the implications for military forces in light of them.

The interface between political and military considerations can evolve over many years. Two very basic examples are constructs that citizens in liberal democracies take for granted today but are historical adaptations: the state monopoly on the legitimate use of force, and the differences between domestic police on the one hand, and armies oriented against external attack on the other.[30] The interface between policy and force can also change quickly. Quick adjustments in American civil–military relations followed the Goldwater-Nichols Act in 1986, which changed the path of military advice to political leaders and created incentives for developing joint institutions from across the military services. Not to be left out are technological developments, as these can affect civil–military relations. Recent advances in information, precision strike, and sensing technologies have enabled heretofore-impossible movements in time and space; some have called these a modern revolution in military affairs (RMA). Innovative weapons and communications systems are altering threat environments (and the importance of populations in war) and very soon may alter the context in which political and military considerations meet.

The ultimate context in which political and military considerations meet is war, and this context is also a site of transformation. The end of the Cold War coincided with declarations of a 'transformation in war' in the strategic studies literature; however, the notion of transformation is more than geopolitical. Scholars compare the pattern of warfare in this century to patterns of previous centuries to unearth differences in conflict purposes, civilian roles in conflict, and institutional manifestations of war. 'Wars of conscience' are of particular interest.[31] The transformation in war is perhaps a 'paradigm shift' – in other words, it is perhaps inherently multidimensional. This transformation includes societal and technological developments that affect definitions of security, locations of threat, and methods of fighting war.[32] Remarkably, the notion that war is changing predates the wave of intrusive UN peace operations in the 1990s and even the end of the Cold War. William Cohen told the U.S. Senate in 1986 that low-intensity conflict as 'a new form of warfare has emerged in recent years, a form of warfare we have not properly understood, and that we have not effectively deterred.'[33]

Transformation writers do not necessarily agree on the direction of the transformation. One hears alternatively of the obsolescence of total war and the obsolescence of the Cold War conception of conflict short of war.[34] At the same time, some academic writers warn of a 'coming anarchy,'[35] whereas others assert an 'emerging right to democratic governance'[36] and a controversial obligation to 'save failed states.'[37]

What is this transformation in war? Many contrast today's wars with the type of war that concerned Clausewitz. The era of Clausewitz was one of massive engagements in total war that predate the technological realities of the modern battlefield.[38] Martin van Creveld argues in *The Transformation of War* that the Clausewitzian differentiation between governments, armies, and peoples is an intellectual relic of a bygone era.[39] Kalevi J. Holsti similarly observes that the Clausewitzian conception of interstate war may fit our mental maps because it was pervasive between 1648 and 1945. However, 'the Clausewitzian image of war, as well as its theoretical accoutrements, has become increasingly divorced from the characteristics and sources of most armed conflicts since 1945.'[40] Conventional conflicts continue to differentiate between military and civilian realms, combatant and non-combatant elements, and the conditions of peace and war. Unconventional conflicts cause havoc with these distinctions. Unconventional conflicts shift the centre of gravity, as for the U.S. forces in Vietnam, 'to the social-political milieu of the opponent's system – a concept evolving out of Sun Tzu.'[41]

However, these critics fail to differentiate the Clausewitzian era from Clausewitzian thought. The latter has acquired meaning over time beyond its historical context. Clausewitz, in advising Prussian leaders on strategy against Napoleon, emphasized the relationship between political and military realms. Warfare was identified as the business of government, as opposed to that of the church, perhaps, or the business of the military alone. The seminal contribution of *On War* is that it defined war as the continuation of policy by other means. That formulation is foundational in two important ways. First, it illustrates the relationship between means and ends in strategy. This relationship was and is essential, a 'permanent injunction.'[42] Second, it serves as a core principle in structuring civil–military relations. The subordination of armed forces to civil authority has acquired greater importance since the time of Clausewitz and constitutes a defining feature of modern liberal democracy. Liberal democracies have no interest in purposeless violence and by definition will not surrender civilian control of their militaries.

Although modern war is described as 'de-institutionalized,'[43] it should be noted that by definition, institutions are highly contested in civil conflicts and that institution building is being emphasized in the aftermath of the conflicts in Bosnia, Kosovo, Cambodia, and elsewhere. Institutions express the nature of community and the organization of social forces; in this sense, wars of conscience or any interventions to change domestic order are trinitarian. In any transition of rule, one authority must replace another or a vacuum thereof.

How should military commanders respond to warfare in which the centre of gravity is civil rather than military? President John F. Kennedy in the early 1960s recognized that a wide range of skills were required for effective execution of 'the other war' in Vietnam:

Pure military skill is not enough. A full spectrum of military, para-military and civil action must be blended to produce success ... To win this struggle, our officers and men must understand and combine the political, economic and civil actions with skilled military efforts in the execution of this mission.[44]

Unfortunately, due in large measure to the perceived failure of the U.S. military in Vietnam in the 1960s and 1970s, U.S. military commanders today are working within an institutional legacy of resistance rather than adaptation to unconventional conflict. The conflict in Vietnam blurred the distinction between combatants and civilians, and the loss of American public support for military operations was painful. As part of a civil–military rapprochement in the United States, the Weinberger Doctrine sought to limit engagements to those with an identified purpose and enemy, public support, sufficient commitment of forces for timely achievement of ends, and likelihood of success.[45] Since Vietnam, some American military thinkers have embraced the idea of military operations other than war; however, the institutional culture favours an all-or-nothing approach to war. That cultural disposition has played an important role in American civil–military debates over peace operations.

According to Carl von Clausewitz: 'It follows that a transformation in the art of war resulted from a transformation in politics.'[46] This section has discussed the historical adjustment to changes in the character of conflict. The adaptation of military institutions to unconventional warfare is part of a broader institutional transformation. Military adaptation can be shaped by developments in civil institutional structures; and can also shape those structures. The construction of a usable peace involves an interface of civil and military considerations. This interface – the civil dimension of strategy – is historically situated. In the next section I look specifically at the institutional expression of the civil dimension in U.S. military terms.

U.S. Civil Affairs

American peace operations as they are formulated today have their roots in U.S. military occupations since the nation was founded, including the Union's occupation of the South during Reconstruction Era following the American Civil War and the grand projects to seal the victory won in the Second World War. It was not very long ago, Martin and Joan Kyre remind us, that peace treaties were replaced by military occupation at the conclusion of hostilities. In 1968 they observed that 'The present generation seems to be observing the replacement of major wars by unconventional limited conflicts within which military civil affairs plays a leading role. It may occur that a modernized hybrid version of military occupation will become a standard vehicle of foreign policy.'[47] The use of military occupation in some form as a 'vehicle for foreign policy' is a use of coercive authority to establish a friendlier and longer-lasting regime in the country that has been defeated.

Two tiers of authority relations merit attention. First, foreign military forces in a successful intervention or a victorious war have established one type of authority with respect to the population. Second, as those troops depart a new or reformed state must establish a legitimate authority with respect to the society. Transitional authority plays a significant role in post-conflict transitions, yet this is difficult to conceptualize under a systemic, state-centric perspective on strategy. External actors can do much to help, but war-torn societies must also be rebuilt from within. U.S. military commanders have an interest in creating conditions for, and managing effectively, the transition to legitimate local authority.

The civil dimension of strategy has been prominent in American civil–military operations in places like Somalia, Rwanda, Haiti, Bosnia, Kosovo, and Afghanistan. The U.S. Department of Defense (DOD) defines civil–military operations as follows:

> The activities of a commander that establish, maintain, influence, or exploit relations between military forces, governmental and nongovernmental civilian organizations and authorities, and the civilian populace in a friendly, neutral, or hostile operational area in order to facilitate military operations to consolidate and achieve U.S. operational objectives.[48]

Since the office was created in the late 1980s, the Assistant Secretary of Defense (Special Operations and Low-Intensity Conflict) has been the principal civilian advisor on American civil affairs policy and planning. The Office of the Assistant Secretary of Defense (OASD) for Special Operations and Low-Intensity Conflict (SO/LIC) reports to the Secretary of Defense and the Under Secretary of Defense for Policy.[49] The Chairman of the Joint Chiefs of Staff provides civil affairs guidance to commanders of geographic Unified Combatant Commands, as well as to the President, the National Security Council, and the Secretary of Defense.

Within the U.S. military, civil affairs is a functional area within the active army and a branch in the U.S. Army Reserve.[50] The U.S. Army has approximately two hundred active component civil affairs soldiers and 5,500 more in the reserve component; another 250 serve in U.S. Marine Corps Civil Affairs Groups.[51] Army civil affairs are designated special operations forces (SOF). The Commander, U.S. Special Operations Command (CDR USSOCOM), is responsible for joint (more than one military service) civil affairs strategy, doctrine, and tactics. In conflict situations, the U.S. military switches to operational command channels. CDR USSOCOM retains combatant command (or command authority) over U.S. Army civil affairs forces, even when forces are under operational control of a theatre commander.[52]

As the name implies, the civil affairs practices of the U.S. military have to do with a civil–military interface in the field. Civil affairs occur in a context of national policy; as such, they evoke other elements of the civil dimension of strategy, including the integration of political and military objectives of operations, military legitimacy at home and abroad, and civil–military relations broadly conceived. Civil affairs or civil–military operations play an important role when the centre of gravity of armed conflict rests in the civil rather than purely military dimension.[53] Civil–military operations are different from war because 'their ultimate objective is not to defeat an enemy with overwhelming force, but to achieve political objectives through public support both at home and in the area of operations.'[54]

U.S. military doctrine confronting the civil dimension is an evolving framework, if not a new one. In the wake of the post–Second World War experience, Americans began to consider seriously a role for the military in shaping the societies in which it was involved through occupation or military intervention.[55] Civil affairs, as a doctrinal referent for U.S. armed forces civil–military operations, developed out of postwar doctrine on military government.

American civil affairs doctrine is a body of teaching about practical aspects of the civil–military interface. Operational requirements of civil affairs may involve considerable authority, exercising executive, legislative, and judicial control, or a lesser degree of authority, involving 'only a relationship between the military forces and the civil population, government and institutions of the area.'[56] Some examples of possible functional areas of activity under the rubric of civil affairs include the following, culled from various U.S. military publications:

- Control of movement of people, for example, by establishing camps for displaced persons and prisoners of war and by issuing identification cards.
- Coordination of public finance by means such as controlling property, making development loans, collecting taxes, controlling currency, controlling prices, rationing, and licensing.
- Supervision of civilian activities, including rallies, demonstrations, and political meetings.
- Determination of labour issues such as the setting of wages and the employment of civilians by the military force.
- Determination of matters relevant to public education, including closing or reopening schools, supervising curricula, and selecting instructors.
- Provision of public security functions, such as by establishing police forces.
- Control of legal institutions, such as courts and prisons.
- Protection of cultural assets, such as, monuments, archives, and works of art.
- Operation of public communications, transportation, and public works, including electricity, water, and sewage treatment plants.
- Provision of public welfare, including that necessary to meet the nutritional and medical needs of the population.[57]

Although all U.S. military services confront the civil dimension, the U.S. Army is the service primarily responsible for civil affairs. In contrast to the Navy and the Air Force, the Army 'moves in an environment that is peopled, and the enemy is immediate, individual, and personal.'[58] The Army is 'the force that protects and controls populations, restores order and facilitates the transition from hostilities to peace.'[59] Army leaders have never welcomed the civil affairs function, instead viewing these operations as necessary to realize victory. 'The Army is not a welfare organization,' wrote a leader of the postwar Allied Military Government in 1943, but then again, 'lack of a condition of social stability in an occupied area would be prejudicial to the success of the military effort.'[60]

Civil affairs in post-conflict environments attempts to complete the Clausewitzian loop. The use of force is an extension of policy; civil affairs and reconstruction bring policy back in. Soldiers may temporarily become governors as part of a deeper transition. This focus situates analysis at an interesting juncture of policy and force. The elements co-mingle in the 1993 U.S. Army Field Manual, which states that 'CA missions are dynamic because they are directly affected by politico-military considerations. A change of national security policy or strategy may alter the nature of a CA mission.'[61]

It is intuitively obvious that the mode of force *after* war should differ from the mode of force *during* war. This proposition applies not only to the 'classical' interstate wars as they were fought between major powers, but also to military interventions, including those labelled peace operations. It remains to be articulated how the mode of force may shift, and under what conditions. For example, environment and intentions are two likely variables affecting the use of force in post-conflict scenarios.

Presumably, characteristics of the *environment* shape the conduct of foreign forces operating in it. The extent of infrastructure damage sustained during conflict, the intensity of the conflict, and the related issue of relations between the host country and the United States in part determine the challenges for U.S. civil affairs. Pre-existing characteristics of the nation's social order also condition the environment. Environmental factors include the following: whether the nation had been hostile or friendly to the intervening power; the physical damage created through the insertion of external military forces; the nation's economic, social, and political structure; and the presence of acceptable and effective leadership within the target country (a defeated state is more likely to possess this attribute than a failed state).[62]

The political *intentions* for which the armed forces are employed presumably govern their conduct.[63] These intentions are set at the highest levels. At one extreme is the intention to conquer, in which case armed forces seek to annex territory. Military operations aim to integrate conquered peoples. At the other extreme is the intention to observe a ceasefire or peace agreement, in which case lightly armed forces seek to remain impartial.[64] In between these extremes are various major interstate wars in the past century. The victors in these wars wished not to permanently govern defeated states, but rather to fashion particular forms of states out of defeated territories. Typically, unilateral interventions are not accompanied by a formal declaration of war or concluded by a peace agreement. But as in the aftermath of interstate war, the actions of intervening troops must fit with the post-conflict objectives of their political masters.

What role do civil affairs efforts play in humanizing the global order? The very fact that such institutional structures exist makes for optimism. But as discussed earlier, one ought to be cautious about any notion of military force as an agent of progress, and the record of the U.S. military as a tool of liberalization is a mixed one. Besides the obvious destruction that one associates with the use of military force, there are more subtle dangers in relying on military policy instruments. The U.S. military during interventions abroad has tended to emphasize foreign internal defence – that is, working to strengthen indigenous military forces. These strengthened local military forces have in the past been countervailing forces to liberalization. If the easy answer seems to be to forgo the use of military force, that is an illusion. Time and again the U.S. military has sought to minimize its involvement when it is greatly needed. The overriding need for security prompts civilian partners in peace processes – including aid workers and local governments working to mend war-torn societies – to seek U.S. military commitment to post-conflict reconstruction. So the final determinant of the military as a humanizing force is the will of civilian policymakers to deploy it, and to conduct appropriate oversight of military activities.

Conclusion

This essay has developed the general idea of a civil dimension of strategy and focused on civil affairs or civil–military operations in that context. These are military operations that translate policy direction into military implementation and push through post–conflict environments toward a returned mode of policy. From the perspective of civil–military relations, civil affairs seem to be two things at once: civil–military in an institutional sense, and civil–military in an operational sense. This relationship moves through time. First, civil–military issues rise and fall within operations; second, the context of these processes shifts over time with the form of conflict.

Conflict is increasingly being expressed in forms other than interstate war with clear differentiation between combatants and civilians. Correspondingly, militarism among the American civilian public is correspondingly not the same as militarism during the major wars of this century. Prevailing political norms as well as evolving military doctrine will affect the character of post-conflict civil–military operations. The intentions of political actors directing military action and the environment in which the military implements policy will affect the prospects for developing a liberal democratic postconflict order.

The reciprocal relationship between policy and force illustrated in this chapter directs our attention to the need, before entering a conflict, to consider issues that have to do with constructing a postconflict order. Civil–military relationships during postconflict transitions acquire special importance but are not especially well understood. for the greater humanization of the global order, paying attention to the civil dimension of strategy is imperative.

NOTES

* This essay is adapted from my doctoral dissertation, Toward a Usable Peace: United States Civil Affairs in Post-Conflict Environments, 1999 University of British Columbia. I am pleased to contribute this chapter to a volume in honour of Ivan Head, who provided me inspiration to seek out and engage the ideas presented here. The views expressed here are my own and do not necessarily represent the views of the Naval Postgraduate School, the U.S. Department of Defense, or the U.S. Government.

1 Ivan L. Head, *On a Hinge of History* (Toronto: University of Toronto Press, 1991), p. 214.
2 This is the focus of the previous chapter by Thomas Franck.
3 There is asymmetry in adherence to the rules of warfare. Professional peace-keeping soldiers who witness the consequences of ethnic violence might wonder whether the rules of war apply only to them. After September 2001 the United States began to reconsider the rules.
4 Franck proposes employing the UN Charter as a quasi-constitutional construct for the use of force, one that adapts 'through the processes of its actual implementation.' Franck calls on scholars to 'measure' and 'map' adaptations. As I see it, the conduct of military forces during such interventions is a vital component of implementation. Franck, p. 93.
5 T. Schelling, *Strategy of Conflict* (Cambridge: Harvard University Press, 1960, 1980) at 1. Schelling's is a game-theoretic rather than a narrow military definition. He distinguishes games of strategy from both games of chance, in which decisions are of little consequence, and games of skill, played against oneself.
6 The metaphor of the center of gravity is generally associated with Carl von Clausewitz. Colonel Robert B. Killebrew wrote that Vietnam taught the military the following:

'The strategic "center of gravity" of any future conflict, for both the United States and its enemies, is American public opinion.' Col. R.B. Killebrew, 'Force Projection in Short Wars,' (March 1991) Military Review at 30 [emphasis in original]. Max G. Manwaring quotes from Sun Tzu in his analysis of limited war: 'Security is the insurgent center of gravity.' M.G. Manwaring, 'Limited War and Conflict Control,' in S.J. Cimbala and K.A. Dunn, eds., *Conflict Termination and Military Strategy: Coercion, Persuasion, and War* (Boulder and London: Westview Press, 1987) 59 at 64.

7 The literature on post-conflict military operations is now growing. Two of the first to deal with the problem of post-conflict transitions after conflict settlement were M.W. Doyle, *UN Peacekeeping in Cambodia: UNTAC's Civil Mandate* (New York: International Peace Academy, 1995) and K. Kumar, ed., *Postconflict Elections, Democratization, and International Assistance* (New York: International Peace Academy, 1998). Some of the first to address the issues that arise from military operations in civilian environments have been writers with U.S. military connections, such as J.T. Fishel, *Liberation, Occupation, and Rescue: War Termination and Desert Storm* (Carlisle Barracks, PA: Strategic Studies Institute, 1992) and *The Fog of Peace: Planning and Executing the Restoration of Panama* (Carlisle Barracks, PA: Strategic Studies Institute, 1992), and L.A. Yates, *Power Pack: US Intervention in the Dominican Republic, 1965–66* (Fort Leavenworth, KA: Combat Studies Institute, 1988). See also R.H. Shultz Jr, 'The Post-Conflict Use of Military Forces: Lessons from Panama, 1989–91' (June 1993) 16 *Journal of Strategic Studies* 2 at 145. Also see by the same author *In the Aftermath of War: U.S. Support for Reconstruction and Nation-building in Panama following Just Cause* (Maxwell Air Force Base, AL: Air University Press, 1993). Although Paul Bracken cites a large body of research on a related issue, war termination, the methodology is largely that of economic bargaining and the context nuclear war. Anthony Lake edited a volume on reconstruction, *After the Wars*, that does not examine the particular role of American military forces. A volume by Yossi Shain and Juan J. Linz on interim governments and the transition to democracy picks up on the theme of reconstruction without explicitly examining U.S. forces. Eva Loser's edited volume, *Conflict Resolution and Democratization in Panama*, hits closer to the mark. See Y. Shain and J.J. Linz, *Between States: Interim Governments and Democratic Transitions* (Cambridge: Cambridge University Press, 1995). Also see A. Lake, *After the Wars: Reconstruction in Afghanistan, Indochina, Central America, Southern Africa, and the Horn of Africa* (New Brunswick, NJ: Transaction Publishers, 1990), and E. Loser, ed., *Conflict Resolution and Democratization in Panama* (Washington, D.C.: Center for Strategic and International Studies, 1992).

8 According to the tradition of American diplomatic thought, the foreign and domestic spheres are distinct. The international sphere is an amoral realm characterized by structural anarchy. There is not yet an international equivalent to the domestic state with a monopoly on the legitimate use of force, governed by rule of law and constitu-

tionalism, containing hierarchically structured authority relations. The domestic
sphere, in contrast, is hierarchical and presumably harmonious. Public policy scholars
may dispute that presumption. Domestic theories of public policy seek to explain policy outcomes with respect to social conflict produced by self-interested policy actors or
group conflict.

9 LTC G. Demarest, 'The Strategic Implications of Operational Law,' U.S. Army, Foreign Military Studies Office, Fort Leavenworth, KA. (April 1995), http://
leav.mil.army.mil/fmso.

10 John Gray in the preface to his volume on liberalism characterizes the perspective as
individualistic, egalitarian, universalist, and meliorist. That is, liberal theory tends to
emphasize the rights of individuals, viewed as equals, irrespective of culture or time,
and perhaps most significantly the possibility of progress for social and political institutions. See J. Gray, *Liberalism* (Minneapolis: University of Minnesota Press, 1986) at
91.

11 This approach effectively extends the domestic analogy – or the democratic procedures
for settling disputes within democratic states – to the international realm. See D.
Held, *Democracy and the Global Order: From the Modern State to Cosmopolitan Governance* (Cambridge: Polity Press, 1995). Idealism of an earlier era resonates in David
Held's recent advocacy of an international governance system based on a model of cosmopolitan democracy.

12 Michael Doyle observes that liberal states create a 'separate peace.' Making reference to
Kant's depiction in an essay on 'Perpetual Peace,' written in 1795, the liberal thesis of
democratic peace holds that war is not thinkable between democratic states. See M.
Doyle, 'Kant, Liberal Legacies, and Foreign Affairs, Part 1' (Summer 1983) 12 *Philosophy and Public Affairs*, 3 and 'Kant, Liberal Legacies, and Foreign Affairs, Part 2' (Fall
1983) 12 *Philosophy and Public Affairs* 4; also see B. Russett, *Grasping the Democratic
Peace: Principles for a Post-Cold War World* (Princeton: Princeton University Press,
1993).

13 F. Fukuyama, 'The End of History?' (Summer 1989) 16 *The National Interest* at 3.

14 Timothy Dunne notes the political consequences of Fukuyama's thesis, in particular
the rationale provided therein for humanitarian intervention and the promotion of
democracy by force. See T. Dunne, 'Liberalism,' in J. Baylis and S. Smith, eds., *The
Globalization of World Politics* (Oxford: Oxford University Press, 1997) 147 at 155.

15 This characterization is made in Commission on Roles and Missions, *Directions for
Defense*, pp. 1–7. The authors do not discuss the promotion of democracy and wealth
as part of the former Cold War strategy. This document's emphasis on free market capitalism is a familiar liberal theme, dating back to the ideological struggle between liberal capitalism and communism. Indeed, early liberals hoped that industry would
replace militarism as society progressed. H. Spencer, *Principles of Sociology*, Vol. 2 (New
York: Appleton, 1898) at 568. See the discussion of Enlightenment thinking about

coercion by W.C. McWilliams, ed., *Garrisons and Government: Politics and the Military in New States* (San Francisco: Chandler, 1967) at 7.

16 United States, White House, *A National Security Strategy of Engagement and Enlargement* (Washington, D.C: February 1995) at 2 [hereinafter 'Strategy of Engagement and Enlargement'].

17 L. Whitehead, 'The Imposition of Democracy,' in A.F. Lowenthal, ed., *Exporting Democracy: The United States and Latin America* (Baltimore: Johns Hopkins University Press, 1991). Also on the United States in Latin America, see R.A. Pastor, *Whirlpool: United States Foreign Policy toward Latin America and the Caribbean* (Princeton: Princeton University Press, 1992).

18 'Bush's Remarks at the Virginia Military Institute,' *The New York Times On the Web*, 18 April 2002, http://www.nytime.com/2002/04/18/international/18FULL-PTEXT.html. James Dao noted that Bush had criticized Clinton-era 'nation building' during the 2000 presidential campaign; therefore his comments on Afghanistan 'seemed to complete a reversal of policy.' J. Dao, 'Bush Sets Role for the US in Afghan Rebuilding,' *The New York Times On the Web*, 18 April 2002 http://www.nytime.com/2002/04/18/international/18PREX.html. The Clinton administration had also employed the Marshall Plan metaphor to describe its approach to 'secure the peace won in the Cold War.' 'Strategy of Engagement and Enlargement' *supra* note 16.

19 Mark Peceny notes that American presidents have combined intervention and democratization since 1898, 'despite the apparent contradictions involved in promoting self-determination through coercion.' In M. Peceny, 'Two Paths to the Promotion of Democracy During U.S. Military Interventions' (1995) 39 *International Studies Quarterly* at 371. Peceny further explains that liberalization is a better description than democratization.

20 Thanks to Robert Wright of the Center for Military History, who pointed out to me that 'Power Pack' and 'Urgent Fury' (the Dominican and Grenada actions, respectively) were randomly generated names. After the appeal of the latter, the randomness was removed and political leaders assigned the operation names.

21 Mark Peceny, *Democracy at the Point of Bayonets* (University Park, PA: Penn State Press, 1999) at 216. F. Kempe, 'The Panama Debacle,' in E. Loser, ed., *Conflict Resolution and Democratization in Panama* (Washington, D.C.: Center for Strategic and International Studies, 1992); in the same volume see E. Loser, 'Conflict Resolution' 1 at 19.

22 T.L. Friedman, 'The Clinton Gamble' *New York Times* (6 December 1995) A25.

23 Peceny, *supra* note 21 at 188.

24 C.E. Magoon, *The Law of Civil Government in Territory Subject to Military Occupation by the Military Forces of the United States*, 3rd ed. Bureau of Insular Affairs, War Department (Washington: Government Printing Office, 1903) at 26.

25 There is in the first instance the damage produced by non-permissive entry of foreign troops. Second, the target population may prefer even indigenous tyranny to foreign

military rule. A discussion of harms of military intervention and alternatives to military means can be found in T.J. Farer, 'The United States as Guarantor of Democracy in the Caribbean Basin: Is There a Legal Way?' (1989) 11 *The Jerusalem Journal of International Relations* 3 at 49.

26 Clausewitz used the term war and I will follow him insofar as the term is synonymous with the use of military force. By his definition, 'war is thus an act of force to compel our enemy to do our will.' Carl von Clausewitz, *On War*, 8th ed., trans., eds., M. Howard and P. Paret (Princeton: Princeton University Press, 1984) at 75. As we know, it is common in this century for organized military action to take place without a formal declaration of war, which is necessary to some definitions of the term.

27 Clausewitz, *supra* note 26. See in particular *Book One: On the Nature of War*, 'Chapter One: What Is War? War is Merely the Continuation of Policy by Other Means' at 87.

28 I owe this insight to Davis Bobrow. His idea is echoed in a report on civil military operations in El Salvador, which concludes that 'civil military operations is an area in which proper actions – taken early – can help prevent an insurgency from developing beyond its latent and organizational stage.' M.G. Manwaring and C. Prisk, 'Civil Military Operations in El Salvador' (Quarry Heights, Panama: United States Southern Command, 1988) at 29. This notion presumes effective timing and action of intervention. Often, what State Department official Todd Greentree calls the 'democratic contradiction' is in effect. As explained by Donald Snow, 'outsiders are unlikely to become adequately sensitive to internal problems until they reach a critical stage at which they are highly visible and troublesome to deal with.' D.M. Snow, *National Security: Defense Policy for a New International Order*, 3rd ed. (New York: St Martin's Press, 1995) at 227.

29 The reciprocal relationship between policy and force is often overlooked but is truly part of the richness of *On War*. My framework takes advantage of a pre-existing circularity in Clausewitzian thought. Edward Luttwak explains that 'in his circularity and indeterminacy Clausewitz captures essential realities which conventional, one-step, unidimensional observation would miss.' E.N. Luttwak, 'Reconsideration: Clausewitz and War' in *Strategy and Politics: Collected Essays* (New Brunswick, NJ, and London: Transaction Books, 1980) at 261. Luttwak describes *On War* at p. 259 as 'one of the most *useful* books ever written,' but one that is 'excessively unread' [emphasis in original].

30 A state monopoly on the legitimate use of force in England, for example, emerged only around 1576 with the demilitarization of the nobility. P. Corrigan and D. Sayer, *The Great Arch: English State Formation as Cultural Revolution* (Oxford: Basil Blackwell, 1985) at 65. This allocation of coercive authority is a form of relationship between civil and military spheres, and is one of the defining features of the modern state. Likewise the distinction of police and armies is, by historical standards, a recent differentiation. C. Tilly, *Coercion, Capital, and European States: A.D. 990–1990* (Cam-

bridge, MA: Basil Blackwell, 1990). The police/army distinction is also a civil/military differentiation.

31 Defence correspondent Christopher Bellamy compares the transformation of war to scientific revolution described by Thomas Kuhn, arguing that 'revolutions in warfare embody all the characteristics of a paradigm shift.' C. Bellamy, 'From Total War to Local War: It's a Revolution,' *The Independent* (23 July 1996) 14. Kuhn wrote: 'When the profession can no longer evade anomalies that subvert the existing tradition of scientific practice – then begin the extraordinary investigations that lead the profession at last to a new set of commitments, a new basis for the practice of science.' See, on paradigm change, T.S. Kuhn, *The Structure of Scientific Revolutions*, in Otto Neurath ed., *International Encyclopedia of Unified Science 2*, No. 2 (Chicago: University of Chicago Press, 1962) at 6.

   See also K.J. Holsti, *The State, War, and the State of War* (Cambridge: Cambridge University Press, 1996) at 27; M. van Creveld, *The Transformation of War* (New York: The Free Press, 1991). At the same time that great power militaries are being re-engineered to become small professional armies preparing to fight medium regional contingencies against other professional armies, most post-1945 conflict have been not between but rather within states. S.J. Cimbala, 'The Role of Military Advice: Civil-Military Relations and Bush Security Strategy,' in D.M. Snider and M. Carlton-Carew, *U.S. Civil-Military Relations: In Crisis or Transition?* (Washington, D.C.: The Center for Strategic and International Studies, 1995) at 88.

32 M.J. Mazarr, 'The Revolution in Military Affairs: A Framework for Defense Planning' (Monograph, U.S. Army War College Strategic Studies Institute, June 1994) at 2.

33 Cohen was then Senator (R-Maine) and later Secretary of Defense. Senator W.S. Cohen, *Congressional Record* (15 May 1986), cited by Col. H.G. Summers, Jr, 'A War Is a War Is a War Is a War,' in L.B. Thompson, ed., *Low-Intensity Conflict: The Pattern of Warfare in the Modern World* (Lexington, MA, and Toronto: Lexington Books, 1989) at 27.

34 On the obsolescence of total war, see Luttwak, 1995, 'Toward Post-Heroic Warfare,' *Foreign Affairs* 74 (May/June 1995) at 109. On the obsolescence of Cold War conceptions of conflict short of war, see S. Metz and J. Kievit, 'The Revolution in Military Affairs and Conflict Short of War' (Carlisle Barracks, PA: US Army War College, 1994)

35 R.D. Kaplan, 'The Coming Anarchy,' *The Atlantic Monthly* (1994) at 44.

36 T.M. Franck, 'The Emerging Right to Democratic Governance' (1992) Am. J. of Int. Law

37 G.B. Helman and S.R. Ratner, 'Saving Failed States' 89 *Foreign Policy* 3.

38 *On War* was written during the dissolution of the monarchical pre-eminence in France and emergence of the First Republic and the Empire. See P. Paret, 1988, 'Continuity and Discontinuity in Some Interpretations by Tocqueville and Clausewitz' (1988) 49

Journal of the History of Ideas 1. Clausewitz described war as a trinity composed of popular passions or social forces it expressed (the people), operational instruments (the military), and political objectives (the government).

39 van Creveld, *supra* note 31 at 43.

40 Holsti, *supra* note 31 at 14.

41 S.C. Sarkesian, J.A. Williams, and F.B. Bryant, *Soldiers, Society, and National Security* (Boulder and London: Lynne Rienner, 1995) at 40. It is not easy for military institutions to maintain means ends and authority demarcations in operations other than war. Strategists might look to Chinese strategist Sun Tzu for advice on the psychology of adversarial relations, but must also maintain clear conceptions of means and ends and clear authoritative relations between military and civil spheres.

42 Luttwak, *supra* note 29 at 263.

43 Holsti, *supra* note 31 at 27.

44 *Public Papers of the Presidents of the United States: The Public Messages, Speeches, and Statements of the President John F. Kennedy, 1962* (Washington, D.C.: U.S. Government General Printing Office, 1963) at 454; quoted in Sarkesian et al., *supra* note 41 at 46.

45 See *Report of the Secretary of Defense to the Congress for Fiscal Year 1987* (Washington, D.C: US Government Printing Office, 1986).

46 Clausewitz, *supra* note 26 at 610.

47 M. Kyre and J. Kyre, *Military Government and National Security* (Washington, D.C.: Public Affairs Press, 1968) at 2.

48 JP 1-02 *Department of Defense Dictionary of Military and Associated Terms* 12 April 2001 (As Amended Through 9 January 2003) available online at www.dtic.mil/doctrine/je1/doddict, at 88.

49 J.M. Deutch, *U.S. Department of Defense Directive 2000.13* (27 June, 1994) at 3.

50 'Civil Affairs Forces. Military units, detachments, or other military organizations that are designated as "civil affairs" organizations and are mission-oriented and trained to plan and conduct civil affairs activities. Also includes personnel who are trained and qualified in civil affairs'; Ibid.

51 D. Mitchell, OASD(SO/LIC)Master (15 May 1995). The 'Total Force' concept in the U.S. military refers to the active/reserve components together.

52 U.S. Joint Chiefs of Staff, *Doctrine for Joint Civil Affairs* (21 June 1995) at ix. When activated, U.S. Marines Civil Affairs Groups are under Command of Commander, US Joint Forces Command (CDR USJFCOM).

53 I use the terms 'civil affairs' and 'civil military operations' interchangeably here. The latter term was previously reserved for operations that handle civilians during combat, but is now used as a general reference to civil affairs. When the U.S. Joint Chiefs of Staff's Joint Warfighting Center assessed joint doctrine on civil affairs, they argued that the concept needed to be broadened beyond a focus on the Army. They suggested renaming the field manual from *Civil Affairs* to *Civil Military Operations*. The U.S.

Army's Civil Affairs and Psychological Operations Command suggested in May 1998
that the Army field manual be split in two.

54 R.C. Barnes, Jr, *Military Legitimacy: Might and Right in the New Millennium* (London:
Frank Cass, 1996) at 1.

55 J.T. Fishel and E.S. Cowan, 'Civil-military Operations and the War for Political Legitimacy in Latin America,' in J.W. De Pauw and G.A. Luz, eds., *Winning the Peace: The
Strategic Implications of Military Civic Action* (New York: Praeger, 1992) at 47. In an
examination of American experience with state-building in Somalia and Panama, Roy
Licklider looked back to post–Second World War occupations and noted that 'as
expected, the United States has developed a doctrine of state building over time.' See
R. Licklider, 'State Building After Invasion: Somalia and Panama' (International Studies Association Annual Convention, San Diego, April 1996) [unpublished]

56 United States Army U.S. Army Military History Institute, Civil Affairs School, *Doctrinal Study on the Theater Army: Civil Affairs Command* (Fort Gordon, GA, 15 August
1959). Annex B Concept of Operation and Organization, B-1.

57 This list might be interestingly compared to the 'Interagency Checklist for Restoration
of Essential Services,' a recent draft Department of Defense document, which identifies well over one hundred services for evaluation as to status and need in civil affairs
operations. My list here reflects reading of numerous editions of Army and Joint field
manuals, but most especially a reading of United States Army U.S. Army Military History Institute, Civil Affairs School *Doctrinal Study on the Theater Army: Civil Affairs
Command* (Fort Gordon, GA: 15 August 1959).

58 J.E. King Jr., *Civil Affairs: The Future Prospect of a Military Responsibility*, Operations
Research Office CAMG Paper, No. 3 (June 1958) at 4. An important exception to
Army responsibility is the administration of islands by the U.S. Navy, for example, in
the Caribbean in the early decades of this century.

59 *Army Vision 2010* cited in K.H. Pritchard, 'Front and Center: The Army and Civil-
Military Operations in the 21st Century' (December 1997) *Army* at 6. The top priority in the Army document is to provide options for military operations short of
war.

60 Ltr. Hilldring to Asst. Secy. of State Acheson, 9 November 1943, CAD files, 400.38
(2-20-43) (I), sec. 3; cited in H.L. Coles and A.K. Weinberg, *Civil Affairs: Soldiers
Become Governors* (Washington, D.C.: Office of the Chief of Military History, 1964)
at 153.

61 FM41-10 Jan. 1993, p. 3-1.

62 A defeated state is more likely than a failed state to possess local human and material
resources for reconstruction.

63 The proposition establishes the role of a nation's military force in the aftermath of conflict as a foreign policy problem. One might inject into this approach another level,
and examine domestic American influences on foreign policy objectives. Marc Peceny,

for example, has weighed the influence of a liberal U.S. Congress against consider-ations of stability in the international system as determinants of American efforts to democratize after intervention. Deborah Avant identified structural characteristics of American and British political systems as influencing the ability of their militaries to adapt to the requirements of operations other than war. Peceny, 'Two Paths.' See also D.D. Avant, *Political Institutions and Military Change: Lessons from Peripheral Wars* (Ithaca, NY, and London: Cornell University Press, 1994).

64 Arguably, states contributing troops to traditional peace-keeping operations employ military force toward a vision of political order in the target territory.

Chapter Seven

Co-opting Common Heritage: Reflections on the Need for South–North Scholarship

KARIN MICKELSON

> *[The] concept of the 'common heritage of mankind' is a fruitful and stimulating one. But while it may reconcile the human race and put the law of solidarity in place of the law of competition which was said to be a characteristic of life itself, nevertheless it carries with it obvious dangers in that it could be applied in one direction only and be 'co-opted' by great powers to their exclusive advantage. If 19th century doctrine considered colonization as an act of civilization on which the 'common good of mankind' depended, modern theory about the 'common heritage of mankind' must not lead to a new historical function which barely conceals another form of domination.*
>
> Mohammed Bedjaoui[1]

> *The South-North matrix is extensive and complex ... It does not respond to simplistic solutions any more than it can be defined in purely statistical terms. Measured against the relentless momentum of current phenomenon, indifference is not benign. Humility is needed, as is sustained dedication, if there is to be any reduction in magnitude of the disequilibria now evident.*
>
> Ivan Head[2]

The 'common heritage of mankind' has provided endless fodder for scholarly comment and debate since its emergence in the late 1960s in the context of discussions on the legal status of the deep seabed.[3] Innovative and unusual approaches abound, some of them bordering on the eccentric. Anyone who seeks to add to an already voluminous body of literature is forced to consider what, if anything, remains to be said. Nevertheless, common heritage offers an irresistible fascination for anyone interested in the South–North dimensions of international law. Its emergence in the heyday of developing country solidarity and its connections with demands for a New International Economic Order make it one of the quintessential 'Third World' doctrines.

It is precisely for that reason that it is worth evaluating some of the ways the concept of common heritage has been interpreted and deployed in international legal scholarship. As the title of this essay indicates, this evaluation veers toward critique. In speaking of 'co-option,' I am not referring to the political and legal shift that occurred with regard to the application of the concept of common heritage to the deep seabed. The changes embodied in the 1994 *Agreement Relating to the Implementation of Part XI of the United Nations Convention on the Law of the Sea* were undoubtedly dramatic.[4] In 1990, when consultations on Part XI were launched, it was openly acknowledged by then UN Secretary General Javier Pérez de Cuellar that the fundamental transformation of international society brought about by the collapse of the Soviet Union required modifications in the applicable legal regime.[5] As a result of those changes, commentators have come to question whether anything of substance remains in the concept of 'common heritage of mankind.'[6] However, there is another phenomenon worth exploring, and that is how the concept of common heritage has been (re)interpreted in the scholarly literature in ways that deprive it of much of its significance. I have chosen to focus on its application in the area of international environmental law, largely because that area has been among the most fertile ground for common heritage scholarship.

I will use this critical evaluation of some of the literature on common heritage as a departure point for some general comments on the current possibilities for South–North scholarship. For many years I have used the term 'South–North' based on the usage employed by Ivan Head in *On a Hinge of History: The Mutual Vulnerability of South and North*.[7] Professor Head expressed a preference for 'South–North' as a more accurate reflection of the international system, asserting that 'North–South' is misleading, 'for it lends weight to the impression that the South is the diminutive.'[8] More recently, however, and partly in response to the challenges that Professor Head's body of work poses, I have come to wonder whether 'South–North' encapsulates something more than an alternative way of referring to the relationship between developed and developing nations – whether in fact it might not embody an alternative way of conceptualizing this relationship. It is this question that I pose in the conclusion to this essay.

The Common Heritage of Mankind and International Environmental Law: Potentials and Pitfalls

As noted above, the idea of common heritage of mankind was brought to prominence in the context of discussions relating to the legal status of the seabed beyond the areas of national jurisdiction. It is most often associated with statements made by Ambassador Arvid Pardo of Malta during debates in the UN General Assembly in 1967.[9] The crucial elements of common heritage as applied to the seabed, as articulated by Pardo and Elisabeth Mann Borgese, are fivefold: non-appropriation by any state; a shared system of management; a sharing of benefits; reservation for peaceful purposes; and transmission substantially unimpaired to future generations.[10] The principle was adopted by the General Assembly in its 1970 *Declaration of Principles Governing the Seabed*,[11] and later incorporated into Part XI of the *United Nations Convention on the Law of the Sea*.[12] In relatively short order, the possibilities of applying the notion of common heritage outside the context of the deep seabed were explored. The other frontier that technology was opening up during the same time period was, of course, that of outer space. The concept, ultimately, was adopted in the *Agreement Governing the Activities of States on the Moon and Other Celestial Bodies*.[13] Despite its incorporation in international legal instruments, however, the concept of common heritage remained highly controversial.[14] The United States, in particular, did not shy away from expressing its scepticism about the concept's legal status.[15] Perhaps industrialized nations' concerns were heightened by the concept's association with proposals for a new international economic order. Pardo and Mann Borgese characterized the oceans as a 'great laboratory for the building of the New International Economic Order.'[16] And common heritage was to play a crucial role in the experiment. As they explain: 'Shared management and benefit sharing ... change the structural relationship between rich and poor nations and the traditional concepts of development aid.'[17]

International environmental law has seemed to be a logical candidate for an extension of the concept of common heritage. The reference to future generations, in particular, resonates with the notion of intergenerational equity. Outside the academic realm, the World Commission on Environment and Development, in its report *Our Common Future*, seemed eager to adopt the concept, albeit with substantial modifications. They put forward a proposal for a '"Species Convention" similar in spirit and in scope to the Law of the Sea Treaty and other international conventions reflecting principles of "universal resources." A Species Convention ... should articulate the concept of species and genetic variability as a common heritage.'[18] The WCED seemed well aware of the spectres it was raising with such language, and attempted to provide reassurance as to its import:

> Collective responsibility for the common heritage would not mean collective international rights to particular resources within nations. This approach need not interfere with concepts of national sovereignty. But it would mean that individual nations would no longer be left to rely on their own isolated efforts to protect species within their borders.[19]

The report went on to affirm that if such a convention were to be concluded, it would require a financial arrangement that would 'not only seek to ensure the conservation of genetic resources for all people, but assure that the nations that possess many of these resources obtain an equitable share of the benefits and earnings derived from their development.'[20]

Nonetheless, the controversy and uncertainty surrounding the concept has had an effect, with scholars taking widely differing stands regarding its potential as a principle of international environmental law. The extremes are illustrated by the stark differences in how the principle is treated in two well-known treatises. Edith Brown Weiss, in her foundational work on intergenerational equity, *In Fairness to Future Generations: International Law, Common Patrimony and Intergenerational Equity*,[21] is extremely cautious about the principle, noting the controversy associated with it and the difficulty of ascertaining its scope and applicability. She cautiously suggests that the common heritage principle can in fact be applied to the environment: 'The doctrine of the common heritage of mankind ... should extend to all natural and cultural resources, wherever located, that are internationally important for the well-being of future generations.'[22] She goes on to point out that 'in the intergenerational context, our planet is a global commons shared by each generation.'[23] On the other hand, in their 1991 treatise on international environmental law, Alexandre Kiss and Dinah Shelton showed confidence in the principle:

> Certain components of the global environment constitute part of the common heritage of mankind, including specific ecosystems like Antarctica or tropical forests, genetic diversity, and, in particular, endangered species. The common heritage notion, which emerged at the beginning of the ecological era in the late 1960s, so far has been seen only as a means of sharing the present benefits of certain natural resources and not as a concept for responsible conservation in the interest of future generations. In other words, the emphasis has been on 'common' and not on 'heritage.' The term itself clearly contains a temporal element and should be reexamined in light of its original intent and phrasing.[24]

Mapping the extensive scholarship on common heritage in international environmental law is a task beyond the scope of this essay. However, it is worth highlighting a recent attempt to read common heritage as a principle of international environmental law. This is found in Prue Taylor's book, *An Ecological Approach to International Law*.[25] Her approach has the virtue of emphasizing the multifaceted nature of the original principle of common heritage of mankind, and the ways in which it went beyond a narrow focus on resource exploitation. Her analysis is detailed and nuanced. Unfortunately, it also illustrates how a principle of this kind can be gutted, purged of many of the elements that make it meaningful from the perspective of the South.

Taylor's view is that common heritage of mankind has significant potential either to be directly incorporated into international environmental law or to be used as the foundation for a new principle that is less anthropocentric. She insists, however, that for such potential to be fulfilled, the principle must be read in a new way. She asserts that common heritage of mankind is currently treated with suspicion by states due to a restrictive interpretation that focuses on particular aspects of the doctrine 'which are not fundamental or indispensable, but which are products of [common heritage's] historical development in particular contexts.'[26]

Which aspects of common heritage is Taylor discarding? Those which fall under the headings of 'property rights, resource exploitation and equitable sharing of benefits.'[27] What would remain would be aspects of intergenerational equity, environmental integrity, and stewardship, all of which are doubtless valuable from an environmental perspective. However, common heritage of mankind was at its very core about global redistributive justice. It was part of an overall package of Third World aspirations and demands for a more equitable international system. Little if anything of that remains in Taylor's formulation. Along with history, it has been discarded for the sake of formulating a principle that will serve narrowly defined environmental interests and be more acceptable to certain states, presumably those of the North.

An interesting counterpoint to Taylor's analysis is offered by Kemal Baslar as part of a recent comprehensive survey of the common heritage concept.[28] Baslar begins his chapter 'International Environmental Law and the Common Heritage of Mankind' by offering the paradox that 'what appeared to be a concept of exploitation of minerals beyond national jurisdiction became a tool for international lawyers to protect the global environment from the early 1980s onwards.'[29] He then undertakes a careful analysis of the differences between the 'exploitation' model of common heritage and the 'environmental' variety, including the fact that the former was championed by the developing countries, was focused on fairness among peoples of the present generation (intragenerational equity), and was applied to resources beyond the sovereign jurisdiction of states, whereas the latter has been embraced mainly by the developed countries, focuses on intergenerational equity, and applies to natural resources within state jurisdiction.[30] In the end, Baslar is quite critical of international environmental lawyers' treatment of common heritage. As he puts it, they 'bear considerable responsibility for debasing the concept into a vulgar recast of the philosophy of saving the planet.'[31]

Nevertheless, Baslar has few concerns about extending the concept to the environmental area per se; what he takes issue with is its indiscriminate application to all parts of the environment. In his view, only 'globally important natural and cultural resources which constitute a physical unity'[32] are logical candidates for consideration as common heritage. Baslar is also critical of the view that common heritage as applied to the environment is inconsistent with state sovereignty over resources, and offers a different interpretation of the relationship between the two doctrines:

The protection of common heritages located within state borders requires states not to give up their national sovereignty but to take account of the interests of the rest of the international community. This is one side of the coin. On the other side, states should be entitled to receive financial, technological and other material help from the international community as a reward for good stewardship of the resource(s) concerned. The common heritage of mankind in this light does not contradict with the [principle of permanent sovereignty over natural resources] in the sense that state sovereignty is sacred as long as the rights and vital interests of mankind are protected.[33]

One might question whether this treatment of 'sovereignty' differs in substance from the more extreme proposals made by international environmental lawyers. Indeed, elsewhere in the book, Baslar undertakes a fairly lengthy discussion of what he openly terms 'eco-intervention.'[34] He terms this 'a first step in the establishment' of common heritage regimes.[35]

Despite surface differences, the approaches taken by Taylor and Baslar dovetail in many respects. Both are critical of the divisiveness that has characterized the debates surrounding common heritage, and both seek to articulate a version that will appeal to North and South alike. However, there is little effort to understand the perspectives that underpin those debates. After setting out the differing perspectives of the developed and developing states on resources outside of national jurisdiction, for example, Taylor simply notes that the 'interpretation of [common heritage of mankind] to meet these differing objectives of resource exploitation often became the focus of common heritage of mankind, at the expense of the objective of environmental protection.'[36] Baslar, on the other hand, is almost comical in his consternation regarding the politicization of the concept:

> What is worse, as it was thought a part of socialist philosophy, the common heritage of mankind has since been perceived as radical, bold and innovative and as a tool of revolutionary transformation on the way to universal socialism and of political antagonism among First (developed), Second (socialist) and Third World (developing countries).[37]

Baslar insists that the 'legal definition of the common heritage of mankind should not be a reflection of a certain ideology or school of thought determined and imposed unilaterally. Rather the concept should reflect the motifs and mores of different civilizations and cultures'[38]

Tellingly, both Taylor and Baslar are implicitly or explicitly critical of Pardo, for what seems to come down to his inability to pull himself out of the position and historical context in which he found himself. Taylor, for example, while noting that protection of the environment was one of the concerns motivating Pardo, refers to the 'pragmatic duality which one would expect of a conservationist,' [for whom] 'protection of the environment is usually inextricably connected to resource exploitation.'[39] Baslar is more blunt. Referring to Pardo's attempts to convince the states of the socialist bloc that support for common concern was in their interest, he expresses disappointment 'that such a noble concept had become a trivial political matter in the hands of a politician.'[40] Taylor, at least, carefully analyses of Pardo's articulation of the concept as the starting point for her treatment. Baslar, it appears, would prefer to bypass the 1960s altogether, going back instead to Grotius and principles of natural law: 'If Grotius had been in Pardo's position, how could he have advocated the common heritage of mankind so that the concept be welcomed [sic] by different interest groups?'[41] His answer: Grotius 'would have set out by saying that the common heritage of mankind was a natural law concept rather than part of a political conflict between East and West and an economic struggle between North and South.'[42]

By way of contrast, it is worth considering the treatment of common heritage by one of the best-known Third World writers, Mohammed Bedjaoui. Bedjaoui is careful to put common heritage in historical context; he characterizes it as the latest in a series of efforts to deal with conflicts over resources. Unlike earlier efforts, such as colonialism and warfare, the notion of common heritage is not based on the idea of the 'conflict of interests ... between industrialized nations striving to control the riches of overseas territories to their own advantage.'[43] The ideal was to put an end to this type of conflict by focusing on the possibilities for 'worldwide solidarity.'[44] Common heritage, then, is a representation of that notion of solidarity.[45]

As indicated in the quotation that serves as one of the epigraphs to this essay, Bedjaoui is all too aware that the idea of common heritage could be co-opted by the 'great powers.' Yet he does not shy away from a radical extension of the common heritage concept. He asks, 'Who has not been made aware of the new, extremely broad horizons which the "common heritage of mankind" is now opening up to mankind, who is not suddenly conscious of the audacious applications whereby this concept can serve to give concrete expression to universal solidarity?'[46] For example, he is quite willing to contemplate an extension of common heritage to resources within national sovereignty – with a proviso. Such an extension must be 'part of a joint pooling of all the riches and resources of the planet, a pooling free of any national self-seeking.'[47] The contrast with Baslar's notion of 'help as a reward for good stewardship' is striking. Bedjaoui goes on to state:

The idea of a 'common heritage of mankind' can therefore only command a significant measure of credibility in so far as it distributes clearly the rights and duties of States in all fairness ... If oil is a common heritage of mankind, it should be so wherever it is found, and not according to its geographic situation. America, British, Norwegian or Soviet oil, just as much as Middle-East oil, should belong to all. Even more than oil, agricultural foodstuffs should be declared the common heritage of mankind, for the north American continent is still, more than anywhere else, the world's granary, and its farmers would become accountable to the international community and particularly to the hungry multitudes of Asia and Africa.[48]

In a short paper published in 1984, Bedjaoui explored the question of whether global food resources could be considered part of the common heritage of mankind.[49] His analysis maintains a resolute focus on the fundamental issues that were included in the concept's original formulation. From the opening paragraph of the piece, in which he refers to the perennial problem of the 'unequal distribution of the world's resources' and 'the scandalous juxtaposition of malnutrition and waste,'[50] to the last paragraphs, in which he discusses the crossroads at which humanity finds itself, the underlying rationale that drove the development of the principle of common heritage remains paramount. Applying the concept of common heritage to food resources is simply the logical extension of its underlying rationale. As he puts it quite simply, humanity 'should not be burdened with the shame of allowing the intolerable tragedy of death through famine to take place, at a time when surplus food is destroyed elsewhere.'[51] Bedjaoui does not disregard the other aspects of common heritage. For example, he refers to the need to take into account ecological limits,[52] and he highlights the aspect of intergenerational equity.[53] Nevertheless, at the heart of the concept – in direct contrast to the approach taken by both Taylor and Baslar – is the notion of responding to unfair and unequal patterns of distribution.

It could, of course, be said that what Bedjaoui is doing is no different from what Taylor and Baslar have attempted to do – take the notion of common heritage and adapt it to other areas and other concerns. However, I would argue that something fundamentally different is going on in the approaches taken by these scholars. Bedjaoui is taking common heritage and trying to extend it beyond its initial focus, but we could say that the extension is being driven by the same impulse that led to the concept's original development and adoption. Taylor and Baslar, on the other hand, along with many others, have in fact 'co-opted' the notion of common heritage. They have wrenched it out of context, pulled it apart, and reassembled it in new incarnations that are little more than hollow mockeries of the original.

The Possibilities for South–North Scholarship

Criticisms of how common heritage has been deployed in the scholarly literature might appear to be an exercise in finger-pointing were it not for the fact that the treatment of common heritage is symptomatic of a perspective that seems widespread. One has become accustomed to reading dismissals of the new international economic order, of the heady optimism of the 1960s and 1970s. What is unusual about common heritage is that instead of merely relegating a Third World doctrine to the dustbin of history, attempts have been made to retool it into a concept that is applicable to a different context. It may seem uncharitable to take issue with such attempts, especially when they are the work of young scholars whose enthusiasm, at least, cannot be faulted. However, I cannot help feeling that these attempts represent a fundamentally problematic approach to international legal scholarship. These writers are able to justify their approach through an elaborate array of reasons and authorities, underlying which is an attitude that verges on contempt for the original rationale of the concept, as well as for its proponents.[54] Even if one were to accept the view that the 'Third World' no longer exists (as I do not), vast disparities of wealth and access to resources are still with us, and these disparities have in fact been increasing over the past decades. This is either missing from the analysis or is mentioned only in passing.

Where, then, does this leave common heritage? My own preference would be to allow the principle to rest in peace rather than have it exist as a simulacrum that not only fails to reflect the content of the original but in fact is almost wholly inconsistent with it. I would argue that politically and legally, such a decision has already been made. Common heritage has not been incorporated into multilateral environmental agreements; in its place, notions such as the 'common concern of humankind' have emerged, which have the benefit of being unaccompanied by the baggage of 'political connotations.'[55] Yet this does not eliminate the underlying dilemma. Common concern, too, along with other principles of international law, must be interpreted and applied in ways that are sensitive and responsive to the needs of the South. And such sensitivity and responsiveness are sorely lacking in the types of analyses I have been considering here.

The failure here is precisely the failure to think this issue through from a South–North perspective. I am *not* saying that the failure is to look at this from the perspective of the South or the Third World, although such a perspective exists. I have argued elsewhere that a 'Third World approach' to international law can be discerned in the work carried out by Third World scholars in the 1960s and 1970s.[56] In recent years, a number of scholars have begun forming a movement known as 'Third World Approaches to International Law' (TWAIL), with the goal of engaging with the dominant discourse of international law and its failure to take into account the perspectives and concerns of Third World peoples.[57] However, it is important to acknowledge that there have been many scholars whose approach to the international system has differed fundamentally from that of the mainstream, who have refused to accept and perpetuate the marginalization of the South, and who have actively worked for a more just and inclusive global order.

One of the enduring legacies of Ivan Head's work, whether in scholarship or in public service, is that it embodies such an alternative approach. His use of 'South–North' is far more than a matter of semantics; it represents a point of view. The excerpt from *On a Hinge of History* that opened this piece might be said to encapsulate what such an approach entails: humility; sustained dedication; the avoidance of simplistic solutions; and the rejection of the view that indifference is benign. The latter two are of particular significance. Despite its broad sweep, the entire book represents the antithesis of oversimplification. Instead of generalizations he offers careful, detailed descriptions and analyses of the various dimensions of South–North vulnerabilities. In place of prescriptions he throws out challenges, emphasizing the need for creativity along with compassion. And he has little patience with those who would seek to offer facile explanations for complex phenomena. Consider, for example, his treatment of the widespread tendency to blame poverty on corruption and incompetence in the South:

> Countries of the South are not by any means free of villains or fools or irresponsible citizens, but I daresay that ratio to population is no greater than in the industrialized countries. Yet in our arrogance or in our laziness, we in the North succumb to the temptation of believing that standards of living in the South are low because values are low, that human pathos and wretchedness is more often than not linked to human moral weakness and human character flaws.[58]

The rejection of indifference may be the ultimate hallmark of Head's work. Head does not address himself to the North alone, but it is for the North that he reserves his most trenchant criticism. This is perhaps most clearly reflected in the closing pages of the same book, in which Head outlines several 'profound truths': the fragility of the environment; the potentially catastrophic consequences of human error in the face of the power we command, such as that of nuclear weapons; and the availability of technology and resources to enhance worldwide human welfare.[59] Our generation, he asserts, has the benefit of this knowledge, and the challenge it presents us with is unmistakable: to accept this knowledge with humility, and to resolve to use it wisely:

> Should we not do so, ours will be the first generation to possess another truth: that we have *consciously* passed to our children a world less wholesome, less humane, less stable, and less promising than the one we inherited. And we will know, too, that it is our greed, our arrogance, and our indifference that are responsible. It is a testament that will be borne most particularly by those now living in the industrialized countries of the North, for we are possessed not only of these truths but possessed as well of the means to ensure a beneficial planetary disposition of the knowledge that

underlies them. To fail this challenge is to commit succeeding generations to the perilous condition of refugees, seeking sanctuary in a world which offers none – not from economic hazard, not from environmental degradation, nor social instability or political upheaval.[60]

Conclusion

Ivan Head poses the challenge of confronting the South–North matrix not as a choice but as a necessity. Similarly, for scholars who choose to work on a concept such as common heritage, a South–North perspective is not merely one of a number of alternatives from which to choose: it is an imperative. This does not presuppose what a South–North analysis of common heritage as a potential principle of international environmental law might look like, or what its conclusions might be. However, I strongly suspect that it would bear little resemblance to the works considered here – including, it is worth emphasizing, that undertaken by Bedjaoui. It would likely give serious consideration and weight to the historical context within which the concept originally developed, although it would not necessarily adopt the rationale and perspective underlying it. It would not, whether explicitly or implicitly, denigrate the hopes that characterized the ideal of common heritage, though it might acknowledge the difficulties of realizing those hopes. Above all, it would not represent the co-option of a Third World doctrine without even confronting the ethical and scholarly dilemmas that such a move represents.

NOTES

1　M. Bedjaoui, *Towards a New International Economic Order* (Paris: Unesco, 1979) at 224.

2　Ivan L. Head, *On a Hinge of History: The Mutual Vulnerability of South and North* (Toronto: University of Toronto Press, 1991) at 22.

3　I use 'emergence' advisedly, given that scholars have identified earlier uses of the term. A recent work that provides an extensive bibliography of works on common heritage is K. Baslar, *The Concept of the Common Heritage of Mankind in International Law* (The Hague: Martinus Nijhoff Publishers, 1998).

4　GA Res. 48/263, reprinted in (1994) 33 I.L.M. 1309.

5　The Secretary-General 'noted that in the eight years that had elapsed since the Convention was adopted certain significant political and economic changes had occurred which had had a marked effect on the regime for deep seabed mining contained in the Convention ... The general economic climate had been transformed as a result of the changing perception with respect to the roles of the public and private sectors. There was a discernible shift towards a more market-oriented economy.' In *Consultations of the Secretary-General on Outstanding Issues relating to the Deep Seabed Mining Provisions of the United Nations Convention on the Law of the Sea: Report of the Secretary-General*, UN Doc. A/48/950 (1994), para. 2, p. 3, available at <http://www.un.org/Depts/los/general_assembly/documents/48_950_English.pdf>.

6 See for example F. Biermann, '"Common Concern of Humankind": The Emergence of a New Concept of International Environmental Law' (1996) 34 Archiv des Volkerrechts 426.

7 Head, *supra* note 2.

8 *Ibid.* at 14.

9 See the discussion by A. Cassese, *International Law in a Divided World* (Oxford: Clarendon Press, 1986) at 379–80.

10 A. Pardo and E.M. Borgese, *The New International Economic Order and the Law of the Sea* (Malta: International Oceans Institute, Occasional Paper No. 4, 1970) at 10.

11 *Declaration of Principles Governing the Seabed and the Ocean Floor, and the Subsoil Thereof, Beyond the Limits of National Jurisdiction*, GA Res. 2749 (XXV), UN GAOR, 25th Sess., Supp. No. 28 at 4.

12 (1982) 21 I.L.M. 1261

13 UN Doc. A/34/664; (1979) 18 I.L.M. 1434.

14 For an overview of the controversy, see A. Cassese, *International Law*, pp. 376–92.

15 See in general M.G. Schmidt, *Common Heritage or Common Burden: The United States Position on the Development of a Regime for Deep Sea-bed Mining in the Law of the Sea Convention* (Oxford: Clarendon, 1989).

16 Pardo and Borgese, The *New International*, p. 142.

17 Pardo and Borgese, *The New International*, p. 10.

18 *Our Common Future* (Oxford University Press, 1987) at 162.

19 *Ibid.*

20 *Ibid.*

21 Edith Brown Weiss, *In Fairness to Future Generations* (Tokyo: United Nations University, 1989).

22 *Ibid.* at 49

23 *Ibid.*

24 A. Kiss and D. Shelton, *International Environmental Law* (Ardsley-on-Hudson, NY: Transnational, 1991) at 379–80.

25 Taylor, *An Ecological Approach*, (London and New York: Routledge, 1998).

26 *Ibid.* at 258.

27 *Ibid.*

28 Baslar, *supra* note 3.

29 *Ibid.* at 277.

30 *Ibid.* at 277–8.

31 *Ibid.* at 314

32 *Ibid.* at 315.

33 *Ibid.* at 286.

34 *Ibid.* at 150–8.

35 *Ibid.* at 150.

36 Taylor, *supra* note 24 at 269.

37 Baslar, *supra* note 3 at 33.

38 *Ibid.* at 37.

39 Taylor, *supra* note 24 at 267.

40 Baslar, *supra* note 3 at 33.

41 *Ibid.* at 34.

42 *Ibid.*

43 M. Bedjaoui, 'Are the World's Food Resources the Common Heritage of Mankind' (1984) 24 Indian J. Int'l L. 459 at 460.

44 *Ibid.* at 461.

45 *Ibid.*

46 *Ibid.* He mentions the possibility of the concept being applied not only to the oceans and to space, but also to the environment, climate, and genetic resources, and even to cultural and artistic achievements.

47 Bedjaoui, *Towards a New International Economic Order, supra* note 1 at 235.

48 *Ibid.* at 235–6.

49 Bedjaoui, 'Are the World's' ... *supra* note 42.

50 *Ibid.* at 459.

51 *Ibid.* at 465.

52 *Ibid.* at 462.

53 *Ibid.*

54 Baslar is quite open about this: 'Despite our coming from a developing country, we were not mesmerized by the high-sounding slogans of the Third World with regard to establishing a new international economic order. Accordingly, our interpretation of the common heritage is not partial. We have sought a theory of justice that will be fair for the rich as well as the poor, and for future generations as well as the present.' Baslar, *The Concept*, p. xxii.

55 Taylor, *An Ecological Approach*, expresses concern that the use of common heritage 'may be greatly limited by political connotations.' (p. 292).

56 Mickelson, K., 'Rhetoric and Rage: Third World Voices in International Legal Discourse' (1998) 16 Wisconsin Int'l L. J. 353.

57 See, for example, M. Mutua, 'What is TWAIL?' (2000) 94 ASIL Proc. 31.

58 Head, *supra* note 2 at 200.

59 *Ibid.* at 193–4.

60 *Ibid.* at 194.

Chapter Eight

Modernization of European Community Competition Law Enforcement for the Twenty-first Century

KIRSTY MIDDLETON

In 1999 the European Commission ('Commission') adopted the 'White Paper[1] on the Modernization of the Rules Implementing Articles 81 and 82 (ex 85 and 86) of the EC Treaty' (the 'White Paper').[2] The Commission proposes *inter alia* to abolish its centralized system of control and give national competition authorities and courts a much greater role in enforcing Community competition rules. The White Paper and the follow-up regulation (adopted by the Council of Ministers on 16 December 2002),[3] have been described by the commissioner for EC competition law, Mario Monti, as 'the most important legislative initiative in the competition field since the 1990 Merger Regulation.' If adopted, there is no doubt that the proposals will radically transform the constitutional, institutional, procedural, and substantive structure of the Community's competition law enforcement process.[4] This will lead, most significantly, to a new, 'rights-based' common culture of competition in the Community.

To achieve general acceptance of a common competition culture in the Community (and indeed beyond), the competition enforcement process needs to be brought closer to the individual. Thus, reform is predicated on decentralization. The Commission has been considering modernizing the current competition law enforcement process for some time, based on greater decentralization of the competition rules through the national courts and competition authorities.[5] The debate has centred on the need to improve the current system of enforcement enshrined in Regulation 17/62, which gives the Commission significant powers of supervision and enforcement of the Community competition rules.[6] Although the system worked well in the early days of the Community, the White Paper notes that a system devised for a group of six member states 'is no longer appropriate for the Community of today with 15 Member States, 11 languages and over 350 million inhabitants.'[7] With new members clamouring for membership in the Community, it is imperative that the necessary institutional and legislative improvements be in place to prepare the Community for its greatest challenge. Accession negotiations formally commenced at the end of March 1999, with Poland, the Czech Republic, Hungary, Estonia, Slovenia, and Cyprus forming the first group of applicants. Talks are continuing with many others, including Turkey. Integration of these countries – some of them with former socialist economies – will place enormous pressure on an already overburdened Commission. The White Paper therefore focuses on various proposals for reforming the present system of competition law enforcement for the twenty-first century.

Globalization and International Cooperation in Competition Law Enforcement

Commerce is no longer at a purely national or even European level; it is increasingly global. As companies expand their commercial activities, geographic and political boundaries are becoming increasingly blurred. The White Paper expressly acknowledges that 'the internationalisation of the European economy has speeded up in recent years, so that competition policy is now for the most part conducted in a global context.'[8] This is demonstrated by the recent increase in competition cases involving more than one competition law system.

Increasingly, global markets are posing a significant challenge to national and regional competition law enforcement processes. Undertakings are more likely to resort to protectionist measures in their attempts to counter the threat of globalization. As a result of corporate mergers, international cartels, and abuses of power in various markets, demand is increasing for effective measures and greater cooperation among the world's competition authorities. Working with other countries to tackle large international cartels is already an important aspect of the Commission's work.[9] The Community's bilateral cooperation agreement with the United States has provided a vital framework for cooperation in tackling international cartels and has prompted new agreements, most recently with Canada.[10] However, the need to devise effective enforcement mechanisms for international competition law will only increase, and the Commission needs to free itself from having to deal with matters that interfere with these demands. At the regional level, this is of particular importance, since in an enlarged Community, transactions with cross-border aspects are likely to increase.[11]

There are also internal, 'technocratic' reasons for reform; not the least of these is the growing burden on commission resources. These are discussed throughout this essay. Certainly, the case for a radical overhaul of Community competition law enforcement processes gathered momentum throughout the 1990s. For example, in 1997 the law on vertical agreements was subjected to substantial review. The Commission published a Green Paper on Vertical Restraints,[12] which resulted in the adoption of a new Block Exemption Regulation in 1999.[13] Regulation 2790/99 revolutionized the block exemption system in the community, specifically, the application of Article 81(3) to vertical agreements;[14] this has important implications for enforcement. It is important to view the White Paper and new Regulation in the context of the Commission's wider program of modernization of Community competition law.

Response to the White Paper

It is widely accepted that the present system of Community competition law enforcement is untenable. However, the Commission's proposed reforms, contained in the White Paper and new Regulation, Regulation 1/2003, have proved controversial because they are so radical. Some view the proposals as an admission ('capitulation,' according to the president of the Bundeskartellamt)[15] that the centralized system of control is beyond the capability of the Commission, whose resources are already stretched.[16] Others – for example, academics, lawyers, and representatives from European industry – have expressed surprise and concern at the extent of the proposals, although they broadly welcome reform.[17] The main areas of concern are the Commission's role in enforcing the competition rules and promoting cooperation with national competition authorities and courts; undertakings' need for legal certainty for commercial investment; the consistent and uniform application of EC competition law throughout the EU; and the ability of judges in national courts to apply economic criteria and weigh policy considerations in court proceedings.

This essay seeks to make a modest contribution – albeit *ex post facto* – to the modernization of Community competition law enforcement processes. Given the far-reaching nature of the Commission's proposals, there has been considerable academic debate on both sides of the Atlantic.[18] This essay does not try to address all the issues raised in the White Paper. Rather, it discusses the main areas of concern, with particular emphasis on the status of individuals, and attempts to place the debate in the wider global context.

Treaty Rules and Procedures

The Community competition rules applicable to undertakings are set out in Articles 81 and 82 (formerly 85 and 86) of the EC Treaty.[19] Article 81 prohibits restrictive practices. However, the same provision states that exemptions are possible where the relevant agreement contains countervailing economic benefits that are shared with consumers. Article 82 prohibits abuse of dominant positions. The competition rules play a key role in the commission's fight against cartels, abusive behaviour, and monopolies in the community and beyond. A strong and effective competition policy is also the foundation of a 'single market' as provided for in Article 2 of the EC Treaty. In this way, the contribution of Articles 81 and 82 to the community's goal of market integration has been vital.[20]

Article 81 of the EC Treaty, paragraph (1) provides that:

> the following shall be prohibited as incompatible with the common market: all agreements between undertakings, decisions by associations of undertakings and concerted practices, which may affect trade between member states and which have as their object or effect, the prevention, restriction or distortion of competition within the common market.

Article 81, paragraph 2, provides that 'any agreements or decisions prohibited pursuant to this article shall be automatically void.'

Article 81(1) sets out the general prohibition; however, the 'provisions of paragraph 1 may be declared inapplicable' by Article 81(3), the exemption provision. Thus, a restrictive practice is null and void if it is caught by paragraph (1) of Article 81, until such time as the Commission authorizes it under paragraph (3).

The procedure for enforcing Articles 81 and 82 is enshrined in EC Regulation 17/62,[21] the first regulation implementing Articles 81 and 82 (ex 85 and 86), which in certain cases requires the Commission to be informed in advance of restrictive practices. Although prior notification of restrictive practices is not compulsory under the Regulation, companies seeking an exemption under Article 81(3) are required to notify the Commission. As a result, many companies have notified Brussels about restrictive practices. Since the Commission has sole power under Article 9(1) of the regulation to declare Article 81(1) inapplicable to restrictive practices,[22] companies have used this centralized authorization system not only to achieve legal security but also to block private actions before national courts and national competition authorities. Moreover, the jurisdiction of the national authorities is removed once the Commission commences proceedings under the regulation (Art. 9[3]); this strengthens the mechanism of centralized control. Although the Commission believes this monopoly is justified in order to ensure the uniform application of Article 81(3) across the Community and thereby contribute to a 'culture of competition' in Europe,[23] it has clearly undermined efforts to promote decentralized application of Community competition laws through the national competition authorities.

Notwithstanding the commission's monopoly over the exemption procedure under Article 9(1) of Regulation 17/62, national courts have also played a part in the enforcement of the Community competition rules. The European Court of Justice has held in a number of cases that Articles 81 and 82 are capable of producing direct effects; thus they do create individual rights that must be protected by national courts.[24] Community competition law is also enforced alongside the competition laws of the member states; many states prefer to apply their domestic competition laws. However, despite the absence of any legal requirement to do so, in recent years there has been a clear trend among the member states toward harmonizing domestic competition law with Articles 81 and 82.[25] In the past few years, member states such as Sweden,[26] Denmark,[27] Ireland,[28] and the Netherlands[29] have introduced national competition legislation based on the Community model; this has reduced the risk of conflict between Community law and domestic law and encouraged competitiveness in international markets.[30] A number of central and eastern European countries such as Romania[31] and Hungary[32] have done the same.[33] The trend toward harmonization undoubtedly influenced the decision of the new British government in 1997 to choose Articles 81 and 82 as appropriate models for its new domestic competition laws.[34] The United Kingdom was the fourteenth member state to harmonize its domestic competition law with the Community model.[35] Clearly, national competition authorities are able to cooperate more efficiently in cases with cross-border implications if the laws and procedures of the countries concerned are broadly similar.[36] Also, cooperation and information sharing with the commission is easier when the national competition authorities are well versed in applying Community competition law concepts. This process of 'soft' harmonization has clearly contributed to the creation of an environment across the Community in which decentralization of the competition law can occur.

Background – the Commission's Role

As guarantor of the Community interest, the Commission has played a pivotal role in enforcing competition policy. This role has expanded over the past thirty-five years to account for the expansion of the Community, greater market integration, and the signing of cooperation agreements with third countries. However, the same procedural rules that were designed for a Community of six are still being applied today. The Commission can no longer cope with the huge numbers of applications received each year. Within five years of the implementation of Regulation 17/62, over 37,000 applications were pending. At present, over 1000 such outstanding cases are pending.

In spite of procedural constraints and limited administrative resources, the Commission has devised a number of pragmatic measures over the years to reduce its reliance on formal decisions under Article 9 of Regulation 17/62.

These include the development of concepts such as 'appreciability,' which allow cases to fall outside the scope of Article 81(1) altogether when the effect on competition is imperceptible.[37] Also, various Commission Notices have been published in order to provide undertakings with guidance on particular Commission policies.[38] These notices are designed to take much of the administrative burden off the Commission by allowing undertakings to decide for themselves whether their agreements have infringed the competition rules.

The Commission has also adopted a number of block exemption regulations, which apply to specific categories of practices, agreements, and joint ventures.[39] Block exemptions offer legal certainty for companies in situations where the particular agreement is compatible with the terms of the regulations. In such cases, the need for a prior assessment is dispensed with, and Article 81(1) is simply declared inapplicable.

Although these measures helped reduce the number of applications, delays in decision making were still common. So the Commission began using administrative letters ('comfort letters') to communicate its decisions. This practice is now the most common method of settling competition cases. The chief advantages of comfort letters are that they obviate the need to publish decisions under Articles 19 and 21 of Regulation 17, and they reduce the amount of translation that a formal decision demands. The White Paper notes that the Commission issues between 150 and 200 comfort letters each year, over 90 per cent of such cases are closed informally.[40] Unfortunately, comfort letters have reduced the transparency of the process, since they are rarely published in the Official Journal. These letters do not provide companies with the same degree of legal protection as formal decisions. Furthermore, the European Court of Justice ruled in the 'Perfumes cases' that comfort letters, being essentially administrative letters, amount to no more than a statement of the Commission's opinion, and thus do not bind national courts.[41]

Another initiative designed to promote the decentralization of Community competition law enforcement followed the European Court's decision in *Automec (No. 2)*.[42] The Commission produced a notice that proposed various means of cooperation between the national courts and the Commission based on the concept of decentralized enforcement.[43] The notice sets out the general legal framework and details the practical measures for increasing the involvement of national courts in applying Articles 81 and 82. This notice was supplemented in 1997 by a subsequent notice, which developed guidelines for allocating cases between the national authorities and the Commission and encouraged companies to approach the national authorities with respect to the enforcement of Articles 81 and 82.[44] The central aim of these notices was to reduce the number of applications for exemption addressed to the Commission; however, their contribution to greater decentralized enforcement has been limited.[45] As previously noted, Article 81(1) can be directly applied by the national competition authorities and courts, but at present only the Commission has the power to grant an exemption under Article 81(3). Companies have therefore been reluctant to approach their national competition authorities in most situations where an infringement of community law has been alleged. The White Paper explicitly recognizes that the 1993 and 1997 notices 'have now reached their limits within the existing legal framework.'[46]

The next section examines the options for reform, and discusses in more detail the proposals articulated in the White Paper.

Options for Reform

The purpose of the White Paper was to encourage a 'wide-ranging debate between the Commission, the Member States and all interested parties.' The Commission considered a number of approaches to achieving more effective supervision of competition policy in an enlarged Community. These were based mainly on the need to improve the existing authorization system. The first of these involved proposals to alter the interpretation of Article 81 to include an analysis of the pro- and anti-competitive effects of an agreement under Article 81(1). The application of the exemption provided for in Article 81(3) would be restricted to those cases in which the need to ensure consistency between competition policy and other Community policies took precedence over the results of the competition analysis.[47] Protagonists of this 'rule of reason' approach argue that this would reduce the number of applications for exemption, since Article 81(3) would not be invoked. The debate would instead focus on whether an agreement 'has as its object or effect, the prevention, restrictions or distortion of competition.' This would bring Community law more in line with the American approach. However, the White Paper rules out greater use of this approach, given the structure of Article 81. The Commission considered that a balancing approach under Article 81(1) would result in Article 81(3) being 'cast aside' and would require revision of the EC Treaty.[48] Such an approach would also run the risk of diverting Article 81(3) from providing a legal framework for the economic assessment of restrictive practices toward allowing 'the application of the competition rules to be set aside because of political considerations.'[49] Thus, a rule-of-reason approach seems to have been ruled out, on the basis that it would rely on policy developments and decision making.[50]

It is clear from an examination of all the Commission's options that the primary objective was to enable the Commission to refocus its resources on the most serious restrictions of competition in the Community, and beyond; hence the dismissal of options that would enable the national competition authorities to apply Article 81(3). The Commission considered that the decentralization of Article 81(3) would not enable it to take stronger action against the most serious infringe-

ments of the competition rules, and would pose a major risk to the uniform application of Community law. The simplification of the procedures laid down by
Regulation 17/62 – for example, the extension of the applicability of Article 4(2)
of Regulation 17 – was also ruled out, for the same reason.[51]

The End of Notification and Authorization

Having considered various options, the Commission has proposed a radical solution to the problem of centralized control based on a fourfold objective: 'rigorous
enforcement of competition law; effective decentralisation; simplification of procedures; and uniform application of law and policy development throughout the
EU.'[52] First, the Commission has proposed that the notification and exemption
system in Regulation 17/62 be abolished and replaced by a Council Regulation
that would render the criteria in Article 81(3) directly applicable without the
prior decision of the Commission. Article 81 would then become '*a unitary norm
comprising a rule establishing the principle of prohibition, unless certain conditions
are met.*'[53] This is the most striking feature of the White Paper. The Commission
would lose its seemingly entrenched monopoly over whether or not an agreement
fulfils the criteria in Article 81(3). Second, since notification would no longer be
required, the decision would be taken by a national court (if the matter was relevant to litigation before it) or by the national competition authority. Thus,
national courts and competition authorities would play a much greater role in the
enforcement of Community competition law. The third strand of this proposal
involves intensified *ex post facto* control by the Commission.

Decentralized Application of the Competition Rules

The Commission has advocated more decentralized application of the Community competition rules for almost a decade. *Automec (No. 2)*[54] was regarded as the
turning point in the Commission's decentralization policy. In that case, the Court
of First Instance held inter alia that the Commission may refuse to investigate a
complaint if there is a perceived lack of Community interest in doing so. This
landmark case paved the way for greater decentralization; it also encouraged individuals to pursue their cases before national courts. In fact, national courts
already had jurisdiction to apply Community competition law, and the number
of national judicial decisions applying Community competition rules has risen
steadily year after year. Articles 81 and 82 in particular are capable of producing
'direct effects in relations between individuals;[55] consequently, they 'create rights
which the national courts must safeguard.' Thus, the Commission has proposed
to abolish its Article 9(1) monopoly; this would give the national competition
authorities the power to apply Article 81 in its entirety. As noted at the beginning

of this essay, the Commission would be free to concentrate on practices with a Community or international dimension; less significant agreements would be left to the national institutions of member states.

I generally welcome the decentralization of the Community competition rules. It is the only realistic solution to the serious resource deficit faced by the Commission, short of a massive boost to its resources. However, decentralization presents particular difficulties to those states which have applied for membership in the Community. The White Paper acknowledges some of the obstacles faced by these former socialist economies in this regard. For example, it has noted.

'Dominant positions held by undertakings which inherited state monopolies are particularly numerous in the applicant countries, and such undertakings might be tempted to abuse those positions so as to make up for their lack of economic competitiveness.' The tradition of the planned economy is also potential danger inasmuch as it encouraged agreements between 'competitors.'[56]

However, the White Paper does not explain how the Commission intends to accommodate the special needs of these former socialist states. It is content to make the rather ambiguous remark that it 'will devote particular attention to the development of competition in the candidate countries and will provide their competition authorities with increased assistance.' Although the Commission is currently assisting the applicant states as part of the overall accession negotiations, it will prove difficult enough for former socialist economies to apply Community competition concepts and embrace a modern 'competition culture' as part of the *acquis communautaire*.[57] On accession, however, it is questionable whether even those applicant states which have domestic competition authorities of their own and which meet the criteria for accession – for example Estonia, Latvia, Lithuania, and Slovenia – have the capacity to deal effectively with the competition cases that will come under their jurisdiction as a result of decentralization. The additional burdens and responsibilities demanded by the Commission following decentralization may even delay accession for some applicant states. For example, the Commission has noted that Cyprus and Malta have yet to develop effective antitrust enforcement procedures; competition negotiations cannot be provisionally closed until they do.[58]

The Role of the National Courts

The Commission has in the past not had close contact with the national courts in the past, and the proposals for increased cooperation are especially sensitive.

The full involvement of the national courts in enforcing Community competition law raises a number of important issues. Most prominent are these: How can consistency and uniformity in decision making be ensured across the Community with particular reference to the courts of the new member states? Will harmonization of national procedures be necessary? Can the criteria articulated in Article 81(3) be judicially determined?

There is real concern that decentralization of competition law enforcement will lead to lack of uniformity across states, and between states and the Commission, in interpretation and decision making. It is almost inevitable that there will be some disharmony between the Commission's interpretation of Article 81(3) and those of the national courts and competition authorities. However, in the event of a conflict between national law and Community law, the doctrine of the supremacy of community law will help resolve matters.[59] The EC Treaty also provides for formal dialogue between the national courts and the European Court by way of the Article 234 (ex. 177) preliminary ruling procedure. The full text of Article 234 reads:

> The Court of Justice has jurisdiction to give preliminary rulings concerning:
> (a) the interpretation of the Treaty;
> (b) the validity and interpretation of acts of the institutions of the Community and of the ECB;
> (c) The interpretation of the statutes of bodies established by an act of the Council, where those statutes so provide.
>
> Where such a question is raised before any court or tribunal of a Member State, that court or tribunal may, if it considers that a decision on the question is necessary to enable it to give judgement, request the Court of Justice to give a ruling thereon. Where any such question is raised in a case pending before a court or tribunal of a Member State, against whose decision there is no judicial remedy under national law, that court or tribunal shall bring the matter before the Court of Justice.

The European Court has stated:

> Article [177] is essential for the preservation of the Community character of the law established by the Treaty and has the object of ensuring that in all circumstances this law is the same in all States of the Community.[60]

It is clear from the text of Article 234 that the national courts may refer to the European Court any question of Community law, if clarification of the matter is essential to the determination of the case.[61] Thus, in cases involving the application of Articles 81 and 82 before the national courts, a request for a preliminary ruling would be competent. Article 234 refers to 'any court or tribunal of a Member State'; however, a further distinction is made between courts and tribunals 'against whose decisions there is no judicial remedy under national law' – which are covered by Article 234(3) – and other national courts and tribunals – which are subject to Article 234(2). The distinction is important because the latter do have some discretion in deciding whether to refer questions of Community law to the European Court. Yet the former – that is, courts of last instance – *must* refer such questions to the Court. For instance, a reference by the House of Lords to the European Court is mandatory.[62]

It is unlikely that the Article 234 procedure by itself will be adequate to ensure uniformity and consistency in the interpretation and application of competition law throughout the Community. First, a request for a preliminary ruling is limited to questions of interpretation of Community law, and national courts will be unable to ask the European Court for assistance in making a judgment based on economic criteria under Article 81(3). Thus, a judge will not be able to ask the European Court whether an agreement contributes to improving the production or distribution of goods or to promoting technical or economic progress. Second, the Article 234 reference procedure has proved cumbersome, and delays are commonplace. The implications for the European Court's workload in an enlarged community are obvious. Moreover, the European Court has rarely declined to exercise jurisdiction under Article 234 despite a dramatic upturn in its caseload in recent years.[63] Some member states' courts have also shown a 'reluctance to refer cases to Luxembourg, fearing that a request for a preliminary ruling will merely result in unnecessary delay.[64]

Of course, as judges in the national courts gain expertise in Community competition matters, and gain confidence in their ability to apply the Article 81(3) criteria, there may well be a reduced need for national courts to refer questions to the European Court. Furthermore, it is hoped that they will draw not only from community jurisprudence but also from the experience of their counterparts in other member states. It is doubtful in any case whether the potential overburdening of the European Court is a legitimate concern of the national courts.[65]

These concerns must be viewed alongside the ongoing reform of the Community's institutional framework to prepare for the accession of new member states. A key issue is how to reduce the caseload of the European Court. One suggestion is that competition cases be referred to the Court of First Instance, which was established in 1989 to hear *inter alia* competition cases.[66] A far more radical solution is to create a Community competition court that would have jurisdiction to challenge national rulings on competition matters. Although this option cannot be ruled out, it is unlikely that it will be chosen in the immediate future.[67]

The Commission proposes steps to 'support' national courts when interpreting and applying EC competition rules. The White Paper accepts that consistency in decision making might be improved by increasing information and cooperation procedures, and suggests that national courts should be obliged to notify the Commission of cases before them that raised competition issues.[68] This is to ensure that the Commission is made aware of 'any problems of textual interpretation or lacunae in the legislative framework.'[69] The Commission would then be able to intervene, with leave of the court, as *amicus curiae*; this would give it a much greater role in national proceedings.[70] Centralized, faceless institutions clearly do not facilitate effective enforcement through the national courts; in this regard the Commission's proposal to become more involved at a national level is a pragmatic response to calls for greater cooperation between national judges and Commission officials. However, it is questionable whether the member states' legal systems would permit this role. Moreover, it envisages a role for the Commission in the national legal systems that would encroach on the hallowed turf of judicial autonomy. The Faculty of Advocates in Scotland, for example, has stated that the Commission's proposal to intervene raises 'delicate questions as to the role of the national courts and seems to envisage a more pro-active or inquisitorial role for domestic courts and judges than has hitherto been the norm within the Anglo-Celtic legal systems of England, Scotland and Ireland.'[71] Moreover, the Commission would face the practical problem of when and when not to intervene. The respective market shares of the various parties to the case would likely play a significant role in such decisions. The White Paper also proposes that Regulation 17 be amended to allow national courts to approach the Commission to ask for 'procedural, legal or economic information.' The rules in the 1993 Notice on Cooperation would also be incorporated in the regulation amending Regulation 17/62. These proposals are radical; they envisage a much greater role for the Commission in national proceedings than has previously been the case. Although designed to alleviate the Commission's burden in Community competition law enforcement, and to promote more effective cooperation between the courts and DGIV, it is clear that these 'solutions' are also resource intensive.

The proposal to involve the national courts in Community competition law enforcement also raises controversial questions of procedural harmonization. Although the White Paper does not explicitly mention the need to harmonize procedures and remedies, it is clear that the integration of national systems is very much on the Commission's agenda. One Commission official, speaking at a conference held shortly after the White Paper was published in 1999, referred to the need for all national courts to be in a position to protect the rights given by Community competition law. For example, in his view, national courts ought to hear declaratory and class actions, to give interlocutory relief, to give remedies against unlawfully obtained advantages, and to proceed without delay.[72] This is a development that many member states may wish to resist.

A related issue is whether the national courts are suitable forums for determining whether the criteria articulated in Article 81(3) have been met. As previously mentioned, the proposal to involve the national courts in the competition law enforcement process has met considerable opposition in certain member states. The concern is that the national courts – especially in the applicant states in central and eastern Europe – will apply the criteria inconsistently. It has been suggested for example, that '[judges] cannot make value judgements except in a very limited field, certainly not in relation to general economic questions.'[73] This view is not credible. Several cases decided in the British courts demonstrate that national court judges are perfectly capable of applying competition law concepts.[74] National courts have, since the very inception of the Community, been empowered to apply Article 81(1) – a provision that arguably involves a much more complex consideration of what a restriction of competition is or is not than the criteria articulated in Article 81(3). The important issue here is not whether Article 81(3) is suitable for judicial determination but rather what the criteria enshrined in Article 81(3) are designed to achieve.[75] This issue is not new, and since the inception of the Community there has been considerable debate concerning the meaning of Article 81(3). Oddly enough, the White Paper seems to reject the consideration of non-economic concerns as part of the balancing test to be carried out under Article 81(3). This statement is puzzling, given the European Court's insistence that the EC competition rules be interpreted in light of the treaty objectives. It is also hard to reconcile with some of the Commission's previous decisions, which confirm the relevance of a broad range of factors under Article 81(3) – not just economic factors but also social, cultural, industrial, and environmental ones. Employment, for example, was considered a relevant factor under the first condition in Article 81(3) in *Metro v. Commission*.[76] Thus, assuming Article 81(3) allows the consideration of non-competition criteria, the question is whether national courts are equipped to take decisions that require the weighing of public and private interests. Given the margin of discretion open to the Commission in deciding cases under Article 81(3), there is a real danger that the criteria would be open to subjective interpretation.

Certainly those member states (like the United Kingdom) that have introduced domestic competition laws that have been modelled closely on the Community system have resisted incorporation of an exemption procedure that requires a national court to make that decision.[77]

These proposals are clearly controversial and raise a number of practical, institutional, and constitutional concerns vis-à-vis the relationship between Community law and national law. There can be no doubt that involving the national courts in the application of Article 81 in its entirety will dramatically alter the culture of Community competition law enforcement. The inability of the national courts to exempt agreements under Article 81(3) has been a significant obstacle to the enforcement of individual rights. Thus, an obvious consequence will be an increase in recourse to the national courts by private individuals. This will bring the Community competition law enforcement process more in line with the position in the United States, where private enforcement of the competition rules is prevalent.[78] Aggrieved third parties who are directly affected by restrictive practices will be able to obtain damages more easily since Article 81 in its entirety would be directly applicable. Although there have been many cases in which the British courts have considered the possibility of obtaining a final award of damages,[79] there has not as yet been any definitive decision on the issue in such domestic forums. The White Paper puts the position beyond doubt: individuals will become full players in the Community competition law enforcement process.

Elevation of the National Competition Authorities

The Commission also proposes a bigger role for the national competition authorities (NCAs) in the application of the Community competition rules.[80] Their role in the enforcement process will be crucial, and their relationship with the national courts and the Commission will be redefined. In practice there is already extensive cooperation between the Commission and the national competition authorities. The Commission intends to formalize this arrangement to 'make better use of the complementarity that exists between the national authorities and the Commission, and to facilitate the application of the rules by a network of authorities operating on common principles and in close collaboration.'[81] As mentioned earlier, Regulation 17, Article 9(1) will need to be amended to remove the monopoly over exemptions and to make it clear that any authority considering a case of application of Article 81 will have to consider whether the tests for exemption have been satisfied. In this regard, each NCA will need to be empowered, as a matter of domestic law, to apply Community law. At present only eight member states have given their NCAs the requisite administrative competence to apply the Community competition rules.[82]

One of the biggest obstacles to decentralization has been the risk of inconsistent application of the competition rules by NCAs throughout the Community. The need for consistency remains a key issue, and the Commission is concerned that the NCAs might diverge from the Community position. Accordingly, the White Paper makes a number of proposals to ensure a maximum of uniformity. For instance, the Commission supports proposals to amend Regulation 17 so as to obligate NCAs to inform the Commission of cases being conducted by them under national law that may have implications for Community proceedings. There is already a precedent for this in German law, which provides that the

Commission must be informed of cases that involve the application of Community law so that the Commission can express its views.[83] Where appropriate, the Commission would have the right to withdraw a case from the jurisdiction of the particular NCA. For example, where the alleged restriction of competition is especially serious or has implications for the 'Community interest,' the Commission would withdraw the relevant case. These pragmatic proposals are designed to ensure that the NCAs reach the same decisions as the Commission would have, had it been dealing with these cases; however, simply informing the Commission of this intention will not be sufficient to ensure the uniform application of Community law. Moreover, although the national courts will be able to make an Article 234 reference to the Court on substantive issues of Community law, the competence of an Article 234 reference from the NCAs is less certain, and merits close study.[84]

In a British context, the Competition Commission (previously the Monopolies and Mergers Commission), in its capacity as an appeal tribunal, will operate within the framework of legal principles, and its decisions will have the same effect as a judgment of a court of law. Appeals will be competent to the English Court of Appeal and the Scottish Court of Session. Clearly, the Competition Commission qualifies as a tribunal under Article 234(2).[85] As such, it would be competent to refer a matter to the European Court for a preliminary ruling.[86]

The position regarding the status of the Director General of Fair Trading, and the respective sector regulators in the United Kingdom is less certain. Community jurisprudence provides that the particular entity must satisfy a number of criteria in order to come within the meaning of Article 234. In *Almelo* the European Court confirmed that the entity must be established by law, must be in permanent existence, must exercise binding jurisdiction, and must apply the rule of law.[87] In *Dorch Consult* the Court extended the criteria to include the requirement of 'independence.'[88] In that case, the European Court held that the German Federal Public Procurement Awards Supervisory Board could refer a question under Article 234 to the European Court, even though not all the relevant criteria had been met.[89] The office of the Director General clearly meets these broad criteria, and a request for a preliminary ruling *may* therefore be favourably received – although not all commentators accept this position. Whether or not the director would exercise his discretion is, however, a policy decision.[90]

The trend toward harmonizing national competition laws with the Community model should alleviate some concern over the need for consistency.[91] For instance, section 60 of the UK Competition Act 1998, the 'Euro-clause,' obliges the national courts and NCAs to consider the Community position on a corresponding issue of Community law to ensure consistency with the domestic rules. The Act is therefore silent on a number of key concepts – for instance, the definition of an 'undertaking' or 'agreement' – and the national courts and competition authorities are to seek guidance on these issues from established Community case law.[92] So it is anticipated that the NCAs will have gained valuable experience in dealing with Community competition law concepts before the White Paper proposals are implemented.

Intensified Ex Post Facto Control

The third and final strand regards intensified *ex post facto* control by the Commission. This inevitably requires reallocation of responsibility for competition law enforcement as between the national competition authorities and the Commission. Although the competition authorities of member states will be able to apply Community law, the Commission will, as guardian of the treaties and guarantor of the Community interest, retain sole competence over legislative initiatives (including block exemptions, notices, and guidelines) in Community competition law. Thus, overall responsibility for competition policy will continue to rest with the Commission. The Commission will continue to adopt 'prohibition decisions' to protect the broader Community interest; this will require delimitation. It is suggested that because the Commission will concentrate on the most serious restrictions of competition, these decisions will assume great importance as Community competition law precedents.[93] It is also anticipated that the number of prohibition decisions that the Commission can take will increase, although, given the other resource pressures it faces, the Commission's claim that the numbers will increase 'substantially' is not credible.

Ex post facto control will make a vital contribution to the attainment of a rights-based common culture of competition in the Community and indeed beyond. A system of *ex post facto* control will place additional responsibilities on undertakings to carry out their own assessment of whether their activities are compatible with the Community competition rules; this will make them more autonomous and accountable in global society.

The trend toward greater autonomy and 'the more responsible' undertaking is of particular importance in the context of the enlargement of the Community. It is doubtful, however, whether the applicant states presently have the expertise to advise undertakings of such risks as previously discussed. Although the Commission expressly recognizes that the introduction of a 'decentralized' notification system 'could prove particularly difficult for the new Member States, whose administrative structures might not be up to such a task,'[94] it fails to mention how it intends to devise a system in the 'context of pre-accession strategy' of preparing new member states for the demands of decentralized EC competition law. The Commission will clearly need to devote more time and energy than the

White Paper seems to envisage in the area of helping the administrations of member states. For example, it may be that some sort of transitional notification system will need to be retained in the new member states requiring undertakings to notify the Commission where they exceed a certain level of market power. This would therefore operate as an exception to the proposals outlined in the White Paper. Of course, an unfortunate consequence of greater autonomy – and one not confined to the enlargement debate – may be a greater inclination to sue professional advisors over matters of compliance. Such practice is already prevalent in American antitrust cases.

Conclusion

The White Paper and the new regulation have been described as 'bold and imaginative' initiatives of the commission.[95] They clearly represent a radical and pragmatic program of reform based on a threefold approach: ending of the notification and authorization procedure and replacing it with a directly applicable exemption system; decentralizing enforcement through the national courts and NCAs and intensifying *ex post facto* control. It is perhaps inevitable that reform is also controversial, and the implications wide-ranging.

Besides the technocratic reasons for reform, the White Paper heralds (to borrow a phrase from a former Competition Commissioner, Professor C.D.Ehlermann) the start of a 'cultural revolution' in the Community competition law enforcement process. As I have stated repeatedly throughout this essay, decentralized application of the Community's competition rules is integral to the creation of a 'rights-based' common culture of competition throughout the Community. This culture cannot be imposed on individuals in the member states, and those aspiring to membership; it must develop from within. Decentralization is the key to that process. Involving the national judiciary in competition law enforcement will mean Community competition norms become less institutionalized and administrative in nature and will consequently assume greater relevance for individuals. However, given the tendency of Europeans to seek redress through administrative and governmental bodies rather than through courts, this 'cultural revolution' will not happen overnight. The draft regulation is not likely to be implemented until 2004, and even then it will be several years before a significant sea change in the culture of competition law enforcement is felt.

As this essay has also sought to demonstrate, the development of a rights-based common culture of competition has particular relevance for the applicant states. Private enforcement of the Community competition rules through the national courts will help the applicant states embrace fully functioning market economies; it will also foster acceptance of competition norms. I welcome the proposals to bring the NCAs and the national courts closer to individuals although for many applicant states is the additional burden and responsibility that decentralization will entail for some applicant states – for example, Cyprus and Malta – remain problematic and may delay accession to the treaties. Arguably, the ending of the centralized notification system will merely shift the administrative burden off the Commission onto the national authorities. The Commission therefore has a duty to help the applicant states prepare for the *acquis communautaire*, and also to help them surmount the additional difficulties that decentralization will bring. Concrete proposals are urgent – for example, training for the various national judiciaries and clearer support for the NCAs will both need to be provided.

Decentralization will also entail a new role for undertakings in the competition law enforcement process. The regulatory burden for undertakings will increase – significantly in some cases, especially among small and medium-sized enterprises – and this will result in greater compliance costs and a loss of some legal certainty. However, decentralization presents undertakings with the opportunity to take on new responsibilities to police their own conduct and ensure compatibility with the competition rules. This new role will encourage undertakings, both by 'carrot and stick,' to become more responsible and accountable in a global economy. The inclusion of the new Charter of Fundamental Rights in the Treaty framework, currently in draft form, will play a vital role in bridging the gap between the new legal remedies proposed – for example, by offering the possibility of awards of damages and interim relief through the national courts, and by ensuring an adequate degree of protection of the rights of undertakings and individuals in the community. It is hoped that undertakings will relish the additional responsibilities that decentralization entails.

The new era is eagerly awaited.

NOTES

* This essay was written in response to the publication of the Commission's White Paper and draft Regulation in 1999 and 2000 respectively. A final amended Regulation was adopted in December 2002, Regulation 1/2003, and will enter into force on 1 May 2004. The timing of this revised Regulation coincided with copy proofs and hence full cognizance of this development has not been possible.

1 A White Paper represents a statement on the part of the Commission as to its policy, whereas a Green Paper merely sets out a number of options as part of a wide consultation process. See Commission of the European Communities, *The Green Paper on Vertical Restraints*, 1996 at 721.

2 Commission of the European Communities, *White Paper on Modernisation of the Rules Implementing Articles 85 and 86 of the EC Treaty,* [1999] 5 C.M.L.R. 208, OJ [1999] C 132/1.

3 Proposals for a Reg. implementing Arts. 81 and 82, (2000) COM 582, 27 Sept. 2000 (the draft Reg).

4 See R. Wessling, 'The Draft Regulation Modernising the Competition Rules: The Commission Is Married to One Idea' (2001) 26 E.L. Rev. 357.

5 Commission Notice of 1997 October 15, [1997] O.J.I. C313/3 on cooperation between national competition authorities and the Commission in handling cases falling within the scope of Article 85 or 86 of the E.C Treaty; Commission Notice on cooperation between National Courts and the Commission in applying Articles 85 and 86 of the E.C Treaty, [1993] O.J.I. C39/6.

6 EC, *Council Regulation No. 17 of 6 Feb 1962 (First Regulation implementing Articles 85 and 86 of the Treaty),* [1962] O.J.L. 35 at 118 (Special Edition 1959-62 at 132).

7 White Paper, *supra* note 1 at para. 40.

8 White Paper, *supra* note 1 at para. 5

9 The Commission has reiterated its commitment to tackle hard-core cartels in recent years. Initiatives range from the creation of a dedicated 'cartel unit' within DG IV in 1998 to the Commission's Leniency Notice, which encourages participants in cartels to blow the whistle on illegal activities as a tradeoff for a reduced fine.

10 Agreement between the Government of the United States and the European Communities Regarding the Application of their Competition Laws, OJ L95/47, 1995, as corrected by OJ L131/38, 1995, and amended by OJ L173, 1998. See, generally, C. Cocuzza, and M. Montini 'International Anti-Trust Cooperation in a Global Economy' [1998] 3 E.C.L.R. 156.

11 The Commission identifies enlargement as one of the essential challenges to the modernization of EC competition policy.

12 Commission of the European Communities, *Green Paper on Vertical Restraints in EC Competition Policy,* [1996] COM 721, *Communication from the Commission on the application of the Community competition rules to vertical restraints – Follow-up to the Green Paper on Vertical Restraints,* [1998] COM 544; *Reg. 1215/1999 of June 10, 1999 amending Reg. 19/65 on the application of Article 81(3) of the Treaty to certain categories of agreements and concerted practices,* [1999] O.J.L. 148/1; *Reg. 1216/1999 of June 10, 1999 amending Reg. No. 17: first Regulation implementing Articles 81 and 82 of the Treaty,* [1999] O.J.L. 148/5.

13 Regulation 2790/99 came into force on 1 June 2000.

14 More recently, the Commission completed a review of its policy on horizontal agreements.

15 Dr D. Wolf, 'Perspektiven des Europaischen Kartellrechets' (Position paper, Frankfurter Institute- Stiftung Marktwirkschuft und Politik, 8 July 1999) [unpublished].

16 The German Monopoly Commission and the German government made it clear that they would not support the Commission's proposals. Although the German government's assent to the new regulation is not crucial – following the Treaty of Amsterdam, under Article 81(3) action may be taken by qualified majority – a legal challenge remains a possibility.

17 Even more surprising is the realization that the Commission's comprehensive and ambitious reform of the block exemption system completed in 1999 will be rendered largely obsolete. The White Paper proposals also affect the enforcement of domestic law – for example, the U.K. Competition Act 1998, which only came into force in 2000. This Act will have to be amended when the new regulation comes into force. See B.J. Rodger, 'The Commission White Paper on Modernisation of the Rules Implementing Articles 81 and 82 of the EC Treaty' (1999) 24 E.L. Rev. 653 at 654.

18 See, for example, R. Wessling, 'The Draft Regulation Modernising the Competition Rules: The Commission Is Married to One Idea' (2001) 26 E.L. Rev. 357; C.D Ehlermann, 'The Modernization of EC Antitrust Policy: A Legal and Cultural Revolution' (2000) 37 C.M.L.R. 537.

19 The Treaty of Amsterdam, which came into force on 1 May 1999, renumbered various treaty articles, including Articles 85 and 86, which became Articles 81 and 82. This essay refers to the new treaty numbering.

20 Article 3(g) of the EC Treaty, for instance, requires 'the institution of a system ensuring that competition in the internal market is not distorted.'

21 Commission of the European Communities, O.J.L. 13, 21.2.62, at 204, *supra* at note 6.

22 Article 9(1) provides: 'Subject to review of its decision by the Court of Justice, the Commission shall have sole power to declare Article 81(1) inapplicable pursuant to Article 81(3) of the Treaty.'

23 White Paper, *supra* note 2 at para. 76.

24 See, for example, *B.R.T v. S.A.B.A.M,* [1974] E.C.R. 51.

25 Article 10 (ex 5) of the Treaty, for example, does not require member states to align domestic laws with community law. It merely establishes an obligation on states not to introduce measures that would impede community objectives. See, however, *INNO v ATAB,* [1977] E.C.R. 2115.

26 The Competition Act 1992 entered into force on 1 July 1992. See, for example, J. Carle and K. Simonsson, 'Competition Law in Sweden' [1993] E.C.L.R. 177.

27 The Competition Act Statute No. 384 of 10 June 1997 entered into force on 1 January 1998. See M. Kofmann, 'The Danish Competition Act' [1998] E.C.L.R. 1.

28 The Competition Act 1991 and the Competition Amendment Act 1996.

29 The Competition Act 1998.

30 Maher suggests that the process of decentralization in the community has contributed to the creation of an environment in which alignment of domestic competition law

with the community rules is more likely. See I. Maher, 'Alignment of Competition Laws in the EC' (1996) 16 *Yearbook of European Law* 223 at 226.

31 Competition Law No.21/1996, adopted by the Parliament of Romania in February 1996, came into force on February 1997. See, for example, U. Zinameister and D. Vasile, 'Romania's New Competition law' [1998] E.C.L.R. 164.

32 See, for example, T. Toth, 'Competition Law in Hungary: Harmonisation towards EU Membership' [1998] E.C.L.R. 358.

33 Prospective members of the European Union are required to introduce competition laws based on the competition provisions of the Community treaty. See K. Van Miert, 'Competition Policy in relation to the Central and Eastern European Countries – Achievements and Challenges' *Competition Policy Newsletter*, Issue 2, June 1998.

34 Despite widespread recognition that substantive reform was necessary, the Conservative government failed to introduce legislation based on the Community model, citing lack of Parliamentary time, and instead made only minor amendments to existing legislation. See *Department of Trade and Industry Consultation Document: Review of Restrictive Trade Practices Policy*, Cm 331, 1988; *Opening Markets: New Policy on Restrictive Trade Practices*, Cm 727, 1989; and *Abuse of Market Power*, Cm 2100, 1992. A more plausible explanation has been suggested for the delay in reform; some commentators have regarded the Conservative Party's stance on Europe as an obstacle to the introduction of pro-European legislation. See S. Wilks, 'The Prolonged Reform of UK Competition Policy,' in G.B. Doern and S. Wilks (eds.), *Comparative Competition Policy: National Institutions in a Global Market*, (Oxford: Clarendon Press, 1996) at 139.

35 Germany is the only member state not to have introduced Community-based rules, most likely because its competition regime was already well entrenched in German commercial culture prior to accession to the European Communities. The German Government has repeatedly expressed concern about the efficacy of the Community model of competition, and it is unlikely that new legislation will be enacted in the near future.

36 Many OECD countries have also adopted the Community model of competition. On 20 February 1998 in Paris, the OECD Committee on Competition Law and Policy agreed a Draft OECD Recommendation based closely on the Community approach to cartels.

37 See *Volk v. Etablissements Vervaecke Sprl* [1969] E.C.R. 295, [1969] C.M.L.R. 273, in which the European Court held 'an agreement falls outside the prohibition in Article 85(1) where it has only an insignificant effect on the market, taking into account the weak position which the persons concerned have on the market of the product in question.'

38 See the recently revised Commission Notice on Agreements of Minor Importance (2003) O.J. No. C368/13.

39 See *Commission Regulation on Exclusive Distribution 1983/84,* [1984] O.J.L. 173/1, *Commission Regulation on Exclusive Purchasing 1984/84,* [1984] O.J.L. 173/5. These block exemptions have now been replaced by the single-umbrella block exemption, Regulation 2709/99.

40 White Paper, *supra* note 1, at para. 34.

41 *Procurer de la Republique v. Bruno Giry and Guerlain* [1981] C.M.L.R. 99.

42 Case T-24/90 *Automec v. Commission* (No.2) (1992) E.C.R. II-2223, [1992] 5 C.M.L.R. 431.

43 *Commission Notice of 23 December 1992 on co-operation between national courts and the Commission in applying arts. 85 and 86 of the EC Treaty,* O.J.I. [1993] C39/6.

44 *Commission Notice on co-operation between the national competition authorities and the Commission in handling cases falling within the scope of arts. 85 and 86 of the EC Treaty,* O.J.I. [1997] C 313 at 25.10.

45 See, generally, A. MacCulloch and B.J. Rodger, 'Wielding the Blunt Sword: Interim Relief for Breaches of EC Competition Law before the UK Courts' [1996] E.C.L.R. 393.

46 White Paper, *supra* note 1 at para. 39.

47 White Paper, *supra* note 1 at para. 56.

48 White Paper, *supra* note 1 at para. 57.

49 For a detailed discussion on the issue of whether non-competition concerns should be taken into account under Article 81(3), see Wessling, *supra* note 4 at 368-374.

50 The Commission acknowledges this concern in the White Paper, *supra* note 1 at para. 57.

51 White Paper, *supra* note 1 at paras. 66, 67, and 68.

52 White Paper, *supra* note 1 at para. 11.

53 White Paper, *supra* note 1 at para. 69.

54 *Case T-24/90* [1992] E.C.R. II-2223.

55 *B.R.T. v. S.A.B.A.M.* [1974] E.C.R. 51.

56 White Paper, *supra* note 1.

57 Prospective members of the European Union are required to introduce competition laws based on the competition provisions of the Community Treaty. See K. Van Miert, 'Competition Policy in relation to the Central and Eastern European Countries - Achievements and Challenges,' *Competition Policy Newsletter,* Issue 2, June 1998.

58 See the Commission's Competition Policy Newsletter, 2002 Number 1, February, at 4.

59 See *Van Gen en Loos* [1963] E.C.R. 1; [1963] 105; *Costa v ENEL* [1964] E.C.R. 585; [1964] C.M.L.R. 425.

60 *Rheinmuhlen-Dusseldorf v. Einfuher-und Vorratsstelle fur Gerreide und Futtermittel (No. 1)* [1974] E.C.R. 33, at 38. See also the opinion of Advocate General Lagrange in *de Geus v. Bosch* [1962] E.C.R. 45, which provides an excellent overview of the function of the Article 234 procedure.

61 See A. Arnull, 'References to the European Court' (1990) 15 E.L.R. 375.

62 Courts of last instance need not refer where the matter has been previously determined by the European Court or the matter is clear. See, for example, *CILFIT v. Ministry of Health* [1982] E.C.R. 3415 and Re Sandhu, *The Times*, 10 May 1985.

63 An exceptional case, in which the European Court declined to exercise jurisdiction, can be seen in *Foglia v. Novello (No. 1)* [1980] E.C.R. 745, [1981] 1 C.M.L.R. 45 and *Foglia v. Novello (No. 2)* [1981] E.C.R. 3045, [1982] 1 C.M.L.R. 585. See generally A. Barav, 'Preliminary Censorship? The Judgment of the European Court in *Foglia v. Novello*' (1980) 5 E.L.R. 443; D. Wyatt, 'Foglia No. 2: The Court Denies It Has Jurisdiction to Give Advisory Opinions' (1982) 7 E.L.R. 186; and G. Bebr, 'The Possible Implications of *Foglia v. Novello* II' (1982) 19 C.M.L.R. 421. In subsequent cases the Court reverted to a policy of non-interference; see, for example, *Walter Rau v. de Smedt* [1982] E.C.R. 3961, [1983] 2 C.M.L.R. 496.

64 This was certainly true until the early 1990s. British courts made approximately five to six references a year. Since 1992 this figure has been slowly rising; twenty-four cases were referred in 1998. See the European Court's website: www.europa.eu.int/cj/en/stat/index.htm.

65 See, for example, the comments of Pennycuick. VC, in *Van Duyn v. The Home Office* [1974] 3 All. E.R. 178 (Ch.D) at 187.

66 See the comments of Professor Richard Whish to the House of Lords Select Committee on the European Communities, Fourth Report, 15 February 2000, H.L. 33 at paras. 85 and 90.

67 *Ibid.*

68 A similar requirement exists in German competition law; paragraph 96 of the German Act against Restrictions of Competition, read in conjunction with paragraph 90, requires the German court to inform the Bundeskartellamt of proceedings in which Community law is applied. White Paper, paragraph 107, footnote 63.

69 White Paper, *supra* note 1, at para. 107.

70 White Paper, *supra* note 1 at para. 107.

71 House of Lords Select Committee [Sub-Committee E] on the European Communities, Session 1999–2000, Fourth Report, 29 February 2000 at para. 87.

72 J. Temple Lang, Paper (Hammond Suddards/UCL conference, London, 17 September 1999) [unpublished].

73 House of Lords Select Committee [Sub-Committee E] on the European Communities, Session 1999–2000, Fourth Report 29 February 2000 at para. 59 per Laddie J.

74 See *Oakdale (Richmond) Ltd v. National Westminster Bank* [1997] E.L.R. 40; affirmed [1997] 3 C.M.L.R. 815.

75 Certainly the U.K. judges who gave evidence to the House of Lords Select Committee on the White Paper concluded that Article 81(3) should not be debated in the national courts. *Supra* note 73, *ibid.*

76 *Metro v. Commission (No. 1)* [1977] E.C.R. 1875, [1978] 2 C.M.L.R. 1 at para. 43.

77 Under the U.K. Competition Act 1998, it is the Director General of Fair Trading who presently makes the decision to grant an exemption.

78 To date, the greatest number of cases in the national courts in the field of competition law concerned a number of beer ties in the U.K. in 1999.

79 See, for example, *Garden Cottage Foods v. The Milk Marketing Board* [1984] A.C. 130.

80 White Paper, *supra* note 1, at para. 91–8.

81 White Paper, *supra* note 1, a para. 91.

82 It is of course arguable the member states are under an obligation to make such powers available to the NCAs in any event under Article 10 (ex 5) of the EC Treaty, which imposes a duty on member states to fulfil their community obligations.

83 See paragraph 50(3) of the Restriction of Competition Act, as amended by the Sixth Amendment, which entered into force on 1 January 1999.

84 On this issue, see, generally, K.G. Middleton, 'Harmonization with Community Law: The Euro-clause,' in B.J. Rodger and A. MacCulloch (eds.), *The UK Competition Act* (Oxford: Hart, 2000). *A New Era?* [forthcoming in 2001].

85 See *Vaassen–Gobbels v. Beammbten-fonds voor het Mijnbedrijf* [1966] E.C.R. 377, [1966] C.M.L.R. 508.

86 The DTI published the *Competition Commission's Tribunal Rules (Consultation on Draft Rules)* in October 1999, 1999 U.R.N. 99/1154. Part IX, paragraph 29, explicitly refers to references to the European Court.

87 *Almelo and Others* [1994] E.C.R. I-1477.

88 *Dorch Consult v. Bundesbaugesellschaft Berlin* [1997] E.C.R. I-4961, at para. 23.

89 See also the opinion of Advocate General Leger in *Mannesmann v. Stohal Rotations-druck* [1998] E.C.R. I-73.

90 This interpretation, however, apparently contradicts the position of the government.

91 Harmonization with Community law of course brings its own set of unique problems. On the topic of harmonization, see K.G Middleton, *supra* at note 84.

92 See, for example, the decision of the Commission in *Polypropylene* O.J., 1986, L230/1; [1988] 4 C.M.L.R. 347.

93 The Commission has also indicated that it 'should be able to adopt individual decisions that are not prohibition decisions.' This might be a decision, for example, where new questions of Community law arise and a declaration of the Commission's position in relation to them is needed. White Paper, *supra* note 1, at para. 88.

94 *Ibid.,* at para. 62

95 House of Lords report, *supra* note 71, para. 145.

Chapter Nine

The Institutional Legitimacy of the International Trade System*

ROBERT SHUM

The International Trade System and Its Alleged Legitimacy Deficit

The international trade system has gone through many changes since the middle of the twentieth century, growing in both membership and activities. Throughout these changes the General Agreement on Tariffs and Trade (GATT) and the World Trade Organization (WTO) have also seen significant shifts in their legitimacy[1] as institutions. Many groups, especially those who feel that they do not have a voice in the WTO, even though it significantly affects their interests, are alleging that the international trade system is suffering from many defects.

Over time, these groups' demands for greater representation, participation, and accountability have grown more insistent. Fundamentally, these demands reflect the perception that the WTO is more a captive bureaucracy than an intergovern-mental arrangement of agreements, understandings, and mechanisms designed to facilitate greater trade and prosperity. These opposing perspectives represent pos-sible organizational destinies that Ivan Head predicted long ago would begin to characterize international organizations as their activities developed and expanded: on the one hand, the international trade system may indeed represent an effort to evolve a 'brilliant patchwork' of laws and other instruments to help nations cope with growing economic interdependence; on the other hand, it may also evolve into a dysfunctional and unaccountable bureaucratic entity, one that is characteristic of so many 'which now rest upon the international community as an increasingly insupportable burden'.[2]

The conflicting points of views regarding the legitimacy of the international trade system go to the heart of the following questions: Is the present system indeed an appropriate institutional instrument for effective global governance?

And can it function effectively in a complex and pluralistic global social environment beset with multiple interests and values that sometimes compete and conflict with one other? As the international trade system has expanded, it has come into increasing contact and occasional conflict with other interests and values – values unrelated to trade and economic efficiency but equally embedded in international law and society. In this essay I examine some of the conflicts that have emerged. I conclude with an analysis of some of the pressures that seem to consistently act on the international trade system, and threaten its legitimacy, and suggest some consequences that these pressures may produce.

Specific Areas and Examples of Conflict

Fundamentally, GATT and the WTO Agreement recognize that states have an interest in trade. The question is whether the international trade system recognizes any other social interests. In the following section I examine the treatment of security, macroeconomic, environmental, labour, and intellectual property concerns in the WTO jurisprudence. The treatment of these issues also reflects potential conflicts that could arise among international organizations, and the consequences those conflicts may have for their legitimacy as institutions in the international legal order. The following cases illustrate potential stresses on the legitimacy of the WTO system, especially those stresses which may arise in the course of the WTO's treatment of broader international interests within its trade-oriented framework. This treatment may conflict with that of other international legal regimes designed primarily to protect and regulate these other international rights and interests, which exist independent of trade priorities.

Security

Security interests are clearly recognized by GATT. Article XXI, titled 'Security Exceptions,' states that when necessary, security interests are to prevail over trade interests. But relatively few countries have used this exception to impose trade sanctions.[3] Article XXI consists of three paragraphs as follows:

> Nothing in this Agreement shall be construed
> (a) to require any contracting party to furnish any information the disclosure of which it considers contrary to its essential interests; or
> (b) to prevent any contracting party from taking any action which it considers necessary for the protection of its essential security interests
>   (i) relating to fissionable materials or the materials from which they are derived;

(ii)   relating to the traffic in arms, ammunition and implements of war and to such traffic in other goods and materials as is carried on directly for the purpose of supplying a military establishment;

(iii)   taken in time of war or other emergency in international relations; or

(c)   to prevent any contracting party from taking any action in pursuance of its obligations under the United Nations Charter for the maintenance of international peace and security.[4]

Regarding these provisions, the most popular subject of GATT panel legislation has undoubtedly been Article XXI(b)(iii). Before examining the jurisprudence, we should also note the presence of Article XXI(c). This last provision is one example of GATT clearly and unequivocally deferring jurisdiction to another instrument – in this case the UN Charter. Under Article 2(7) of the Charter, it is left to the Security Council to determine what constitutes a threat to international peace and security. Thus, no conflict in jurisdiction is ever likely to arise between GATT and the Security Council regarding security measures taken by the latter that also affect trade. This is because GATT clearly defers to the Security Council in this respect and does not reserve any right for the WTO to review Security Council decisions. Article XXI(c) is therefore the basis for the 'GATT legality' of all trade sanctions authorized by the Security Council under Chapter VII of the UN Charter.

It is also worth noting that Article XXI(c) does not apply to the International Court of Justice (ICJ) and that GATT has not deferred to the ICJ on security matters. It has been argued that ICJ decisions should be taken into account by GATT panels when the validity of an Article XXI defence is being determined. For instance, when Nicaragua complained that the American embargo on it constituted a violation of GATT that was unjustifiable by reference to Article XXI(b), it cited the ICJ's judgment in its favour regarding American actions in Nicaragua.[5] This argument, however, was found to be inapplicable given the panel's terms of reference, which had been set according to a strict view of the references to self-judgment in Article XXI(b), which will be discussed further below.[6] It would seem that only sovereign states and the Security Council have the power to assess the validity of a claim that 'essential security interests' may justify trade measures.

Article XXI also seems to permit unilateral trade sanctions for political and security reasons. Article XXI(b) applies the security exception to measures taken by any contracting party 'which *it* [i.e., that party] considers necessary for the protection of its essential security interests.' A GATT panel seems to have no jurisdiction at all to consider or review an invocation of security interests as justification for a breach of GATT obligations. The bar on GATT review of national security justifications for trade restrictions was in particular reinforced by the precedent set by the 1986 *Trade Measures Affecting Nicaragua* panel; here the GATT

Council expressly denied to the panel any jurisdiction to adjudicate the substantive legal validity of the American defence.[7]

Overall, however, optimism may be derived from the exceptional nature of the Nicaragua case. It seems that informal restraints on the use of Article XXI(b) have been largely effective to date: states appear to be well aware that unrestrained invocations of Article XXI(b) would pose a threat to their credibility. Because of all the pressure that could be brought to bear on states, which have an interest in maintaining both their own credibility and that of the GATT/WTO system; abuses of Article XXI(b) have largely been averted. At the same time, attacks have been avoided on the legitimacy of the WTO based on the perception that that body is a threat to a country's security interests (as might be thought to be a likely reaction to WTO actions seeking to limit trade-related security measures). Nonetheless, the WTO's legitimacy as it affects national security interests can still become a live political issue when sharply defined ideological interests come into play, as in the case of relations between the United States and Cuba under the U.S. Helms–Burton legislation.

Monetary Policy

It seems that next to the Security Council, the International Monetary Fund (IMF) receives the greatest amount of recognition in the text of the GATT treaty. GATT recognizes that trade restrictions can provide relief from balance-of-payment difficulties, and it reserves the WTO's right to investigate the imposition of such measures. Thus, the mere assertion of a 'balance-of-payment difficulty' is not sufficient for trade restrictions.[8] Exchange measures can also affect international trade, although they seem to be more clearly under the purview of the IMF.[9] Article XV(1) sketches out the broad outlines of jurisdiction in these areas:

> The Contracting Parties shall seek co-operation from the International Monetary Fund to the end that the Contracting Parties and the Fund may pursue a co-ordinated policy with regard to exchange questions within the jurisdiction of the Fund and questions of quantitative restrictions and other trade measures within the jurisdiction of the Contracting Parties.[10]

The relationship between the GATT–WTO and the IMF is one of cooperation and coordination rather than hierarchy or primacy. This is quite different from the hierarchical relationship between the UN Charter and GATT in matters of international peace and security.

Where there is an overlap in jurisdiction, this cooperative relationship between the IMF and the GATT–WTO appears to demand consultation between the two organizations.[11] Provision for consultation is made under Article XV(2):

> In all cases in which the Contracting Parties are called upon to consider or deal with problems concerning monetary reserves, balances of payments or foreign exchange arrangements, they shall consult fully with the International Monetary Fund. In such consultations, the Contracting Parties shall accept all findings of statistical and other facts presented by the Fund relating to foreign exchange, monetary reserves and balances of payments, and shall accept the determination of the Fund as to whether action by a contracting party in exchange matters is in accordance with the Articles of Agreement of the International Monetary Fund ...

Thus, it seems that GATT defers to the IMF's judgment on factual and technical points concerning monetary policy, but in no way cedes to the IMF the right to determine the GATT legality of measures affecting monetary and/or trade policy. An exchange measure is subject to scrutiny by GATT, and is still subject to GATT's standard that no measure shall nullify or impair the benefits that accrue under GATT.[12]

This requirement for consultations has at times been met informally – for example with regard to the measures imposed by Italy at a time of acute balance-of-payment difficulties requiring importers to make temporary foreign exchange deposits.[13] This measure is a typical example of an action that essentially reduced the profitability of imports yet also seemed to be a legitimate exchange control measure designed to make up balance-of-payments shortfalls.[14] With regard to the design of exchange controls, the outer limits of creativity have surely not yet been tested, so the issues this incident raises are certainly interesting. This particular measure was discussed in GATT, IMF, and EEC committees, but it was never subject to a GATT panel since it was simply a temporary measure and no formal complaint was ever brought.

GATT panels have also had to deal with balance-of-payments justifications for trade restrictions. This justification has often seemed rather desperate and has been used only in situations where the party invoking it appears to have no real case at all. Parties seem to avoid whenever possible having to rely on this defence. The GATT panel report on *Japanese Measures on Imports of Leather* is a prime example.[15] This case concerned a quantitative restriction that had been justified on balance-of-payments grounds when it was enacted. Before the panel, however, Japan chose to focus its arguments solely on social concerns for its disadvantaged leather-working caste. One can imagine that they did so because they knew that defences based on Article XV were unlikely to persuade. In the *Korean Restrictions on Imports of Beef* cases,[16] Korea did attempt to argue a balance-of-payments justification. It did so in part because of the massive public debt that its government owed, which, it was argued, placed Korea's currency and balance-of-payments situation in a position of extreme vulnerability, despite the large balance-of-payments surpluses the country was running at the time. Korea lost the argument largely because of this last fact. On that point, the panel relied on the IMF's factual and statistical submissions in making a determination in accordance with Article XV.[17] Thus, in practice, while almost any trade restriction could perhaps be justified by balance-of-payment concerns, to be legitimate, such restrictions would likely have to be temporary in nature, and would have to be removed as soon as a balance was restored. GATT complaints tend to concern long-term trade barriers, and the use of balance of payments as a justification is perhaps an accurate indicator of a losing cause. There appears to be no large loophole for trade barriers based on the separateness of monetary policy from trade policy, and no real opportunity for conflict between the IMF and GATT. Their jurisdictions, while at times concurrent and overlapping, do not in any inherent fashion represent opposing state interests, policies, or imperatives.

Environmental Treaties

Neither GATT nor the WTO agreement makes explicit reference to international environmental treaties or organizations. There is no conclusive provision in the GATT/WTO treaties for applying international environmental agreements within the GATT/WTO framework. We may, however, turn to general principles of international law for guidance regarding how these two sets of treaties – the one trade related, and the other environmentally focused – are to interact. Here we encounter two relevant principles of international law: *lex posterior* and *lex specialis*. The former is described in Article 30(3) of the Vienna Convention on the Law of Treaties.[18] According to that provision, when two agreements signed by the same parties are in conflict, the agreement that is earlier in time applies only to the extent that its provisions are compatible with those of the later treaty. *Lex specialis* is the basic principle of legal interpretation which presumes that of two agreements, the more specific is meant to control. Under these principles, it may be reasonable to expect that obligations deriving from environmental treaties will be recognized by the GATT/WTO system, insofar as they deal with specific problems, and insofar as most if not all such treaties postdate the original 1947 GATT agreement. It would indeed be difficult to consider the 1994 WTO agreement as an entirely novel regime intended to be a specific waiver of environmental obligations, rather than to assume the reverse.[19] These principles might therefore outweigh the potential conflict between the GATT principle of non-discrimination[20] and the obligation in several international environmental treaties to discriminate against non-parties in the course of restricting trade in certain environmentally hazardous substances. An obligation of this sort is contained in Article 4 of the Montreal Protocol on Substances That Deplete the Ozone Layer,[21] which prohibits trade with non-parties in specified controlled substances.[22] Similar provisions restricting trade with non-parties also appear in the Basel Convention on the Control of Transboundary Movements of Hazardous Wastes and Their Disposal,[23] and in the Convention on International Trade in Endangered Species of Wild Flora and Fauna (CITES),[24] regarding trade in hazardous wastes and endangered species, respectively.

An additional problem relates to the status of non-parties to the environmental treaties who are, however, parties to GATT. Article 30(4) of the Vienna Convention provides that 'as between a State party to both treaties and a State party to only one of the treaties, the treaty to which both States are parties governs their mutual rights and obligations.'[25] In such an event, an obligation under an environmental treaty could indeed come into conflict with the principle of non-discrimination. As a result, GATT could, according to the interpretative rules of the Vienna Convention, decide that the obligation it imposes must prevail and thereby rule the relevant environmental obligation to be GATT illegal; thus a state that is party to an environmental treaty could theoretically find itself in violation of GATT by virtue of its treaty-obligated refusal to trade with another GATT member that is non-party to the environmental treaty.

However, the environmental obligation might still be saved in such cases under provisions within GATT itself. In particular, Article XX of GATT may be effective in this regard despite the pessimism that has been generated by the *Tuna/Dolphin* panel's ruling on this provision.[26] In this panel report, Article XX(b)'s exception from GATT scrutiny for bona fide measures 'necessary to protect human, animal, or plant life'[27] was interpreted as requiring a measure to be necessary in the sense of there not being any less GATT-inconsistent means available to accomplish the measure's ends. The essence of Article XX(b)'s requirement that restrictions be 'necessary' was defined by the *Tuna/Dolphin* panel as requiring the exhaustion of 'all options reasonably available' to the restricting party. Of special note is the statement that such GATT-legal options include those 'in particular through the negotiation of international cooperative arrangements.'[28] In the context of the specific measures at issue in the *Tuna/Dolphin* panel report, unilateral environmental measures were deemed unnecessary. There is no indication that a multilateral international regime would not be considered 'necessary' under Article XX. The evidence, however, is to the contrary. GATT has never denied that the international community has the right to defend itself against environmental threats by whatever means it may find fit. It appears that we must distinguish between the environmental judgments of individual states and those of the international community (as expressed through international organizations and international agreements). In this area there is not as yet any reason to fear a lack of cooperation between international organizations. Even those whose interests appear to be as disparate *prima facie* as those of GATT and the international environmental regimes[29] are likely to cooperate in this area. Given the benefit of the doubt, there is little foundation for criticizing the WTO system as an *over-reaching* and *inherently* hostile threat to legitimate multilateral environmental agreements.

Domestic Environmental Regulations

In the *Tuna/Dolphin* case the GATT/WTO dispute settlement mechanism applied the idea that environmental regulations might only govern production 'processes.' This being so, the regulations would be viewed as discriminatory and as a barrier to free trade that might be subject to trade sanctions. The *Tuna/Dolphin* case has for this reason become the focus of opposition to the WTO – specifically, to its tendency to view social norms and institutions as production 'processes' that are secondary to the main priority of ensuring the free movement of goods.

The GATT panel report on this case, formally known as *United States Restrictions on Imports of Tuna,*[30] considered the GATT legality of an American restriction on foreign tuna. This restriction was applied on the basis of whether or not there existed in a given exporting country sufficient regulation of certain dolphin-unsafe tuna-harvesting practices. This prompted a challenge by Mexico, which viewed the legislation as a violation of GATT trade obligations.

The United States argued that its legislation did not violate any trade obligations under GATT and that even if it did, it was still legal as an example of measures excepted by Article XX.[31] Article XX recognizes concerns that may ground exceptions to GATT's trade obligations, in such a way that such trade obligations are not to prevail over legitimate domestic measures intended to protect certain public-policy interests.[32] The environment is one such interest. Article XX is headed 'General Exceptions'; under it, paragraphs (b) and (g) might conceivably be interpreted as encompassing most environmental policy interests:

> Subject to the requirement that such measures are not applied in a manner which would constitute a means of arbitrary or unjustifiable discrimination between countries where the same conditions prevail, or a disguised restriction on international trade, nothing in this Agreement shall be construed to prevent the adoption or enforcement by and contracting parties of measures: ...
>
> (b) necessary to protect human, animal or plant life or health; ...
>
> (g) relating to the conservation of exhaustible natural resources if such measures

are made effective in conjunction with restrictions on domestic productions or consumption;'.[33]

Paragraphs (b) and (g) themselves may be a source of controversy in terms of defining what is 'necessary' and what constitutes 'domestic' measures. Another source of controversy involves the qualification contained in the introductory section of Article XX regarding 'arbitrary or unjustified discrimination where the same conditions prevail, or a disguised restriction on international trade.' Questions may arise as to the standards to be applied in the course of inquiring into the arbitrariness and underlying purposes of such a measure.

Returning to the *Tuna/Dolphin* case, Mexico argued that Article XX did not apply to the American legislation, because of the international scope of the measures it entailed:

> [N]othing in Article XX entitled any contracting party to impose measures in the implementation of which the jurisdiction of one contracting party would be subordinated to the legislation of another contracting party. It could be deduced from the letter and spirit of Article XX that it was confined to measures contracting parties could adopt or apply from within or from their own territory. To accept that one contracting party might impose trade restrictions to conserve the resources of another contracting party would have the consequence of introducing the concept of extraterritoriality into the GATT, which would be extremely dangerous for all contracting parties.[34]

Mexico contended that the American measures were outside the exception in Article XX since they were not 'necessary' as required by Article XX(b), insofar as other GATT-legal measures were available, the scope of which could have been confined within American territory, enabling them to have maintained GATT legality. Mexico also argued that the American measures constituted 'arbitrary discrimination' in terms of their unilateral nature, and were therefore not covered by Article XX according to the article's preamble.[35] The United States replied that Article XX provided exceptions for the simple and unqualified protection and conservation of animal life and resources. It further suggested that since the subjects of protection in this case 'roam the high seas,' it indeed 'could protect imports of tuna produced in a manner resulting in the needless death of dolphin outside the jurisdiction of the United States and of any country.'[36] The concern here related to the ineffectiveness of merely domestic measures to protect the environment while unsafe practices were continuing elsewhere unabated and while the products of these practices received unimpeded access to the domestic market. The result would be ineffective protection whose only beneficiaries would be for-

eign producers, who would be gaining a competitive advantage against the regulated producers of the importing state.

The *Tuna/Dolphin* panel report reveals what might be at stake for environmentalists and developing countries with regard to trade-related environmental obligations. Environmentalists are concerned about the potential for environmental
free-riding, environmental dumping, and the externalization of environmental
costs by producers in developing countries; in contrast, developing countries are
deeply concerned about measures that make trade conditional on the adoption of
developed countries regulatory standards – measures that might indeed be characterized as 'extraterritorial.' The panel decision reflected these concerns by agreeing with Mexico that unilateral and extraterritorial measures could not be
justified under Article XX:

> The Panel considered that if the broad interpretation of Article XX(b) suggested by
> the United States were accepted, each contracting party could unilaterally determine
> the life or health protection policies from which other contracting parties could not
> deviate without jeopardizing their rights under the General Agreement. The General
> Agreement would then no longer constitute a multilateral framework for trade
> among all contracting parties but would provide legal security only in respect of trade
> between a limited number of contracting parties with identical internal regulations.[37]

Such a result could lead to the imposition of developed countries standards on
the governments of developing countries, and enforce measures taken by developed countries to govern resources that do not belong to them. Indeed, some
might argue that such measures represent a kind of 'eco-imperialism,' or a 'green
variant of the nineteenth-century's white-man's burden.'[38] Developing countries
have alleged that environmental measures are a form of the 'disguised protectionism' that the Preamble to Article XX anticipated: the *Tuna/Dolphin* panel report
included a submission by Indonesia which pointed out that the Americans' environmentally justified restrictions on tuna were merely the latest in a series of
twenty-three restrictions on tuna imports.[39] In sum, developing countries fear
that environmental justifications may not be genuine, and may simply be a disguised form of protectionism.

All of this highlights some of the tensions and contradictions that exist
between the international trade system and its critics. The case shows why 'the
opponents of trade liberalisation decry the secretiveness and "nondemocratic"
nature of the WTO, and the disproportionate influence of corporate interests in
rule making.' They see 'a trading system that privileges business over labour
rights, the environment, and consumer safety.'[40] These widespread perceptions,
encouraged by decisions such as in the *Tuna/Dolphin* case, show that the WTO

can easily lose its public legitimacy. Citizens may not feel directly represented in the WTO. Their lack of a sense of participation can develop into anger when combined with the perception that certain constituencies do indeed have privileged access to the organization. The fear that the WTO is not accountable to public interests is further amplified when WTO decisions seem to affect policies designed primarily to address public issues and values unrelated to trade. These actions are then perceived as outrageous and illegitimate. These problems are especially acute given the diffuse and abstract nature and benefits of the relevant trade principles that the WTO endeavours to uphold and protect.

Overall, the issue of environmental regulation seems to be a flashpoint for conflicts and concerns regarding the legitimacy of the international trade system. Pressure for institutional reform has continued to build despite indications that WTO panels have begun to leave more room for countries to impose environmental regulations on widely traded products in a non-discriminatory manner, as in the more recent appellate decision on the *Shrimp/Turtle* case.[41] In this 1998 case the WTO's Appellate Body revisited the Article XX(g) exception and ruled that an American import ban on shrimp that had been harvested according to processes harmful to sea turtles could *prima facie* be a WTO-legal measure relating to the conservation of exhaustible natural resources as contemplated in Article XX(g). This decision accepts that states can impose trade-restrictive measures relating to animal species outside of the regulating country[42] – including measures relating to processes – as WTO-legal measures relating to the conservation of exhaustible natural resources, subject to the general prohibitions on arbitrary and unjustifiable discrimination and on disguised restrictions of international trade. In the specific case at issue, however, implementing procedures relating to the American legislation to protect sea turtles were found to be discriminatory and thus WTO illegal. The outcome of this case seems to indicate that the balance between the two imperatives of conservation and non-discriminatory trade will remain a point of contention for some time to come. This highlights the challenges facing the international trade system in terms of the need to address perceived defects in the legitimacy of its treatment of environmental concerns as they relate to the movement of goods across borders.

Labour

Trade-restrictive labour regulations are excepted from trade obligations. The one narrow exception is for trade-restrictive measures 'relating to the products of prison labor,' which are explicitly covered by Article XX(e) of GATT.[43] Arguments have also been made that this provision can and should be interpreted to cover products of forced labour generally.[44]

Beyond this, however, one rapidly enters a domain where labour regulations might be considered 'process' factors that cannot be invoked in order to restrict trade. This is so despite the existence of the International Labour Organization (ILO) and its work in supporting labour regulations around the world.

There is a general distaste everywhere for forced labour. Beyond this, however, there is no international consensus on labour standards, and arriving at one will be difficult at best. Within the trade framework, there is also a fundamental divergence of perspectives between developing and developed countries. Where developing countries perceive disguised attempts at protectionism and the diminution of their comparative advantage, developed countries see subsidies to industry by governments as an outgrowth of low labour standards.

This is why efforts by developed countries to establish labour standards often seem illegitimate to developing countries. Conversely, certain sectors in developed countries regard free trade without harmonized labour standards as unfair. To address the concerns of the relevant parties, careful negotiations will have to be conducted and conscientious policy mechanisms will have to be developed. Since this area of international concern relates to interests and values falling outside strictly trade-related questions, it may be most appropriate to increase action and organizational development outside the WTO. As it happens, the ILO is a legitimate institution designed specifically to address labour concerns. It has the specialized expertise to help build capacity for developing and enforcing labour standards in developing countries. This shift in focus onto the ILO may not, however, eliminate the pressure to include labour standards in the WTO's mandate. This pressure may well bear fruit, given the WTO's perceived effectiveness in approving trade sanctions. Legitimacy in this area is likely to remain contested for some time to come. The possible upside to this kind of continuing conflict is that institutions will have an incentive to serve dissatisfied constituencies as a means of gaining legitimacy for themselves.

Nonetheless, in the area of minimum labour standards, the international trade system faces pressure to take steps that may undermine its long-term legitimacy. In the developing world, legitimacy will probably require that protection of social norms and institutions be implemented without imposition of national standards. Failure to prevent the imposition of foreign standards would undermine the legitimacy of the international trade system by threatening domestic norms and self-determination through the unrestrained exercise of unilateral power.

Intellectual Property

Among the arguments against recognizing labour and environmental concerns in the international trade system is the supposed need to maintain a strictly trade-oriented focus. This is belied, however, by the inclusion of intellectual property rights in the international trade system. Intellectual property does not directly generate any efficiency gains from trade. The pharmaceutical industry is a good example of how the international enforcement of intellectual property rights serves only to transfer monopoly rents from developing countries to companies in developed countries.[45] For many, the inclusion of intellectual property rights and the exclusion of labour and environmental concerns are evidence that the trade system's agenda favours commercial interests.

The international regime for intellectual property rights has been administered since its inception by the World Intellectual Property Organization (WIPO).[46] GATT had no provisions at all concerning intellectual property rights. However, the Final Act Embodying the Results of the Uruguay Round of Trade Negotiations included an Agreement on Trade-Related Aspects of Intellectual Property Rights (TRIPS).[47]

The WIPO's objectives are listed under Article 3 of its founding treaty. They are the following:

(i)   to promote the protection of intellectual property throughout the world through co-operation among states and, where appropriate, in collaboration with any other international organization,
(ii) to ensure administrative cooperation among the Unions.[48]

The 'Unions' referred to in paragraph (ii) are defined in Article 2 (v–vii) as those organs which were established by the Paris and Berne Conventions, as well as any other intellectual property organs and agreements the administration of which the WIPO might assume. While the WIPO Convention expressly refers in its objectives to the agreements that preceded it, the TRIPS Agreement states its objectives generally:

The protection and enforcement of intellectual property rights should contribute to the promotion of technological innovation and to the transfer and dissemination of technology, to the mutual advantage of producers and users of technological knowledge and in a manner conducive to social and economic welfare, and to a balance of rights and obligations.[49]

Thus TRIPS seems intended to be self-standing, encompassing its own finite set of goals and objectives. Although cooperation with the WIPO is mentioned in the preamble,[50] the TRIPS agreement is in none of its essential operations in any way contingent on or built on existing WIPO activities. In the TRIPS agreement itself, the WIPO is merely referred to in the context of negotiations for potential joint projects, such as the establishment of a common register of intellectual property laws and regulations.[51]

TRIPS is an interesting example of the international trade system taking on overlapping functions that have already been covered by an existing international institution. This development has certainly been criticized as evidence that powerful private interests in the developed world are able to influence the WTO's agenda and take advantage of its near monopoly on the use of trade sanctions, in effect using the WTO to enforce those rights which are in their interests, to the exclusion of others. The procedural legitimacy of WTO negotiations and the processes for setting the agenda for trade talks have perhaps been harmed to an extent unforeseen by the interested parties. Nonetheless, the parallel TRIPS/WIPO regime may also serve as an example of a way forward – one that includes multiple and partially competing institutional arrangements within the international system. Greater variety and institutional pluralism may well encourage institutions to compete for legitimacy by seeking broader representation and by serving a wider range of constituencies and interests across the international community. The result would be greater legitimacy for the system as a whole.

Conclusion: Processes for Gaining Legitimacy through Competitive Pluralism in the International Institutional Setting

In this essay I have considered the contesting of jurisdiction, express or implied, that has arisen in a number of GATT/WTO panel reports. Over its history, GATT and the WTO have formalized and streamlined their procedures; they have also grown in effectiveness and proven their worth.[52] As a result, aggrieved parties have shown more willingness to pursue claims within a trade framework and to push the limits of the jurisdiction of this relatively effective mechanism. An obvious example of this trend is the inclusion of the Agreement on Trade-Related Aspects of Intellectual Property Rights (TRIPS) as a result of the Uruguay Round of negotiations.

The WTO's relative effectiveness has contributed to its legitimacy as an effective policy instrument and functional international institution. In particular, it has legitimacy among many governments, who see the WTO as fulfilling its mandate, which is to facilitate openness and cooperation in international trade within a multilateral framework. The WTO has also gained legitimacy among certain private constituencies, whose interests have been furthered by the WTO's activities. Other groups, however, question the WTO's basic purposes and objectives as well as its overall legitimacy. For these groups, the WTO's effectiveness is more of a threat than a source of legitimacy. Among these alienated constituencies the WTO has yet to develop sufficient legitimacy in terms of its representation and its procedures for determining its goals and consequences.

The development of the international trade system is representative of the general expansion and entrenchment of international law as a whole. With such an increase in prominence, however, comes new demands. The international system will have to come to terms with the prospect that conflicts and contradictions will arise among international regimes and organizations. In the WTO's encounters with security, macroeconomic, environmental, and intellectual property issues, we see indications that the call will grow louder for international organizations to recognize and balance conflicting interests.

This may require an increase in cooperation among international organizations, as well as the development of more mechanisms to facilitate cooperation. Consultations such as we have seen in the Italian deposit case, between the IMF and GATT, may well become more common as well as a normal part of the business of international organizations. Such overlaps in authority may have other effects besides that of heightening the requirement for coordination. Alternative legal procedures may develop among separate institutions (recall the case of the WIPO and the WTO). Competition as well as coordination may arise as a result. Overlaps in authority may spur innovations in institutional procedures and developments in substantive international law as international organizations compete for legitimacy and resources. Institutional pluralism and competition could thereby exert additional pressure on institutions to widen participation and increase accountability. In this way, among others, their legitimacy may be enhanced.

Without the assurance of such increases in institutional legitimacy, the hope that the global order will become more humanized will more likely than not turn out to be forlorn.

NOTES

* I would like to thank Ivan Head and Janet Lam for their comments on earlier versions of this chapter. Any remaining mistakes and inaccuracies are solely my own.

1 International organizations like the WTO are, of course, structurally legitimate in the contractarian sense of being the product of concrete treaty agreements between sovereign states. These institutions may, however, find their legitimacy challenged as a result of the rules and decisions they promulgate while exercising their legally delegated powers. These decisions may be considered unfair on the basis of underlying values and justifications external to the narrow rule itself. For example, unfairness and illegitimacy can be alleged in terms of process (e.g., lack of transparency, access, or representativeness), fundamental or substantive unfairness (as in unequal distribution of benefits or inconsistent application of rules), inappropriate jurisdiction, or otherwise troubling conflicts with the animating values of the institution concerned (or indeed

of other institutions as well). On legitimacy in the international system, see T.M.
Franck, 'Legitimacy in the International System' (1988) 82 *American Journal of International Law* 705, and *The Power of Legitimacy among Nations* (New York: Oxford
University Press, 1990); and O.C. Okafor, 'The Global Process of Legitimation and
the Legitimacy of Global Governance' (1997) 14 *Arizona Journal of International and
Comparative Law* 117.

2 Professor Head writes of the need for 'brilliant patchworks' in *On a Hinge of History:
The Mutual Vulnerability of South and North* (Toronto: University of Toronto Press,
1991) at 22. In 'The Contribution of International Law to Development,' 1987
Canadian Yearbook of International Law 29 at 36, he writes the following:

> What is advocated here is the enhancement of legal rules and processes, not the creation of ever more numerous institutions and bureaucratic structures, so many of
> which now rest upon the international community as an increasingly insupportable
> burden, structures that quickly take on such a political character that in many
> instances they mask effectively the purpose for which they were created. In recent
> years, the reach of international organizational activity has exceeded by far the grasp
> of substantive international law. If Robert Browning is correct, there may well be
> some sort of organizational heaven somewhere. From the perspective of an international lawyer, however, the absence of adequate legal underpinnings is more reminiscent of T.S. Eliot.

3 Article XXI has been invoked a number of times in direct political disputes such as
those between the United States and Czechoslovakia, Cuba and Nicaragua during the
Cold War; between Argentina and Britain's supporters during the Falkland Islands War;
between the Arab League and Israel; and between Ghana and Portugal with regard to
the latter's colonial policies. Besides these bilateral political disputes, only two restrictions that were justified by 'national security' have generally affected other GATT members as opposed to a particular political target: an American restriction from the pre-
OPEC era and a brief 1975 Swedish restriction on shoes that – according to Sweden's
GATT representative – was justified on the basis that the 'decrease in domestic production had become a threat to the planning of Sweden's economic defence. This policy
required the maintenance of a minimum domestic production capacity in vital industries.' Only in the Nicaragua case did a panel report result. See R.S. Whitt (Note), 'The
Politics of Procedure: An Examination of the GATT Dispute Settlement Panel and the
Article XXI Defense in the Context of the U.S. Embargo on Nicaragua' (1988) 19 *Law
and Policy in International Business* 603 at 617–20; R.E. Hudec, 'GATT Legal
Restraints on the Use of Trade Measures against Foreign Environmental Practices,' in J.
Bhagwati and R.E. Hudec, eds., *Fair Trade and Harmonization: Prerequisites for Free
Trade?*, Vol. 2: *Legal Analysis* (Cambridge, MA: MIT Press, 1996) 95 at 148.

4 General Agreement on Tariffs and Trade, *Basic Instruments and Selected Documents* 38.

5 'Panel Report on Trade Measures Affecting Nicaragua,' GATT Doc. L/6053 (13 October 1986), online: LEXIS, Library: *INTLAW,* File: *GTTWTO.*

6 Ibid., para. 5.15: 'The Panel wishes to note that in the course of the Panel proceedings Nicaragua had maintained that GATT could not operate in a vacuum and that the GATT provisions must be interpreted within the context of the general principles of international law taking into account inter alia the judgment by the International Court of Justice and United Nations resolutions. While not refuting such argumentation, the Panel nevertheless considered it to be outside its mandate to take up these questions because the Panel's task was to examine the case before it "in the light of the relevant GATT provisions," although they might be inadequate and incomplete for the purpose.'

7 Ibid.

8 Art. XIV, General Agreement on Tariffs and Trade, *Basic Instruments and Selected Documents* 23–4.

9 Art. XV(9) states in particular that the use of 'exchange controls or exchange restrictions in accordance with the Articles of Agreement of the International Monetary Fund' shall not be precluded by the GATT. Ibid., 26.

10 Art. XV, ibid., 24.

11 Aside from the provisions in Article XV(2), recognition of the possibility of overlap also appears in the form of a general exhortation under Article XV(4): 'Contracting parties shall not, by exchange action, frustrate the intent of the provisions of this Agreement, nor, by trade action, the intent of the provisions of the Articles of Agreement of the International Monetary Fund.' Ibid.

12 Art. XXIII, ibid., 39.

13 See D.L. Guider, '1981 Italian Deposit Requirement' (1983) 14(3) *Law and Policy in International Business* 927.

14 It did so by requiring 30 per cent of the lire value of exchange transactions to be deposited without interest for ninety days with the Bank of Italy; this reduced the purchasing power of importers, thereby decreasing the volume of imports and thus the balance-of-payment deficit. The result for trade and importers was essentially to increase the cost of imports by requiring a forfeiture of the interest on the deposit.

15 GATT Doc. L/5623 (2 March 1984), in *Basic Instruments and Selected Documents,* 31st Supp. (1985) 94–114.

16 GATT Docs. L/6504 (24 May 1989), L/6505 (24 May 1989), and L/6503 (24 May 1989), in *Basic Instruments and Selected Documents,* 36th Supp. (1990) 202–306.

17 See *Ibid.,* GATT Doc. L/6503, paras. 121–3.

18 *Vienna Convention on the Law of Treaties,* 1155 U.N.T.S. 331.

19 Some have claimed, however, that under Art. II, para. 4, of the Agreement Establishing the World Trade Organization, the WTO is to be considered 'legally distinct from the GATT,' and that GATT/WTO obligations should therefore be considered to now

postdate all pre-1994 treaties. See for example, S. Hudnall, 'Towards A Greener Trade System,' in (2000) 29 *Columbia Journal of Law and Social Problems* 175 at 192. The fact remains, however, that the GATT obligations most relevant to the enforcement mechanisms of environmental treaties were established in 1947, and that these obligations remain fundamentally unaltered by the WTO Agreement.

20 Art. I, General Agreement on Tariffs and Trade.

21 26 I.L.M. 1541.

22 It should be noted that Article 4.8 of the Montreal Protocol does allow for non-parties to be accorded favoured treatment if they nonetheless can be determined to be in full compliance with the terms of the Protocol.

23 Article 4.5; 28 I.L.M. 649.

24 Article X; 12 I.L.M. 1085.

25 *Vienna Convention on the Law of Treaties*, 1155 U.N.T.S. 331.

26 'United States Restrictions on Imports of Tuna (Tuna/Dolphin),' *Basic Instruments and Selected Documents*, 39th Supp. 155 (1993).

27 Art. XX(b), 4 *Basic Instruments and Selected Documents* 37.

28 *Tuna/Dolphin, supra* note 26, para. 5.28.

29 The best way to confront hostile 'faceless international bureaucrats,' it would appear, is to mobilize your own friendly international bureaucrats. This seems especially applicable in dealings with GATT, which has become habituated to having to keep a close watch on national governments, which never seem to tire of attempting bad-faith unilateral manoeuvres for circumventing international objectives in pursuit of short-term gains. There is no reason to believe that GATT is at all hostile to environmental measures taken cooperatively and in good faith, and no indication that it would not work constructively alongside the relevant international organizations.

30 GATT Doc. DS21/R, in *Basic Instruments and Selected Documents*, 39th Supp., 155.

31 Ibid., para. 3.27.

32 Many of these exceptions have been largely uncontroversial, since they deal with such measures as those for 'public morals,' para. (a); 'importation or exportation of gold or silver,' para. (c); and 'national treasures,' para. (f). See GATT, 4 *Basic Instruments and Selected Documents* 37–8.

33 *Ibid.*

34 *Supra* note 26, para. 3.31. Questions about this line of argument remain as to where exactly the 'letter or spirit of Article XX' is to be found. If anything, the exceptions in para. (e) regarding prison labour and paragraph (f) regarding national cultural treasures reflect precisely a concern for the practices and resources of other countries – a concern that seems quite expressly recognized by Article XX despite the fearsome connotations conveyed by Mexico's invocation of the spectre of 'extraterritoriality.'

35 *Ibid.*, para. 3.34

36 *Ibid.*, para. 3.36.

37 *Ibid.*, para. 5.27. Cf. 'United State Restrictions on Imports of Tuna (II),' GATT Doc. DS29/R (20 May 1994), 33 I.L.M. 839, para. 5.38, where the Panel agreed with the arguments of the European Community with regard to the effects of the American restrictions on their trade: 'If ... Article XX (b) were interpreted to permit contracting parties to impose trade embargoes so as to force other countries to change their policies within their jurisdiction, including policies to protect living things, and which required such changes to be effective, the objectives of the General Agreement would be seriously impaired.' The emphasis here is on the nature of the American measures as intending to 'force' a change in policy by other states, and on the measure's exclusive reliance on such coercion to achieve its objectives, since it 'required such changes to be effective.'

38 See for example, D. Lal, 'Trade Blocs and Multilateral Free Trade' (1993) 31 *Journal of Common Market Studies* 356.

39 *Tuna/Dolphin* panel report, *supra*, note 26, para. 4.15.

40 See for example, D. Rodrik, '5 Simple Principles for World Trade,' *The American Prospect*, 17 January 2000.

41 Report of the Appellate Body on U.S. Import Prohibition of Certain Shrimp and Shrimp Products, WTO Doc. WT/DS58/AB/R, 12 October 1998.

42 It should be noted that the Appellate Body seems to be aware of the issues of extraterritoriality raised by the *Tuna/Dolphin* panel, since the Appellate Body is careful to observe that sea turtles migrate through American territory, so that there is a sufficient nexus between the migratory and endangered marine populations involved and the United States for purposes of Article XX(g). See *ibid.*, para. 133.

43 GATT, 4 *Basic Instruments and Selected Documents* 38.

44 K.A. Elliot, 'Getting Beyond No ...! Promoting Worker Rights and Trade,' in J.J. Schott, ed., *The WTO After Seattle* (Washington: Institute for International Economics, 2000).

45 See, e.g., D. Rodrik, *The New Global Economy and Developing Countries: Making Openness Work* (Washington: Overseas Development Council, 1999) at 148.

46 828 U.N.T.S. 3; 6 I.L.M. 782.

47 33 I.L.M. 1197.

48 828 U.N.T.S. 3; 6 I.L.M. 782.

49 TRIPS Agreement, *supra* note 47, art. 7.

50 The preamble states that the Contracting Parties are 'Desiring to establish a mutually supportive relationship between the WTO and the World Intellectual Property Organization as well as other relevant organizations.' TRIPS Agreement, *supra* note 44, Preamble.

51 TRIPS Agreement, *supra* note 47, Arts. 63 and 68.

52 See R.E. Hudec, *Enforcing International Trade Law: The Evolution of the Modern GATT Legal System* (Salem: Butterworth Legal Publishers, 1993) at 11–15.

Chapter Ten

The International Seabed Authority: Challenges and Opportunities

RONALD ST J. MACDONALD

The purpose of this essay[1] is to contribute to the debate about the role of the International Seabed Authority ('the Authority') and its evolutionary development as envisaged by the Implementation Agreement of the Law of the Sea Convention.[2] The challenge is to bring new activities that have arisen as a result of scientific, technological, economic and political developments within the scope of the mandate of the Authority and organize them in a manner that will benefit all stakeholder states, other regimes, the Biodiversity and Climate conventions, and other major groups. I will outline a few of the complex interconnections between the Seabed Authority, the UNCED 1992 instruments (namely, the Biodiversity[3] and Climate conventions),[4] seafloor observations and the laying of submarine cables, and open ocean fertilization. This essay's theme is the need for a more active Authority and for greater harmonization of its activities with the related mandates and activities of international bodies.

Genetic Resources and Biodiversity

Even though the Law of the Sea Convention (UNCLOS)[5] generally limits its mandate to the exploitation of the mineral resources of the deep seabed (the 'Area'), the Authority has some responsibility for the conservation and orderly utilization of newly discovered resources in the Area. Article 145 of UNCLOS states that necessary measures shall be taken with respect to the mining 'activities in the Area to ensure effective protection for the marine environment from harmful effects which may arise from such activities.' Subparagraph (b) says that these measures must include 'the protection and conservation of the natural resources [biodiversity] of the Area, and the prevention of damage to the flora and fauna of the marine environment.' If the Authority is to protect these resources, it must first know something about them. And it must be in a position to monitor activities in the Area that may have harmful effects.

At present this responsibility is shared with the secretariats established under the Biodiversity and Climate conventions. As Dr Salvatore Arico has recently observed, the contracting parties to the Convention on Biological Diversity (CBD) have responsibilities for the overall conservation of biodiversity, and these responsibilities may include the international seabed area.[6]

Article 4 of the CBD provides that regarding the components of biodiversity, the convention applies only within the areas of national jurisdiction of contracting parties. Regarding 'processes and activities,' the convention applies in areas both within and outside national jurisdiction. At the same time, Article 5 promotes international cooperation among the parties to the treaty 'directly or, where appropriate, through competent international organizations [such as the Authority] in respect of areas beyond national jurisdiction [which would include the Area] and on other matters of mutual interest, for the conservation and sustainable use of biological diversity.'[7] Article 6, paragraph 4, of the same convention provides that 'each Contracting Party shall take legislative, administrative or policy measures, as appropriate, with the aim that the private sector facilitates access to joint development and transfer of technology referred to in paragraph 1 above for the benefit of both governmental institutions and the private sector of developing countries.'[8]

The reference in Article 6 to 'joint development and transfer of technology' should be emphasized. This provision is reinforced by Article 17, paragraph 5, which states that 'the Contracting Parties shall, subject to mutual agreement, promote the establishment of joint research programs and joint ventures for the development of technologies relevant to the objectives of this Convention.'[9] Finally, Article 22 represents the essential bridge between the Biodiversity Convention and the Convention on the Law of the Sea. That provision states that 'Contracting Parties shall implement this Convention with respect to the marine environment consistently with the rights and obligations of States under the law of the sea.'[10] These responsibilities are reinforced by the Jakarta Mandate on Marine and Coastal Biological Diversity, which provides a framework for implementating these provisions.

Article 4 refers to 'processes and activities' affecting biodiversity, and in Article 5 to cooperation with respect to areas beyond national jurisdictions; in practice, however, activities have been restricted to areas under national jurisdiction and to exclusive economic zones regulated mainly by bilateral agreements based on the convention. This is partly because at the present time, access to genetic resources in the Area is essentially unregulated.

It was in this context that in 1995 the Conference of the Parties to the CBD, at its second meeting, commissioned a study on the overlapping responsibilities arising from the Law of the Sea and Biodiversity conventions. Because the political climate at that time was not favourable, the study had to be postponed. But the political situation has changed. Cooperation in the field of genetic resource bioprospecting is ongoing between the CBD Secretariat and UNDOALOS, for the purpose of completing this study. Furthermore, the CBD Secretariat has been following with interest the work of the Authority, as well the ongoing discussions on the possible expansion of the latter organization's mandate. In this spirit, the CBD has asked the Authority for observer status and been granted it. If the mandate is expanded to cover issues relating to genetic resources, this will require close cooperation with the CBD and with the relevant processes that are taking place in its context, such as the work of the CBD Expert Panel on Access to Genetic Resources and Benefit Sharing.

Dr Arico has indicated that many questions – for example, questions regarding *ex situ* conservation – remain unresolved and will have to be dealt with at future meetings of contracting parties. The conservation and sustainable use of genetic resources in international waters, including the deep seabed, and the sharing of benefits arising from them, constitutes a sort of legal vacuum. Clearly, programs of action to conserve biodiversity in international seabed areas will have to be carried out in cooperation with the Authority, which under Article 145 of UNCLOS also has responsibility for the 'prevention of damage to the flora and fauna' in the Area (including its genetic resources).

It is apparent that a potentially strong legal framework already exists for cooperation between the CBD and the International Seabed Authority. The success of this interorganizational cooperation will depend partly on the future work of the ISA and partly on the deliberations of the Conference of the Parties on the issue of bioprospecting for marine and coastal genetic resources, including those in the Area. The debates at this conference will be based on the findings of the abovementioned study, as well as on the knowledge base that the secretariat has been acquiring with the assistance of the convention's experts on marine and coastal biological diversity.

At present there seems to be agreement only on broad principles. Genetic resources in international waters, including the deep seabed, are freely accessible and are not regulated in any way. In fact, the existence of these resources was unknown at the time UNCLOS was drafted. That is why no reference is made to them in the text of that convention.

Today, more and more of these resources are being discovered. It seems that millions of species await discovery and DNA sequencing. Technologies for commercially exploiting the enzymes they produce are already at advanced stages of development. Some of the bacteria found in the deep seabed possess unique qualities, such as resistance to extremely high temperatures and high pressures – qualities that make them suitable for certain bioindustrial and pharmaceutical applications. Some of these bacteria possess medicinal properties, such as anticancer or antiviral properties. Many industries could benefit from these genetic resources, for example, the pharmaceutical, waste treatment, food processing, oil extraction, paper processing, and mining industries. It is estimated that the exploitation of genetic resources already generates billions of dollars in annual revenues.

So far, little has been done to implement the Biodiversity Convention and protect biodiversity in international waters, including the seabed beyond national jurisdictions. This lack of regulation of international waters is jeopardizing the effectiveness of protective measures that *have* been taken under national jurisdiction. The different sectors of ocean space are closely interrelated and need to be regulated in a much more holistic way. The relevant genetic resources overlap the territorial waters within national jurisdictions and the high seas outside them. As long as these resources can be taken freely from the high seas, without any obligation to share their benefits, why would any industrial state bother to conclude 'access agreements' with relevant coastal states?

Methane Hydrates of the Seep Aeabed, Climate, and Climate Change

Hydrates are found in abundance in marine sediments. They store immense amounts of methane, and their exploitation will have major implications for the energy generation capacities of states, as well as for the stability of the global climate. In physical appearance, methane hydrates resemble ice. They are common in the Arctic and Antarctic permafrost zones and in seafloor sediments below 500 metres. The zone of the seabed in which these hydrates are stable in marine sediments extends from the sea floor down for hundreds and even thousands of metres.

Seabed hydrates were discovered in the early 1970s, but only in the past five years has serious research has been carried out regarding their potential use. In February 1999 the U.S. Department of Energy's Office of Fossil Energy released a Draft National Methane Hydrate Multi-Year R&D Program Plan. This detailed plan to remove technological barriers preventing resource extraction by 2010, and to provide guidelines for commercial development of the resource by 2015, contains information of very great interest to the International Seabed Authority. Energy resource enhancement, hazard and seafloor destabilization prevention, and the impact of methane hydrates on climate change will be the three main aspects of future methane research.

Hydrate research is being carried out in several countries besides the United

States. India and Japan have initiated national programs to recover methane from oceanic hydrates within their territorial waters. Participants in hydrate research programs include the Japan Petroleum Exploration Company (JAPEX), the U.S. Geological Survey, the Geological Survey of Canada, and a number of universities. It should be noted that cooperation between hydrate researchers and oil companies, utilizing the latter's technologies and infrastructures, is cost-effective and mutually advantageous. Cooperation with the fibre-optic cable companies would be equally advantageous and would reduce risks of cable breakage arising from the destabilization of the sea floor and from landslides on continental margins. The Indian government launched its program of resource evaluation in 1996 and is already offering hydrate development leases to private industry.

Some may consider methane an excellent *transition* fuel in the gradual movement toward non-polluting energy sources. Methane, however, is a 'greenhouse gas.' Although there is much less methane in the atmosphere than there is carbon dioxide, each methane molecule has a much greater heating effect. For example, the global warming potential of methane over a twenty-year period is calculated to be fifty-six times greater than that of carbon dioxide. Scientists are concerned about what might happen if large volumes of methane were released abruptly from the gas hydrate reservoir. In such a thing happened, the changes in the global climate could be enormous. The increase in the carbon dioxide content of the atmosphere has so far been continuous and predictable; in contrast, the increase in the methane content of our global atmosphere is highly unpredictable and could be catastrophic.

To exploit gas hydrates, exploration and research will be required to locate concentrations of these resources and to understand the natural processes at those sites where methane can be extracted economically. The technologies required are known and are fairly simple but they have not yet been developed on a commercial scale. Some places where methane hydrate is concentrated have been identified, but little intensive exploration has so far been carried out.

Just as with the Biodiversity Convention, the Framework Convention on Climate Change (FCCC) covers the hydrosphere (including the oceans and seabed), the biosphere, and the geosphere. This latter convention also deals with the deep seabed – a fact that calls for cooperation between the FCCC Secretariat and 'competent international organization[s]' (including the Authority). Article 5 exhorts the parties to the convention 'to support and further develop, as appropriate, international and intergovernmental programs and networks or organizations aimed at defining, conducting, assessing and financing research, data collection and systematic observation, taking into account the need to minimize duplication of effort.'[11]

The FCCC contains numerous other articles relating to the need for cooperation between the secretariat it establishes and the Authority. We can hope that the FCCC Secretariat will follow the precedent set by the CBD Secretariat and request observer status with the Authority. This could be done by establishing joint programs linking the two organizations. In the South China Sea, cooperation between the Parties to the Law of the Sea Convention, the Biodiversity Convention, and the Climate Convention is already well developed.

Methane has affected the world's climate throughout geological history, and its impact is even greater today. A better understanding of the methane cycle will be needed if we are to respond intelligently to the greenhouse effects of this otherwise useful gas resource. Those who drafted the FCCC could not have been aware of research undertaken during these last five years; furthermore, like the Biodiversity Convention, the FCCC does not pay sufficient attention to methane's impact on climate change in international waters, including the seabed. However, the parties to the FCCC are aware of the valuable analytical work being done on climate change and of the important contributions being made by the World Meteorological Organization, the UN Environment Program, and other organizations and bodies of the UN system, as well as by other international and intergovernmental bodies. The Authority should take its proper place among these organizations and contribute its share to this research.

The parties to the FCCC have made a commitment to 'promote sustainable management, and promote and cooperate in the conservation and enhancement, as appropriate, of sinks and reservoirs of all greenhouse gases not controlled by the Montreal Protocol, including biomass, forests, and oceans as well as other terrestrial, coastal and marine ecosystems.'[12] With regard to the methane reservoirs in the deep ocean, the FCCC could best fulfil this commitment through cooperation with the Authority. It is instructive that the FCCC lists the duty 'to ensure the necessary coordination with the secretariats of other relevant international bodies' as among the functions of its secretariat.[13]

Clearly, then, the Biodiversity Convention, the FCCC, and the Authority have complementary responsibilities in the management of the resources of the deep seabed. These responsibilities can best be discharged through cooperation among the institutions of all three regimes. All three regimes will be strengthened by these cooperative activities. Where the state parties to the three conventions coincide, the first step on the road to cooperation would be a tripartite Memorandum of Understanding establishing the purpose and scope of the envisaged cooperative endeavours.[14] After that it would be up to the Authority to lay down the rules and regulations for exploration and R&D and for the safe, efficient, and economic recovery of methane from ocean gas hydrates. The third step would be to elaborate a common project advancing the purposes and goals of all three convention regimes.

The near-term benefits of all this would include the following: (1) a better understanding of the potential hazards posed by the exploitation of hydrate deposits, and of ways to mitigate the effects of those hazards; (2) a clearer understanding of the location and volume of methane hydrate resources; (3) the development of improved seismic and other geophysical instruments for use by, for example, the petroleum industry; and (4) more accurate data on ocean and atmospheric changes for use in global climate modelling.

Long-term benefits would include the following: (1) the development of engineering concepts for the production of gas from natural gas hydrate deposits; (2) a better understanding of potential safety and environmental issues associated with natural gas hydrate deposits and production; (3) an increased supply of cleaner fuel through the development of technologies required to produce methane commercially; (4) technology transfer as a result of the active involvement of industries and universities in developed and developing countries; and (5) savings in national investments in methane hydrate research and development.

With regard to technology cooperation, the FCCC specifies clearly the financial responsibilities of the industrialized countries. Article 4, paragraph 5, provides that developed country parties shall 'promote, facilitate and finance, as appropriate, the transfer of, or access to, environmentally sound technologies and know-how to other Parties, particularly developing country Parties, to enable them to implement the provisions of the Convention.'[15] Seabed research and R&D is as relevant to the Climate Convention as it is to the Biodiversity Convention. In this regard, the interactions between the deep seabed and adjacent volcanic activities, and adjacent atmospheric and water conditions, are determinants of the global carbon cycle.

Cooperation between the Authority and the Biodiversity and FCCC regimes is just now beginning. This cooperation will be extremely important and will advance the work of all three conventions.

Submarine Cables and Alternative Sources of Funding Ocean Development and Conservation

In a 1998 article in the *Herald Tribune*, a knowledgeable commentator noted that the fibre-optic cable industry was 'one of the most crucial components of today's communication-based global economy.' Question arise from this: Does the traditional freedom to lay cables under the high seas mean that the Authority has no right to control this activity? And should the Authority be compensated for any services it renders in this area?

One could argue that the laying and maintenance of cables across international seabeds constitutes an intensive activity that must be harmonized with other activities in the Area. However, this regime would have to be quite different from the one governing the resources of the Area, because cables are not a 'resource' – rather, they are a 'service.'

If the Authority were to take the task of controlling and coordinating cable laying activities so as to prevent conflict with other uses and harm to cables and other installations, it would be only fair to compensate the Authority its services. Compensation might be in proportion to the length of cables passing through the Area, or might be in proportion to the revenues generated by the cable, or it might be in the form of a 'Tobin tax' levied on financial transfers passing through the cable.

The Tobin tax was generally rejected when it was first proposed by Noble laureate James Tobin; but it has since been widely endorsed by intergovernmental organizations such as UNDP and the World Bank, as well as by academics, non-governmental organizations, and world commissions (including the Independent World Commission on the Oceans and the Commission on Global Governance). Considering that the revenues generated by these cables amount at present to something in the order of $1 trillion annually, even a 0.001 per cent 'tax' or 'user fee' would be quite substantial.

Another possibility would be to establish a Common Heritage Fund, which could be administered by the Global Environmental Facility and used for sustainable ocean development and for the enhancement of marine science and technology in developing countries. Such a fund, based on a small tax on the commercial use of ocean space and resources, was proposed by Nepal during UNCLOS III; the idea was not favourably received. It was rejected for two reasons: an international tax might infringe on the principle of national sovereignty; and the proposal came too late, at a time when UNCLOS III had almost completed its work and had decided against further changes. The idea of international taxation, under whatever name, has since been widely accepted and would be one way of responding to the regular demands by the UN and its agencies and programs for alternative sources of funding for international projects and development cooperation.

Regarding new means of generating 'new and additional and predictable funding,' curious shifts took place between the 1970s (when the LOS Convention was drafted) and the 1990s (when the UNCED process took place). It is now generally recognized that states, through their governments, lack the very substantial means required to implement the multitude of new conventions, agreements, and programs that have been established, and that 'innovative' methods for generating new, additional, and predictable funding must be found. The methods suggested in the relevant documents are not especially innovative. The most detailed projection of needs is found in Agenda 21. The most detailed list of possible sources of supply is in the Global Program of Action, but this list is far from innovative.

UNEP's GEO 2000 reminds us that a start has been made–studies conducted within the framework of the Commission on Sustainable Development have led to several new proposals, including Tobin-type taxes, which would raise money for the environment through an international tax on financial transactions. Canada has taken this idea a step farther; in March 1999 its House of Commons voted to authorize the federal government to promote the Tobin tax internationally. In addition, many banks and lending organizations, including the World Bank, have incorporated environmental considerations into their operations.

International taxation may indeed be an idea whose time has come, since states are no longer the only actors in international law. 'Civil society,' economic and social actors, municipalities, and non-governmental organizations ('major groups') are playing an increasingly important, recognized, and structured role in international negotiations. The duty to make financial contributions should follow this new right. A Tobin tax would be even more efficient today than it would have been two decades ago, since the amounts transferred have grown by several orders of magnitude, as have the technologies through which such transfers can be controlled.

In August 1999, in Jamaica, in the introduction to the proceedings of a leadership seminar organized by the International Ocean Institute, Elisabeth Mann Borgese proposed a 0.001 percent tax on business (including e-commerce) transacted through fibre-optic cables traversing the international seabed, which is the Common Heritage of Mankind. This tax would be so small that it would not be a significant burden, but one must consider that the transactions involved already amount to around $1 trillion per year, and that the revenues generated would be sufficient to change the entire structure of global sustainable development. One should also bear in mind that the Authority is the only existing international institution that, under international law already has the authority to collect taxes from seabed miners, both in the international area and in areas under national jurisdiction (i.e., on the continental shelf). Synergies with the International Telecommunications Union (ITU) would be necessary where that body exerts technical control over fibre-optic cables and transmissions.

In the negotiations that preceded the adoption of the Law of the Sea Convention (UNCLOS) in the 1970s, the developing countries sought financial support and technology transfer as part of the new international economic order they were trying to achieve, and as a corollary of the Common Heritage of Mankind. If certain resources are part of the common heritage to be shared, the technologies to get at those resources must also be shared. The industrialized countries grudgingly made a few concessions, only to take most of them back through the instruments of the UNCLOS Implementing Agreement of 1994.

When environmental agreements were being negotiated in the 1990s, the situation was quite the opposite. It was the industrialized countries that realized that conservation of the environment, of biodiversity, and of the climate required the participation of all states if it was going to succeed. If the poorer countries needed technologies and financial support in order to cooperate, it would have to be provided. The financial and technology transfer obligations imposed on the industrialized countries under the new conventions, agreements, and programs are, in fact, far greater than they were under the Law of the Sea Convention. In practice, of course, not much has changed.

Seafloor Observatories

Today's technology makes it possible to place permanent scientific observatories on the ocean floor to monitor the state of health of the oceans and to advance our understanding of the processes that occur on the ocean floor. The technologies that have made these observatories possible include electro-optical cables, remotely operated vehicles, and connectors for completing electrical and optical circuits in the water. Experimentation and monitoring in the ocean is quite expensive, since the equipment must be protected against pressure and corrosion and must also be supplied with electrical power and the means of storing and/or transmitting data. This usually requires batteries and computer hardware – items with a limited life on the ocean floor.

Observatories can reduce the costs and complexeties of installing systems on the ocean floor; they can also provide a common power and communications infrastructure for a large number of instruments. They can support a considerable variety of monitoring systems, and they make it possible to add experiments to the ocean floor and later remove them. In the present day, several ocean observatory projects are being conducted in Japan, Europe, and the United States. More observatories are being planned.

Considerable effort is being put into the design and installation of ocean observatory systems; many of these will be wired to the shore by means of submarine cables. These observatories will enable countries around the world to take part in deep-ocean monitoring; often these countries will be helping operate observatories for the world community. The installation and utilization of seafloor observatories, and the monitoring and managing of decommissioned cables, are activities that must be harmonized with other uses of the Area. The Authority could benefit greatly from these observatories; it could use those already in place, and those to be built in the future, for the long-term monitoring of the environment and resources. IRIS and the Authority should open a dialogue as soon as possible; one can hope that a delegation will recommend this to the Authority.

From an industry standpoint, collaboration with the ISA would be highly desirable. No other institution can ensure harmonization with other users of the seabed as effectively as the Authority, or establish international standards for cable installation, protection, and maintenance. For its part, the Authority would benefit from sharing the comprehensive cable fault database to be developed by the committee. The committee has an obvious interest in monitoring the development of international treaties and national legislation, as well as promoting ongoing compatibility and uniformity of the law with industry requirements. Sharing the seabed in harmony with others can be achieved only through the Authority, which has a mandate to harmonize 'activities in the Area' with other uses. A recommendation that should be made to the Authority is to commence a dialogue with the committee, the ITU, and the most important cable companies as soon as possible.

Carbon Dioxide (CO_2) Sequestration

There is mounting evidence that anthropogenic carbon dioxide is contributing to global change; this could have a negative impact on human activities. This concern has prompted many efforts at mitigation. Energy conservation and efficiency programs being established, the use of lower-carbon fuels is being encouraged (e.g., natural gas instead of coal), alternative energy sources are being developed (e.g., renewables), and research being carried out on carbon storage (terrestrial, geological, and ocean).

The case for ocean sequestration is as follows: The ocean contains roughly sixty times more carbon than the atmosphere. This means that the additional carbon dioxide that would cause a doubling of atmospheric concentrations – with attendant risks for global change – would cause less than a 2 per cent increase in average ocean concentration. Thus the impact on the ocean should be small. Furthermore, about 85 per cent of the carbon dioxide we are currently discharging into the atmosphere will ultimately enter the ocean indirectly though biological or physical processes. These processes, however, are slow, with the result that atmospheric concentrations are well above equilibrium. The argument, then, is why not pump some of the carbon dioxide into the ocean directly, thus short-circuiting the harmful atmospheric step?

Since other options (e.g., energy conservation, efficiency, fuel switching, and renewables to some degree) are less expensive in the short term, ocean sequestration is not seen as a viable option at present. But it is important to conduct research on the concept before there is any real urgency, so that there will be an adequate basis for evaluation if such an urgent situation arises.

A number of injection scenarios have been suggested, each with different costs, risks, and environmental implications. The scheme that could be realized most easily with existing technology would be to release carbon dioxide as a buoyant liquid from a bottom-mounted pipeline terminating below the ocean thermocline at a depth of about 1000 metres. Another idea is to create a 'carbon dioxide lake.' Since liquid carbon dioxide is more compressible than seawater, it becomes negatively buoyant at depths greater than about 3000 metres. Thus, carbon dioxide delivered to a seafloor depression at depths greater than about 3000 metres would be gravitationally stable.

Since carbon dioxide sequestration may have an environmental impact on the seafloor, as well as on the superjacent waters, the Authority must monitor this research and share its results, and, most desirably, involve these research groups in the environmental impact studies to be undertaken in the Area. Collaboration with UNEP would be desirable if not necessary.

Open Ocean Fertilization

Recent discoveries by oceanographers, along with a growing concern about decreasing fish stocks and increasing carbon dioxide in the atmosphere, have led to unprecedented proposals for fertilizing the oceans to promote the growth of phytoplankton. It is thought that blooms of phytoplankton will draw carbon dioxide from the atmosphere and store it in the ocean, in the process promoting the production of fish.

Phytoplankton, the microscopic plant life that feeds the ocean, is responsible for roughly half the photosynthesis on earth. These tiny plants grow by cell division. New cellular material comes from carbon dioxide as well as from nutrients, such as the nitrogen and phosphorus, that are dissolved in seawater. The proliferation of phytoplankton in surface waters fuels marine food webs; this in turn supports the growth of higher trophic levels.

By late 1989 the oceanographic community was well aware of John Martin's ideas about controlling climate change. If his hypothesis was accepted, proposals to fertilize the ocean in order to mitigate greenhouse gas increases would follow. His ideas generated widespread concern because the 'iron hypothesis' had not been tested in an ecologically relevant context and it was obvious that any widespread fertilization of the ocean would have unknown consequences, many of which could be detrimental to marine ecosystems.

In 1991 an international symposium was organized by the American Society of Limnology and Oceanography (ASLO). The resulting consensus statement 'urg[ed] all governments to regard the role of iron in marine productivity as an area for further research and not to consider [large scale] iron fertilization as a policy option that significantly changes the need to reduce emissions of carbon dioxide.' Research and discussions leading to this resolution revealed significant uncertainties and ecological risks involved in large-scale ocean fertilization. Moreover, models of successful fertilization scenarios forecast relatively small reductions in the rate of increase of atmospheric carbon dioxide.

The ASLO resolution also called for small-scale, *in situ* fertilization experiments for studying the regulation of ocean productivity. Three such experiments were performed, and the conclusions supported John Martin's hypothesis of iron limitation in high-nutrient regions of the open seas. These experiments shed little light on the feasibility of using ocean fertilization as an option in the global management of carbon dioxide emissions; even so, their results have been used by industry and in the media to promote the idea of fertilizing the ocean to sequester atmospheric carbon.

In a recent development, entrepreneurs have been receiving patents for ocean fertilization processes for enhancing fish production and increasing the ocean sink for carbon dioxide. Dr Michael Markels, Jr, of Ocean Farming, Inc., comments:

> When applied to large areas of the barren tropical seas, ocean farming can increase the phytoplankton, the base of the food chain, bringing the productivity up to the level that occurs naturally off the coast of Peru. This can result in an increase in fish catch by a factor of 400 or more. A 53,000 square mile ocean area might see the fish catch up to 50 million tons per year. The carbon dioxide absorbed initially could exceed the production by the United States from burning of fossil fuels.

Another company, Carboncorp USA, is publicizing an ambitious program to equip ships with fertilization modules that will enrich commercial shipping lanes with micronutrients. They claim that the resulting blooms of phytoplankton will safely sequester atmospheric carbon in deep sea sediments. The potential for commercial gains through obtaining carbon credits is highlighted: 'With support of world leaders, already a dynamic market is developing for trade in these carbon offset emission credits like those which result from the use of OCS [their patented technology/methodology] and other CO_2 sequestration technologies.'

There are profound scientific uncertainties associated with plans to increase ocean productivity through fertilization. The ecological consequences of frequent or sustained fertilization are unknown; it is, however, recognized that successful stimulation of the biological pump can only be achieved through a fundamental alteration of marine food webs. The phytoplankton species composition will change, and this change will propagate up the food web to the higher organisms, including fish and birds, with unpredictable consequences. In addition, reductions of oxygen concentration in the deep sea (which compliments the enhanced delivery of organic matter from surface layers) can cause increases in the biological production of methane and N_2O, both of which are potent greenhouse gases. Finally, there is no scientific consensus on how the sequestration of carbon can be quantified.

Conversations with top researchers indicate that groups from the private sector are forming partnerships with oceanographers to conduct ocean fertilization experiments. Other experiments are also being planned through national research agencies. At this time we are unable to say how many experiments are planned or whether any private-sector entity plans to claim carbon offsets for intentional fertilization of the ocean.

No guidelines, political or scientific, have been developed to deal with the inevitable proposals to fertilize international waters for commercial benefit, such as carbon tax credits. There is a desperate need for open and meaningful discussion of these options among scientists and stakeholders, if we are to make the best use of scientific knowledge to develop sound international agreements on the future use of the oceans. As the ASLO Workshop of 2001 emphasized: 'Review and oversight of intentional ocean fertilization should occur through an international mechanism.'

Conclusion

In 1999 the General Assembly decided to establish an open-ended informal consultative process to facilitate the annual review by the General Assembly of developments in ocean affairs. This is consistent with the legal framework provided by the UN Convention on the Law of the Sea and the goals of Chapter 17 of Agenda 21. This process was charged with the task of considering the Secretary General's report on oceans and the law of the sea and suggesting particular issues to be considered by it, with an emphasis on identifying areas where coordination and cooperation at the intergovernmental and interagency levels should be enhanced.

The General Assembly decided that this 'process' should be open to all state members of the UN, all state members of specialized agencies, all parties to the convention, entities that have received a standing invitation to participate as observers in the work of the General Assembly, and intergovernmental organizations with competence in ocean affairs. These meetings, which take place for one week each year, began on 30 May 2000 and may propose items for consideration by the General Assembly. This process provides opportunities to receive inputs from representatives of the major groups as identified by Agenda 21.

The establishment of this process marks a major breakthrough in the evolution of a global system of ocean governance. It had become clear to all that only the UN General Assembly was competent to consider the closely interrelated problems of ocean space as a whole, since such problems transcend the interests of the state parties to the UN Convention on the Law of the Sea and include parties to all the conventions, agreements, and programs adopted by the UN Conference on Environment and Development (UNCED, 1992) and are areas of concern to all UN members. However, since the General Assembly did not have sufficient time to devote to this complex task, it was essential to create some new process to assist it.

The need now is to find logical and effective ways to deal with overlaps between the conventions. These overlaps are clearly recognized in the documents themselves. One idea worthy of attention is that of joint development zones established between an international agency, such as the ISA, and a coastal state. As suggested in *The Oceanic Circle*, the principles and procedures described in Article 142 could form the basis for a joint development regime between interested states and the International Seabed Authority, as well as between two or more states. Another possibility would involve seeking cooperation through the development of memoranda of understanding between ISA and parties to the Framework Convention on Climate Change. In any event, the full potential of the ISA has yet to be exploited, both within the Authority and outside it. One can hope that the Authority will play an active role in strengthening cooperation between the relevant agencies for the future of the ocean.[16]

NOTES

1 This paper has benefited tremendously from the work of Elisabeth Mann Borgese, whose inspiring leadership in the search for good ocean governance deserves the highest praise. See in particular E. Mann Borgese, *The Oceanic Circle: Governing the Seas As a Global Resource* (Tokyo: United Nations University Press, 1998); and the mimeographed papers collected and edited by the International Ocean Institute, *The International Sea-Bed Authority: New Tasks*, Part I, 1999, Part II, 2000 (Proceedings of Leadership Seminar in Jamaica, 1999).

On the subject generally, see M.C. Wood, 'International Sea-bed Authority: The First Four Years' (1999) 3 *Max Planck Yearbook of United Nations Law* 173; R.C. Ogley, *Internationalizing the Seabed* (Hampshire: Gewer Publishing, 1984); W.B. Jones, 'The International Sea-bed Authority Without U.S. Participation' (1983) 12 *Ocean Development and International Law Journal* 151; K.W. Schoonover, 'The History of Negotiations Concerning the System of Exploitation of the International Seabed' (1977) 9 *International Law and Politics* 483; P. Bautista Payoyo, *Cries of the Sea: World Inequality, Sustainable Development and the Common Heritage of Humanity* (The Hague: Martinus Nijhoff, 1997); UNEP, 2001, *International Environmental Governance: Multilateral Environmental Agreements (MEAs)* (2001) [unpublished].

2 Agreement Relating to the Implementation of Part XI of the United Nations Convention on the Law of the Sea (1994) 33 I.L.M. 1309.

3 Convention on Biological Diversity (1992) I.L.M. 822.
4 United Nations Framework Convention on Climate Change (1992) I.L.M. 851.
5 The United Nations Convention on the Law of the Sea, UN Doc. A/CONF.62/122 (1982).
6 International Ocean Institute at note 1 at 6.
7 *Ibid.* at 7.
8 *Ibid.* at 10.
9 *Ibid.* at 12.
10 *Ibid.* at 18
11 International Oceanic Institute, *The International Sea-Bed Authority*, Part I, note 1, *supra*, at 31, and M. Markels, Jr, and R.T. Barbver, 'The Sequestration of Carbon Dioxide to the Deep Ocean by Fertilization,' American Chemical Society Symposium on CO_2 Capture Utilization and Sequestration, 20–4 August 2000 at 1.
12 Online: http://research.com/carboncopr/execsummary 2.html.
13 'The Scientific and Policy Uncertainties Surrounding the Use of Ocean Fertilization to Transfer Atomspheric Carbon Dioxide to the Oceans,' Summary Statement (ASLO, Washington, 25 April 2001) [mimeographed].
14 *Ibid.* at 2; also online at www.aslo.org
15 Borgese, *The Oceanic Circle, supra* note 1 at 185.
16 See, generally, the UNEP study on international environmental governance, *supra* note 1.

Appendix

Ivan Head: Résumé

Born in Calgary, Alberta, 28 July 1930. Primary and secondary education received in Calgary and Edmonton.

Attended University of Alberta 1947–52; B.A. – 1951, LL.B. – 1952. (Chief Justice's Silver Medallist, 1952).

Frank Knox Memorial Fellow, Harvard Law School, 1959–60; LL.M. – 1960; (dissertation – 'Canadian Claims to Territorial Sovereignty in the Arctic Regions').

Called to the Bar of Alberta, 1953. Practised law in Calgary, 1953–9, in partnership with S.J. Helman, Q.C., and R.H. Barron, Q.C.

Foreign Service Officer, Department of External Affairs, 1960–3, serving in Ottawa and Kuala Lumpur.

Associate Professor of Law, University of Alberta, 1963–6; Professor, 1966–73. (On leave, 1967–73).

Associate Counsel (Constitution) to the Minister of Justice, Canada, 1967–8.

Legislative Assistant to the Prime Minister of Canada, 1968–70; Special Assistant to the Prime Minister, 1970–8, with special responsibility for foreign policy and the conduct of international relations.

President and Member of the Board of Governors, International Development Research Centre, 1978–91 (appointed 1978; reappointed 1983 and 1988).

Professor of Law, University of British Columbia, 1991–2000; Emeritus, 2000 to date;

Chair in South-North Studies, 1991–2000; Founding Director, Liu Centre for the Study of Global Issues, 1997–2000, Senior Fellow, 2000 to date.

Honours

Appointed Queen's Counsel by the Government of Canada, 1973.

Recipient of Queen's Jubilee Medal, 1977.

Elected Fellow of The World Academy of Art and Science, 1982.

Inscribed on Global 500 Honour Roll by United Nations Environment Program, 1988.

Grand Cross, Order of the Sun, Peru, 1989.

Officer, Order of Canada, 1990.

Recipient of Commemorative Medal, 125th Anniversary of Confederation, 1992.

Inducted University of Alberta Sports Wall of Fame, 1993.

Conferred Honorary Doctorates:
– University of Alberta, 1987
– University of the West Indies, 1987
– University of Western Ontario, 1988
– University of Ottawa, 1988
– University of Calgary, 1989
– Beijing Forestry University, 1990
– St Francis Xavier University, 1990
– University of Manitoba, 1991
– University of Notre Dame, 1991
– Carleton University, 1996

Honorary Graduate – National Defence College, 1991.

Biographical Entries

Canadian Who's Who
Who's Who in America
Who's Who in the Commonwealth
Who's Who in the World
Who's Who in the West
The Canadian Encyclopedia
The Canadian Establishment
The Collins Dictionary of Canadian History

Offices

Member, Board of Editors, *Canadian Yearbook of International Law,* 1965–96; Honourary Editor, 1997 to date.

Member, Advisory Committee, *University of Toronto Law Journal,* 1966–70.

Member, National Council, Canadian Branch of the International Law Association, 1966–8; Vice-President 1968–1990; Director 1994–2000.

Member, Executive Council, American Society of International Law, 1968–71.

Member, Executive Committee, International and Constitutional Law Section, Canadian Bar Association, 1968–72.

Member, Steering Committee, The Atlantic Conference (of the Chicago Council on Foreign Affairs), 1970–90.

Member, Board of Trustees, International Food Policy Research Institute, Washington, D.C., 1978–88.

Member, Advisory Council, Kellogg Institute for International Studies, University of Notre Dame, 1983–2000.

Member, Board of Directors, The Inter-American Dialogue, Washington, D.C., 1983–98.

Member, Board of Directors, International Aviation Management Training Institute, Montreal, 1984–93 (Chairman, 1984–6).

Member, Board of Overseers, International Centre for Economic Growth, San Francisco, 1987 to date.

Member, Board of Directors, North American Management Council, New York, 1988–91.

Member, Governing Council, Society for International Development, Rome, 1991–6.

Member, Board of Directors, The Salzburg Seminar, Salzburg, Austria, 1992–6 (Senior Fellow, 1996 to date).

Member, Board of Directors, International Ocean Institute, Valletta, Malta, 1992–6.

Member, Board of Directors, Canadian Institute of International Affairs, Toronto, 1992–5.

Member, Board of Governors, National Defence College of Canada, Kingston, Ontario, 1993–4.

Member, Board of Directors, International Centre for Sustainable Cities, Vancouver, 1994–2000.

Member, Board of Directors, Academy for Educational Development, Washington, D.C., 1997 to date.

Member, Board of Directors, Canadian Academy for the Advancement of Science, Vancouver, 1998–2000.

Member, Board of Directors, International Livestock Research Institute, Vancouver, 2001 to date.

Professional Associations

Member: Law Society of Alberta, Canadian Council on International Law, International Law Association (Canadian Branch), Canadian Institute of International Affairs, American Society of International Law, Canadian Association of Law Teachers.

Special Activities

Secretary of Law Society of Alberta Benchers' Special Committee on Mineral Titles, 1955–6.

Secretary to Federal Electoral Boundaries Commission for Alberta, 1965–6.

Executive Member, Banff Conference on World Affairs, 1964–8.

Member, North American Sponsoring and Policy Review Council, World Law Fund, World Order Models Project, 1967–75. (23 members, including George W. Ball, Douglas Dillon, Justice Arthur Goldberg).

Member, Special Advisory Committee of the University of the West Indies considering the establishment of a Faculty of Law, 1969–70. (3 advisers; others – Professors Zelman Cowen, Australia, and L.C.B. Gower, Britain).

Co-Chairman, Jamaica Symposium on the Mobilization of Technology for World Development, January 1979 (with Mahbub Ul-Haq).

Moderator, Aspen Institute for Humanistic Studies, Executive Seminar, 1980, 1982, 1984, 1986, 1989, 1991.

Member, Panel of Eminent Persons, United Nations Institute for Training and Research (UNITAR), 1982–5. (19 members, including Felipe Herrera, Idris Jazairy, Saburo Okita).

Member, Aspen Institute East-West Study Group, 1983–4. (27 members, including James Callaghan, George Kennan, Helmut Schmidt, Cyrus Vance).

Member, the Independent Commission on International Humanitarian Issues, 1983–7. (25 members, including Manfred Lachs, Robert McNamara, Leopold Senghor, Hassan bin Talal, Simone Veil, Gough Whitlam).

Member, High Level Review Committee, Inter-American Development Bank, 1988. (10 members, including Arthur Brown, Carlos Manuel Castillo, John Petty, Mario-Enrique Simonsen, Jésus Sylva-Herzog).

Chairman of the Steering Group and Conference Chairman, Vth International Conference on AIDS, Montreal, 1989.

Conference Chairman, Conference on University Action for Sustainable Development, Halifax, Nova Scotia, 1991.

Member, Evaluation Team, The International Foundation for Science, Stockholm, Sweden, 1993. (3 members; others – Gelia Castillo, Narciso Matos).

Co-Chairman, Chancellor's Commission on the Governance of the University of the West Indies, 1993–4 (co-chairman, Sir Neville Nicholls).

Chairman, Canada 21 Council on Canadian Foreign and Defence Policy, 1992–3 (20 members, including Robert Falls, Arthur Hara, Donald S. Macdonald, Sylvia Ostry, Gerard Pelletier, Robert Stanfield).

Chairman, Rapid Assessment Team, United Nations International Fund for Agricultural Development, 1994 (other members – Ali Attiga, Martin Pineiro).

Canadian Coordinator, Canada-China '3x3' University Consortium (Universities of British Columbia, McGill, Montreal, and Toronto).

Member, Task Force on Education, Equity and Economic Competitiveness in the Americas (PREAL), Washington, D.C. and Santiago, Chile, 1996 to date.

Member, Conflict Analysis and Management Program Advisory Board, Royal Roads University, Victoria, B.C., 1997 to date.

Member, United Nations Environment Program International Group of Experts on Environmental Dispute Avoidance and Settlement, 1998–9.

Member, Advisory Board, Vancouver Economic Development Commission, Vancouver, 2000 to date.

Member, Advisory Board, International Commission on Intervention and State Sovereignty, Ottawa, Ontario, 2000 to date.

Representational Activities

Special emissary of the Prime Minister of Canada to engage in consultations with the Prime Minister or President of each of the following countries: Nigeria (1968, 1969, 1970, 1972, 1973), Tanzania (1969, 1970, 1972, 1973), Zambia (1970, 1972, 1973),

Jamaica (1972, 1973, 1974, 1976), Western Samoa (1973), Tonga (1973), Fiji (1973), Australia (1973, 1974), New Zealand (1973), The Gambia (1973), Sierra Leone (1973), Ghana (1973), Uganda (1973), Kenya (1973), Malawi (1973), Swaziland (1973), Botswana (1973), Lesotho (1973), Mauritius (1973), Britain (1973), Malta (1973), India (1973, 1975), Sri Lanka (1973), Bangladesh (1973), Malaysia (1973), Singapore (1973), Trinidad and Tobago (1973), Guyana (1973), Barbados (1973), Bahamas (1973), Japan (1974).

Member of the Canadian Delegations to the Commonwealth Heads of Government Meetings: London, 1969; Singapore, 1971; Ottawa, 1973; Kingston, 1975; London, 1977; to the NATO summit meetings: Brussels, 1975; London, 1977; to the Conference on Security and Cooperation in Europe: Helsinki, 1975.

Senior Adviser to the Prime Minister of Canada on his official visits to the United Nations (1968, 1969), to the United States of America (1969, 1971, 1974, 1976, 1977), Britain (1969, 1972, 1975), New Zealand (1970), Australia (1970), Malaysia (1970), Singapore (1970), Japan (1970, 1976), Pakistan (1971), India (1971), Indonesia (1971), Ceylon (1971), Iran (1971), the Soviet Union (1971), the People's Republic of China (1973), France (1975), Belgium (1975), Holland (1975), Italy (1975), Germany (1975), Luxembourg (1975), Denmark (1975), Ireland (1975), Mexico (1976), Cuba (1976), Venezuela (1976), Iceland (1977).

Personal Representative of the Prime Minister of Canada to the 1976 (Puerto Rico) and 1977 (London) Economic G-7 Summits.

Publications

Books

'This Fire-Proof House': Canadian Speak Out about Law and Order in the International Community. New York: Oceana, 1966, pp. 169 (editor and contributor).

International Law, National Tribunals and the Rights of Aliens. Syracuse Univ. Press, 1971, pp. xvi, 334 (with Frank Griffith Dawson).

Pierre Elliot Trudeau, *Conversation with Canadians.* Toronto: University of Toronto Press, 1972, pp. vi, 214 (editor).

On a Hinge of History: The Mutual Vulnerability of South and North. Toronto: University of Toronto Press, 1991, pp. xii, 244.

The Canadian Way: Shaping Canada's Foreign Policy 1968–1984. Toronto: McClelland & Stewart, 1995, pp. xi, 361 (with Pierre Elliott Trudeau).

Articles

R. v. Guay (case comment) (1952) 30 Canadian Bar Review 741–6.

'Theories of Ownership of Oil and Gas' (with J.H. Laycraft) (1953) 31 Canadian Bar Review 382–91.

Re Prudential Trust Co. (case comment) (1956) 34 Canadian Bar Review 736–44.

'The Torrens System in Alberta: A Dream in Operation' (1957) 35 Canadian Bar Review 1–37.

'Some Aspects of Canadian Constitutionalism,' Rand (report) (1956) Harvard Law School Bulletin 7, 10–11.

'ADIZ, International Law, and Contiguous Airspace' (1960) 2 Harvard International Law Journal 28–51; reprinted in (1963) Alberta Law Review 182–96, in Bourne and Jahnke, 'Cases and Materials on Public International Law,' 127–39, and in 2001 China Legal Science, vol. 6, 145–58.

'Canadian Claims to Territorial Sovereignty in the Arctic Region' (1963) 9 McGill Law Journal 200–26; reprinted in Castel, 'International Law, Chiefly as Interpreted and Applied in Canada,' 236–56.

'The Stranger in Our Midst: A Sketch of the Legal Status of the Alien in Canada' (1964) 2 Canadian Yearbook of International Law 107–140 (quoted by LaForest, J., Supreme Court of Canada, in *Law Society of British Columbia et al. v. Andrews et al.*, [1989] 2 W.W.R. 289 at 330–1.

'A Strategy of Interdependence'; Rock (Commentary) (1965) 3 Canadian Yearbook of International Law 355–60.

'The Legal Clamour over Canadian Off-Shore Minerals' (1967) 5 Alberta Law Review 1–16.

'A Fresh Look at the Local Remedies Rule' (1967) 5 Canadian Yearbook of International Law 142–58.

'The Canadian Offshore Minerals Reference: The Application of International Law to a Federal Constitution' (1968) 18 University of Toronto Law Journal 131–57.

'International Standards of Civil Procedure: The Alien in the Courts of Ghana' (1968) Saint Louis University Law Journal 392–417.

'Regional Developments Respecting Human Rights: The Implications for Canada,' in A.E. Gotlieb (ed.), '*Human Rights, Federalism and Minorities*' (Toronto: Canadian Institute of International Affairs, 1970), 228–43.

'The Foreign Policy of the New Canada' (1972) 5 Foreign Affairs 237–52.

'Canada's Pacific Perspective' (1974) Pacific Community 8–21.

'The Social Dimension of Development' (1981) Asia Pacific Commentary 75–87.

'The Contribution of International Law to Development' (1987) Canadian Yearbook of International Law 29–46; reprinted in Yves Le Bouthillier et al. (eds.), *Selected Papers in International Law* (The Hague, Kluwer Law International, 1999), pp. 59–78.

'South-North Dangers,' 68 Foreign Affairs (1989) 71–86.

'Diefenbaker's World' (review of book by Basil Robinson), Bout de papier, vol. 7, no. 2, 7–9.

'Roots and Values Inherent in Modern Development,' in Howard Coward (ed.), *Traditional and Modern Approaches to the Environment on the Pacific Rim: Tensions and Values* (Albany, NY: State University of New York Press, 1998), 13–27.

Published Addresses

'The Contribution of the International Court of Justice to the Development of International Organizations,' Annual Meeting of the American Society of International Law, Washington, D.C., April 1965 (published in 1965 Proceedings, American Society of International Law 177–82).

'The "New Federalism" in Canada: Some Thoughts on the International Legal Consequences,' Annual Meeting of the Canadian Bar Association, Toronto, September 1965 (published in 1965 Canadian Bar Papers 87–93); reprinted in (1966) 4 Alberta Law Review 389–94, and in Vaughan, Readings in Canadian Government (1969).

'The Alien's Access to Local Legal Remedies: The Experience in African Commonwealth States,' Regional Meeting of American Society of International Law, Syracuse, N.Y., February 1968 (published in (1968) Vanderbilt Law Review, 701–11).

'Who Owns the Bed of the Sea?' Annual Meeting of the American Society of International Law, Washington, D.C., April 1968 (published in 1968 Proceedings, American Society of International Law 241–3).

'Resources Scarcity and International Relations,' The Atlantic Conference, Taormina, Italy, 1974 (published in Resources and International Politics 71–85 and in 1975 Europa Archiv 261–8).

'Perceptions and Perspectives,' The Soviet Institute of U.S.A. and Canadian Studies, Moscow, July 1977 (excerpted in the Institute Journal 1977, vol. 10, 89–90).

'North-South As Seen from the North,' United Nations Economic Commission for Latin America, Santiago, Chile, April 1981 (published in Estudios Cieplan, vol. 5, 159–66).

'The Issue Is Survival,' American Association for the Advancement of Science, Washington, D.C., January 1982 (published in Bulletin of the Atomic Scientists, 39(5): 20–2; excerpted in R&D Mexico, 2(8): 35).

'April Thoughts from Home,' 20th Anniversary, Norman Paterson School of International Affairs, Carleton University, Ottawa, Ontario, April 1986 (published as an occasional paper by the Norman Paterson School).

'Opportunities in Developing Countries,' 29th Annual Conference, Canadian Institute of Food Science and Technology, Calgary, Alberta, June 1986 (published in Can. Inst. Food Sci. Technol. Journal, 20(1): vii–x).

'Resolving Global Problems: The Role of Science,' Canadian National Conference of Students, Pugwash, Ottawa, Ontario, June 1987 (published in *Resolving Global Problems in the 21st Century: How Can Science Help* (1989), 7–22).

'North-South: The Dangers of Disequilibria,' Fifteenth Plenary Session of the Trilateral Commission, Tokyo, Japan, April 1988 (excerpted in Trialogue 40: 54–6).

'Water and World Development,' Sixth World Congress on Water Resources, Ottawa, Ontario, May 1988 (published in 13 Water International 193–8)

'Challenges to Governments and to Governance,' Conference on the Public Service and the Needs of Changing Societies, Montebello, Quebec, September 1988 (published in Policy Options, July–August 1989, 13–15).

'AIDS in a Global Contest: Conclusions,' Fifth International Conference on AIDS, Montreal, Quebec, June 1989 (published in Conference Proceedings).

'The Economics of Peace,' Walter Gordon Forum, Massey College, University of Toronto, May 1991. Other participant, John Kenneth Galbraith (published as 'The Walter Gordon Series in Public Policy, Second Lectures,' Massey College, University of Toronto, 1991).

'Canada as a Hemispheric Neighbour,' University of Notre Dame, South Bend, Indiana, September 1991 (published in North-South 2:22, University of Miami).

'A World Turned Upside Down,' Vancouver Institute, Vancouver, September 1991 (published in Cleo Mowers, ed., *Towards a New Liberalism*, Victoria, B.C.: Orca, 1991).

Keynote Address, Conference on University Action for Sustainable Development, Dalhousie University, Halifax, Nova Scotia, December 1991 (published in Higher Education Policy 5(1): 9–13).

'The Evolving Foreign Service in the Trudeau Era,' University of Saskatchewan, Saskatoon, March 1992 (published in Donald C. Storey (ed.), *The Canadian Foreign Service in Transition*, Toronto: Canadian Scholars Press, 1993, pp. 23–35).

'Africa's Quest for Dignity,' International Conference, Dakar, Senegal, November 1992 (published Adedeji, Adebayo, ed., *Africa within the World: Beyond Dispossession and Dependence*, London: Zed Books, 1993, pp. 133–40).

'What Kind of World Do We Live In?' National Defence College, Kingston, Ontario, September 1993 (published as NDC Occasional Paper No. 1).

'Knowledge in the Third Dimension,' National Global Education Teachers' Conference, Edmonton, March 1994 (published in Global Education 2: 2–5).

'Environment: The Melding of Concept and Reality,' Keynote Address to Inter-Disciplinary Conference on the Environment, Social Sciences Federation of Canada, Ottawa, February 1994 (published in Louise Quesnel, ed., *Social Sciences and the Environment*, Ottawa: University of Ottawa Press, 1995, chap. 2).

'The Debris of Ancient Lies,' Keynote Address to the Commonwealth Symposium: Curatorship: Indigenous Perspectives in Post-Colonial Societies, University of Victoria, Victoria, May 1994 (published in Proceedings, Commonwealth Association of Museums, 1996, chap. 3).

'Shaping Canada's Foreign Policy 1968–1984,' Vancouver Institute, Vancouver, November 1995 (published in Peter N. Nemetz, ed., *The Vancouver Institute: An Experiment in Public Education*, Vancouver: JBA Press, University of British Columbia, 1998, pp. 576–91.

'Protective Jurisdiction: The Arctic, Fisheries, New Challenges,' Annual Conference, Canadian Council of International Law, Ottawa, October 1997 (published in Proceedings, 'Lessons from the Past, Blueprints for the Future,' pp. 129–38).

Book Reviews

Published in The Canadian Bar Review, International Journal, The Alberta Law Review, Pacific Affairs, The Canadian Yearbook of International Law, Environment and Planning.

Selected Unpublished Papers

'The Limitations of Co-Existence,' Stanley House Conference on International Law, Gaspé, PQ, July 1964.

'A Plea for an Articulate Canadian Foreign Aid Policy,' Prairie Conference on National Problems, Saskatoon, September 1964.

'International Criminal Law,' Annual Meeting of Alberta Magistrates Association, Edmonton, May 1965.

'Offshore Mineral Resources in Canada,' Annual Meeting of the Law Society of Alberta, Edmonton, February 1966.

'Asia: Revolution and Response,' Banff Conference on World Affairs, Banff, August 1966.

'Southeast Asia: Peril in Paradise,' Vancouver Institute, Vancouver, November 1966.

'Constitutional Review in Canada,' Annual Meeting of the Alberta Branch of the Canadian Bar Association, Jasper, May 1968.

'Toward a Normative Canadian Foreign Policy,' Council on Foreign Relations, New York, February 1970.

'Extraterritoriality: The United States and Canada,' Annual Meeting of the Canadian Bar Association, Halifax, September 1970.

'The Moulding and Management of Canadian Foreign Policy,' Calgary Bar Association, Calgary, September 1971.

'The Canadian-American Relationship,' Symposium of Canadian-American Relations, New York University, New York, December 1971.

'Is It Really a New Canada?' Council on Foreign Relations, New York, March 1972.

'Defining the New Canadian Nationalism: The Economics and Political Mix,' Chicago Council on Foreign Affairs, Chicago, December 1972.

'The Commonwealth of Nations, 1973 Version,' Annual Meeting of the Canadian Institute of International Affairs, Toronto Branch, Toronto, June 1973.

'Canadian-American Relations: The View from the North,' Foreign Policy Association. New York, November 1973.

'Canada and the United States – A View from Canada,' Council on Foreign Relations, New York, April 1974.

'The Canada-United States Relationship,' Detroit Council on Foreign Relations, Detroit, November 1974.

'Current Canadian Pre-occupations,' Council on Foreign Relations, New York, March 1977.

'The Canadian Stake in Development,' Annual Meeting of the United Nations Association of Canada, Montreal, May 1978.

'Challenge for Change in Third World Agriculture,' Alberta Association of Agrologists, Edmonton, September 1978.

'Canada and the Third World,' Canadian Club, Calgary, February 1979.

'Science as a Factor in Development,' The Ralph Bunche Institute, City University of New York, New York, March 1979.

'World Food Security,' York University, Toronto, March 1979.

'The World We Live In,' National Defence College, Kingston, September 1979.

'Development as a Policy Issue,' Mid-Continent Dialogue on the Changing World Economy, Minneapolis, September 1979.

'The Social Dimension of Development,' International Development Centre of Japan, Tokyo, November 1979.

'Surviving,' CARE World Conference, West Point, NY, May 1980.

'Today's Commonwealth,' Annual Meeting, Royal Commonwealth Society, Ottawa, March 1981.

'Development and Armaments,' 31st Pugwash Conference, Banff, August 1981.

'North-South: The Issue is Survival,' Canadian Club, Lethbridge, August 1981.

'Energy Issues: Canada and the Developing World,' University of Manitoba, Winnipeg, November 1981.

'La Recherche pour le Développement du Tiers-Monde,' Université du Québec à Trois-Rivières, avril 1982.

'Science and Technology for Development,' 96th Annual Congress, The Engineering Institute of Canada, Vancouver, June 1982.

'The World We Live In: 1982,' National Defence College, Kingston, September 1982.

'Water, Nutrition and Demography,' Royal Academy of Morocco, Marrakech, November 1982.

'Science, Culture, and Development,' Jamaican Society of Scientists and Technologists, Kingston March 1983.

'Health as an Ingredient of Development,' 94th Annual Meeting, Canadian Public Health Association, St John's, June 1983.

'Awareness and Understanding,' Conference on Development Education, University of Calgary, July 1983.

'The World We Live In: 1983,' National Defence College, Kingston, September 1983.

'One World, or Three?' Public Issues and Philosophy Conference, Simon Fraser University, Vancouver, October 1983.

'The Worldwide Refugee Issue,' Annual Meeting, Canadian Bar Association, Winnipeg, August 1984.

'The World we Live In: 1984,' National Defence College, Kingston, September 1984.

'Competence as a Factor in Development,' Research for Third World Development Conference, University of Waterloo, May 1985.

'Present at the Creation,' Annual Meeting, Canadian Orthopaedic Association, Hamilton, June 1985.

'Is It Really a Global Village?' 25th Anniversary Conference, Westminster College, University of Western Ontario, October 1985.

'The African Famine,' National Forum Africa, Ottawa, February 1986.

'The World We Live In: 1986,' National Defence College, Kingston, September 1986.

'The 1986 Keys Memorial Lecture,' Trinity College, University of Toronto, October 1986.

'Graduation Address,' University of the West Indies, Mona, Jamaica, November 1987.

'South-North,' AUCC Conference on International Cooperation, Montreal, April 1988.

'Some Watcher of the Skies,' Annual Meeting of the Canadian Association of African Studies, Queen's University, May 1988.

'Convocation Address,' University of Western Ontario, June 1988.

'Convocation Address,' University of Ottawa, October 1988.

'"North-South" or "South-North"?' Canadian Club of Hamilton, April 1989.

'Major Unstated Premises,' Annual General Meeting, the Group of 78, Ottawa, September 1989.

'No Common Faith?' General Meeting of the Association of University and Colleges of Canada Toronto, October 1989.

'A Way Out for the South?' Nigerian Institute of International Affairs, Lagos, June 1990.

'What Kind of World Will we Live In?' National Defence College, Kingston, June 1990.

'The Three Dimensions of Knowledge,' International Symposium on Development Cooperation, Tokyo, October 1990.

'The Developing World,' Business Week/IMD CEO Roundtable, Lausanne, November 1990.

Convocation Address, Beijing Forestry University, Beijing, November 1990.

Convocation Address, St Francis Xavier University, Antigonish, December 1990.

The Leonard S. Klinck Memorial Lecture, Agricultural Institute of Canada, 20 Canadian venues, February–April, 1991.

Convocation Address, University of Manitoba, Winnipeg, May 1991.

Graduation Address, National Defence College of Canada, Kingston, June 1991.

'The World We Live In,' National Defence College, Kingston, August 1991.

'A World Turned Upside Down,' Vancouver Institute, Vancouver, September 1991.

'Is Sustainable Development an Appropriate Paradigm for Society?' Sustainable Development Research Institute, University of British Columbia, September 1991.

Distinguished Lecture, University of Victoria, January 1992.

Address, World of Opportunity Banquet, University of British Columbia, Vancouver, May 1992.

Conflict and Cooperation, International Summer Institute, Whistler, B.C., August 1992.

'The Policy of Denuclearization,' Conference on Canada and the Politics of the Nuclear Era, Queen's University, September 1992.

'Artificial Horizons,' GIS '93 Symposium, Vancouver, February 1993.

Keynote Address, Beyond NAFTA Symposium, Vancouver, March 1993.

Opening Address, CONSULTEX China Beijing, April 1993.

'In Quest of Community,' 5th Asian and Pacific University Presidents' Conference, University of British Columbia, May 1995.

Address, Royal Commonwealth Society, Vancouver, March 1996.

Address, The 21st Century Forum, Beijing, September 1996.

Address, International Conference on the Helms-Burton Law: Its Implications for Cuba and the International Community, Havana, September 1996.

Keynote Address, 1996 World Food Day Ceremony, United Nations, New York, October, 1996.

Convocation Address, Carleton University, Ottawa, November 1996.

Address, Inter-American Development Bank Felipe Herrera Seminar, 'Culture and Development,' Santiago, Chile, May 1997.

Address, Model United Nations, Vancouver, January 1988.

Address, The 1998 Assembly of the World Academy of Art and Science, 'The Global Economy,' Vancouver, November 1998.

'China in the Global Policy Universe,' First International Symposium on Soft Science, Sanshui, People's Republic of China, November 1999.

'Economic Migrants or Refugees? Trends in Global Migration,' Keynote Address to a conference of that name organized by the Maytree Foundation and the Canadian Institute for International Affairs, Toronto, January 2000.

Keynote Address, Conference on Occasion of 30th Anniversary of the Entry into Diplomatic Relations between Canada and China, Association of Canadian Studies in China, Dalian, People's Republic of China, September 2000.

'Judicial Independence in the New Democracies,' The 1701 Conference: the 300th Anniversary of the Act of Settlement, Vancouver, May 2001.

'On a Hinge of History,' Academy for Education Development 40th Anniversary Celebrations, Washington, D.C., December 2001.

Bibliography

Books

Avant, D.D., *Political Institutions and Military Change: Lessons from Peripheral Wars* (Ithaca and London: Cornell University Press, 1994).

Barnes, Jr, R.C., *Military Legitimacy: Might and Right in the New Millennium* (London: Frank Cass, 1996).

Baslar, K., *The Concept of the Common Heritage of Mankind in International Law* (The Hague: Martinus Nijhoff, 1998).

Bautista Payoyo, P., *Cries of the Sea: World Inequality, Sustainable Development and the Common Heritage of Humanity* (The Hague: Martinus Nijhoff, 1997).

Beyerlin, U., and T. Marauhn, *Law-Making and Law-Enforcement in International Environmental Law after the 1992 Rio Conference* (Berlin: E. Schmidt, 1997).

Bichler, G., ed., *Federalism against Ethnicity?* (Zurich: Verlag Ruegger AG, 1997).

Bloed, A., ed., *The Challenge of Change: The Helsinki Summit of the CSCE and its Aftermath* (Dordrecht: Martinus Nijhoff, 1994).

– *The Conference on Security and Co-operation in Europe: Analysis and Basic Documents, 1972–1993* (Dordrecht: Kluwer Academic Publishers, 1993).

Borgese, E.M., *The Oceanic Circle: Governing the Seas As a Global Resource* (Tokyo: United Nations University Press, 1998).

Cassese, A., *International Law in a Divided World* (Oxford: Clarendon Press, 1986).

Cohen, J., *Conflict Prevention in the OSCE: An Assessment of Capacities* (The Hague: Netherlands Institute of International Relations, Clingendael, 1999).

Coles, H.L., and A.K. Weinberg, *Civil Affairs: Soldiers Become Governors* (Washington, D.C.: Office of the Chief of Military History, 1964).

Corrigan, P., and D. Sayer, *The Great Arch: English State Formation as Cultural Revolution* (Oxford: Basil Blackwell, 1985).

Crocker, C.A., F.O. Hampson, and P. Hall, *Herding Cats: Multiparty Mediation in a Complex World* (Washington, DC: United States Institute of Peace, 1999).

De Smet, P.A.G.M., *Herbs, Health, and Healers: Africa As Ethnopharmocological Treasury* (Netherlands: Afrika Museum, 1999).

Doyle, M.W., *UN Peacekeeping in Cambodia: UNTAC's Civil Mandate* (New York: International Peace Academy, 1995).

Dunay, P., 'Concerns and Opportunities: The Development of Romanian-Hungarian Relations and National Minorities,' in G. Bichler, ed., *Federalism against Ethnicity?* (Chur, Zurich: Verlag Ruegger, 1997).

Eide, A., 'Territorial Integrity of States, Minority Protection, and Guarantees for Autonomy Arrangements: Approaches and Roles of the United Nations,' in *Local Self-Government, Territorial Integrity and Protection of Minorities* (Strasbourg: Council of Europe Publishing, 1996).

Estibanez, M.A., and G.L. Kinga, *Implementing the Framework Convention for the Protection of National Minorities* (Flensburg: European Centre for Minority Issues, 1999).

Fenet, A., et al., eds., *Le droit et les minorites: analyses et textes* (Bruxelles: Etablissements Emile Bruylant, 1995).

Fishel, J.T., *Liberation, Occupation, and Rescue: War Termination and Desert Storm.* (Carlisle Barracks, PA: Strategic Studies Institute, 1992).

Franck, T.M., *Fairness in International Law and Institutions* (New York: Oxford University Press, 1995).

– *The Power of Legitimacy among Nations* (New York: Oxford University Press, 1990).

Fuller, L.L., *The Morality of Law* (New Haven: Yale University Press, 1969).

Gal, K., *Bilateral Agreements in Central and Eastern Europe: A New Inter-State Framework for Minority Protection* (Flensburg: European Centre for Minority Issues, 1999).

Ghébali, V.Y., *L'OSCE dans l'Europe post-communiste, 1990–1996: Vers une identite paneuropenne de securite,* (Bruxelles: Etablissement Emile Bruylant, 1996).

Gray, J., *Liberalism* (Minneapolis: University of Minnesota Press, 1986).

Held, D., *Democracy and the Global Order: From the Modern State to Cosmopolitan Governance* (Cambridge: Polity Press, 1995).

Holsti, K.J., *The State, War, and the State of War* (Cambridge: Cambridge University Press, 1996).

Horowitz, D., *Ethnic Groups in Conflict* (Berkeley: University of California Press, 1985).

Hudec, R.E., *Enforcing International Trade Law: The Evolution of the Modern GATT Legal System* (Salem: Butterworth Legal Publishers, 1993).

International Ocean Institute. *The International Sea-Bed Authority: New Tasks*, Part I, 1999, Part II, 2000 (Proceedings of Leadership Seminar in Jamaica, 1999).

Johnston, D.M., *Consent and Commitment in the World Community: The Classification and Analysis of International Instruments* (Irvington-on-Hudson: Transnational Publishers, 1997).

Keck, M.E., and K. Sikkink, *Activists Beyond Borders: Advocacy Networks in International Politics* (New York: Cornell University Press, 1998).

Kemp, W., ed., *Quiet Diplomacy in Action: The OSCE High Commissioner on National Minorities* (The Hague: Kluwer Law International, 2001).

Kempe, F., 'The Panama Debacle,' in E. Loser, ed., *Conflict Resolution and Democratization in Panama* (Washington, D.C.: The Center for Strategic and International Studies, 1992).

Kinga, G.L., *Bilateral Agreements in Central and Eastern Europe: A New Inter-State Framework for Minority Protection?* (Flensburg: European Centre for Minority Issues, 1999).

Kiss, A., and D. Shelton, *International Environmental Law* (Ardsley-on-Hudson, N.Y.: Transnational, 1991).

Koskenniemi, M., *From Apology to Utopia, The Structure of International Legal Argument* (Helsinki: Finnish Lawyers' Publishing Group, 1989).

Kuhn, T.S., 'The Structure of Scientific Revolutions,' in Otto Neurath ed., *International Encyclopedia of Unified Science 2*, No. 2 (Chicago: University of Chicago Press, 1962).

Kumar, K., ed., *Postconflict Elections, Democratization, and International Assistance* (New York: International Peace Academy, 1998).

Kyre, M., and J. Kyre, *Military Government and National Security* (Washington, D.C.: Public Affairs Press, 1968).

Lake, A., *After the Wars: Reconstruction in Afghanistan, Indochina, Central America, Southern Africa, and the Horn of Africa* (New Brunswick, NJ: Transaction Publishers, 1990).

Loser, E., ed., *Conflict Resolution and Democratization in Panama* (Washington, D.C.: The Center for Strategic and International Studies, 1992).

Luttwak, E.N., 'Reconsideration: Clausewitz and War,' in *Strategy and Politics: Collected Essays* (New Brunswick, NJ, and London: Transaction Books, 1980).

Manahan, S.E., *Environmental Chemistry* (Chelsea, Michigan: Lewis Publishers, 1991).

Mbanefo, L.N., *Essays on Nigerian Shipping Law* (London: Professional Books, 1991).

Magoon, C.E., *The Law of Civil Government in Territory Subject to Military Occupation by the Military Forces of the United States*, 3rd ed. Bureau of Insular Affairs, War Department (Washington: Government Printing Office, 1903).

Manwaring, M.G., and C. Prisk, *Civil Military Operations in El Salvador* (Quarry Heights, Panama: U.S. Southern Command, 1998).

Mazarr, M.J., 'The Revolution in Military Affairs: A Framework for Defense Planning' (Monograph, U.S. Army War College Strategic Studies Institute, June 1994).

Metz, S., and J. Kievit, *The Revolution in Military Affairs and Conflict Short of War* (Carlisle Barracks, PA: US Arm War College, 1994).

Mbiti, J.S., *African Religions and Philosophy* (London: Heinemann, 1969).

McWilliams, W.C., ed. *Garrisons and Government: Politics and the Military in New States* (San Francisco: Chandler, 1967).

Ogley, R.C., *Internationalizing the Seabed* (Hampshire: Gewer, 1984).

Ojo, G.U., *Ogoni: Trials And Travails – Report of the Environmental Rights Action* (Lagos: Civil Liberties Organization, 1996).

Ollennu, N.A., *Principles of Customary Land Law* (London: Sweet and Maxwell, 1962).

Pardo, A., and E.M. Borgese, *The New International Economic Order & the Law of the Sea* (Malta: International Oceans Institute, Occasional Paper No. 4, 1970).

Pastor, R.A., *Whirlpool: United States Foreign Policy toward Latin America and the Caribbean* (Princeton: Princeton University Press, 1992).

Peceny, M., *Democracy at the Point of Bayonets* (University Park, PA: Penn. State Press, 1999).

Peck, C., *Sustainable Peace: The Role of the UN and Regional Organizations in Preventing Conflict* (Lanham: Rowman & Littlefield, 1998).

Phillips, A., and A. Rosas, eds., *Universal Minority Rights* (Turku and London: Abo Akademi University Institute for Human Rights, 1995).

Raikka, J., ed., *Do We Need Minority Rights?* (The Hague: Kluwer Law International, 1996).

Rodrik, D., *The New Global Economy and Developing Countries: Making Openness Work* (Washington: Overseas Development Council, 1999).

Rousso-Lenoir, F., *Minorites et droits de l'homme: l'Europe et son double* (Bruxelles: Etablissement Emile Bruylant, 1994).

Sarkesian, S.C., J.A. Williams, and F.B. Bryant, *Soldiers, Society, and National Security,* (Boulder and London: Lynne Rienner, 1995).

Schelling, T., *Strategy of Conflict* (Cambridge: Harvard University Press, 1960, 1980).

Schmidt, M.G., *Common Heritage or Common Burden: The United States Position on the Development of a Regime for Deep Sea-bed Mining in the Law of the Sea Convention* (Oxford: Clarendon, 1989).

Shain, Y., and J.J. Linz, *Between States: Interim Governments and Democratic Transitions* (Cambridge: Cambridge University Press, 1995).

Shapiro, I., and W. Kymlicka, eds., *Ethnicity and Group Rights* (New York: New York University Press, 1997)

Sipry, E., *Pratique francaise du droit international des droits de l'homme – le cas des minorites,* (University of Geneva Graduate Institute of International Studies, 1998) (unpublished).

SIPRI Yearbook 2000: Armaments, Disarmament and International Security (Oxford: Oxford University Press, 2000).

Snow, D.M., *National Security: Defense Policy for a New International Order* 3rd ed. (New York: St Martin's Press, 1995).

Spencer, H., *Principles of Sociology* II (New York: Appleton, 1898).

Taylor, P., *An Ecological Approach to International Law* (London and New York: Routledge 1998).

Tilly, C., *Coercion, Capital, and European States: A.D. 990–1990* (Cambridge, MA: Basil Blackwell, 1990).

U.S. Army Military History Institute, Civil Affairs School, *Doctrinal Study on the Theater Army: Civil Affairs Command* (Fort Gordon, Georgia, 15 August 1959).

van Creveld, M., *The Transformation of War* (New York: The Free Press, 1991).

von Clausewitz, Carl, *On War*, 8th ed., trans. and ed. M. Howard and P. Paret (Princeton: Princeton University Press, 1984).

Weiss, E.B., *In Fairness to Future Generations: International Law, Common Patrimony and Intergenerational Equity* (New York: Transnational Publishers, 1989).

Whitehead, L., 'The Imposition of Democracy,' in A.F. Lowenthal, ed., *Exporting Democracy: The United States and Latin America* (Baltimore: Johns Hopkins University Press, 1991).

Yates, L.A., *Power Pack: US Intervention in the Dominican Republic, 1965–66* (Fort Leavenworth: Combat Studies Institute, 1988).

Zaagman, R., *Conflict Prevention in the Baltic States: The OSCE High Commissioner on National Minorities in Estonia, Latvia and Lithuania* (Flensburg: European Centre for Minority Issues Monograph, 1999).

Cases

Allar Irou v. Shell-BP Petroleum Development Company (Unreported, Suit No. W/89/71 High Court of Warri, Nigeria).

Almelo and Others [1994] E.C.R. I-1477.

Automec v. Commission (No.2) [1992] E.C.R. II-2223, [1992] 5 C.M.L.R. 431.

B.R.T v. S.A.B.A.M, [1974] E.C.R. 51.

B.R.T. v. S.A.B.A.M. [1974] E.C.R. 51.

Case Concerning the Gabcikovo-Nagymaros Project (Hungary v. Slovakia), (1998) 37 *I.C.J.* Rep. 162.

Case T-24/90 [1992] E.C.R. II-2223.

CILFIT v. Ministry of Health [1982] E.C.R. 3415.

Costa v. ENEL [1964] E.C.R. 585; [1964] C.M.L.R. 425.

de Geus v. Bosch [1962] E.C.R. 45.

Dorch Consult v. Bundesbaugesellschaft Berlin [1997] E.C.R. I-4961.

Foglia v. Novello (No 1) [1980] E.C.R. 745, [1981] 1 C.M.L.R. 45.

Foglia v. Novello (No 2) [1981] E.C.R. 3045, [1982] 1 C.M.L.R. 585.

Garden Cottage Foods v. The Milk Marketing Board [1984] A.C. 130.

INNO v. ATAB, [1977] E.C.R. 2115.

Kennedy v. Mendoza-Martinez, 372 U.S. 144 (1963).

Mannesmann v. Stohal Rotationsdruck [1998] E.C.R. I-73.

Metro v. Commission (No.1) [1977] E.C.R. 1875, [1978] 2 C.M.L.R. 1.

Oakdale (Richmond) Ltd v. National Westminster Bank [1997] E.L.R. 40.

Polypropylene O.J., 1986, L230/1; [1988] 4 C.M.L.R. 347.

Procurer de la Republique v. Bruno Giry and Guerlain [1981] C.M.L.R. 99.

Rheinmuhlen-Dusseldorf v. Einfuher-und Vorratsstelle fur Gerreide und Futtermittel (No.1) [1974] E.C.R. 33.

The Cases Concerning North Sea Continental Shelf (Federal Republic of Germany v. Denmark and v. Netherlands), [1969] I.C.J. Rep. 3.

Vaassen-Gobbels v. Beammbten-fonds voor het Mijnbedrijf [1966] E.C.R. 377, [1966] C.M.L.R. 508.

Van Duyn v. The Home Office [1974] 3 All. E.R. 178 (Ch.D).

Van Gen en Loos [1963] E.C.R. 1.

Volk v. Etablissements Vervaecke Sprl [1969] E.C.R. 295, [1969] C.M.L.R. 273.

Walter Rau v. de Smedt [1982] E.C.R. 3961, [1983] 2 C.M.L.R. 496.

Articles

Adewale, O., 'Customary Environmental Law,' in M.A. Ajomo and O. Adewale, eds., *Environmental Law and Sustainable Development in Nigeria* (Lagos: Nigeria Institute of Advanced Legal Studies, 1994).

Alfredsson, G., and M.G. Goran, 'A Compilation of Minority Rights Standards' (1997) 24 Raoul Wallenberg Inst. H.R. & Hum. L. R.

Arnull, A., 'References to the European Court' (1990) 15 E.L.R. 375.

Asiema, J.K., and F.D.P. Situma, 'Indigenous Peoples and the Environment: The Case of the Pastoral Maasai' (1994) 5 Colorado J. of Int'l Env'tl. Law & Policy 149.

Barav, A., 'Preliminary Censorship? The Judgment of the European Court in Foglia v. Novello' (1980) 5 E.L.R. 443.

Bebr, G., 'The Possible Implications of Foglia v. Novello II' (1982) 19 C.M.L.R. 421.

Bedjaoui, M., 'Are the World's Food Resources the Common Heritage of Mankind' (1984) 24 Indian J. Int'l L.

Bellamy, C., 'From Total War to Local War: It's a Revolution,' *The Independent* (23 July 1996) 14.

Biermann, F., 'Common Concern of Humankind.' The Emergence of a New Concept of International Environmental Law (1996) 34 Archiv des Volkerrechts 426.

Bodansky, D., 'The Legitimacy of International Governance: A Coming Challenge for International Environmental Law?' (1999) 93 Am. J. Int'l L. 596.

Bowman, M.J., 'The Multilateral-Treaty Amendment Process – A Case Study' (1995) 44 Int'l & Comp. L. Q. 540.

Brady, J., 'The Huaorani Tribe of Ecuador: A Study in Self-determination for Indigenous Peoples' (1997) 10 Harvard Human Rights Journal 291.

Brunnée, J., 'A Fine Balance: Facilitation and Enforcement in the Design of a Compliance Regime for the Kyoto Protocol' (2000) 13 Tulane Envtl. L.J. 223.

– 'Coping with Consent: Lawmaking Under Multilateral Environmental Agreements' (2002) 15 Leiden J. Int'l L. 1.
– 'Toward Effective International Environmental Law – Trends and Developments,' in S.A. Kennett, ed., *Law and Process in Environmental Management* (Calgary: Canadian Institute of Resources Law, 1993) 217.

Brunnée, J., and S.J. Toope, 'Interactional International Law' (2001) 3 Int'l L. Forum 186.
– 'International Law and Constructivism: Elements of an Interactional Theory of International Law' (2000) 39 Col. J. Trans. L. 19
– 'The Changing Nile Basin Regime: Does Law Matter?' (2002) 43 Harv. J. Int'l L. 105.

Camdessus, J., 'The IMF and the Beginning of the Twenty-First Century: Can we Establish a Humanized Globalization?' (2001) *Global Governance* 363.

Carle, J., and K. Simonssom, 'Competition Law in Sweden' [1993] E.C.L.R. 177.

Charnovitz, S., 'Two Centuries of Participation: NGOs and International Governance' (1997) 18 Mich. J. Int'l L. 183.

Churchill, R., and G. Ulfstein, 'Autonomous Institutional Arrangements in Multilateral Environmental Agreements: A Little-Noticed Phenomenon in International Law' (2000) 94 Am. J. Int'l L. 623.

Cimbala, S.J., 'The Role of Military Advice: Civil-Military Relations and Bush Security Strategy,' in D.M. Snider and M. Carlton-Carew, *U.S. Civil-Military Relations: In Crisis or Transition?* (Washington, D.C.: The Center for Strategic and International Studies, 1995) 88.

Cocuzza, C., and M. Montini, 'International Anti-Trust Cooperation in a Global Economy' (1998) 3 ECLR, 156.

Crawford, J., and S. Marks, 'The Global Democracy Deficit: An Essay in International Law and Its Limits,' in D. Archibugi et al., eds., *Re-imagining Political Community Studies in Cosmopolitan Democracy* (California: Stanford University Press, 1998) 72.

Danspeckgruber, W., 'Self-determination, Self-governance and Security' *International Relations* 15 (April 2000) 1.

Deutch, J.M., *U.S. Department of Defense Directive 2000.13* (27 June 1994).

Downs, G.W., K.W. Danish, and P.N. Barsoom, 'The Transformational Model of International Regime Design: Triumph of Hope or Experience?' (2000) 38 Col. J. Transnat'l L. 465.

Doyle, M., 'Kant, Liberal Legacies, and Foreign Affairs, Part 1' (Summer 1983) 12 *Philosophy and Public Affairs* 3.

Dunne, T., 'Liberalism,' in J. Baylis and S. Smith, eds., *The Globalization of World Politics* (Oxford: Oxford University Press, 1997) 147.

Ehlermann, C.D., 'The Modernization of EC Antitrust Policy: A Legal and Cultural Revolution' (2000) 37 C.M.L.R. 537.

Elliot, K.A., 'Getting Beyond No ...! Promoting Worker Rights and Trade,' in J.J. Schott, ed., *The WTO After Seattle* (Washington: Institute for International Economics, 2000).

Falk, R., and A. Strauss, 'On the Creation of a Global Peoples' Assembly: Legitimacy and the Power of Popular Sovereignty' (2000) 36 Stan. J. Int'l L. 191.

Farer, T.J., 'The United States as Guarantor of Democracy in the Caribbean Basin: Is There a Legal Way?' (1989) 11 *The Jerusalem Journal of International Relations* 3.

Fishel, J.T., and E.S. Cowan, 'Civil-military Operations and the War for Political Legitimacy in Latin America,' in J.W. De Pauw and G.A. Luz, eds., *Winning the Peace: The Strategic Implications of Military Civic Action* (New York: Praeger, 1992) 47.

Franck, T.M., 'The Emerging Right to Democratic Governance' (1992) Am. J. of Int. Law.

– 'Legitimacy in the International System' (1988) 82 Am. J. Int'l L. 705.

Franck, T.M., and G. Nolte, 'The Good Offices Function of the UN Secretary-General,' in A. Roberts and B. Kingsbury, *United Nations, Divided World*, 2nd ed. (New York: Clarendon Press, 1993).

French, D., 'Developing States and International Environmental Law: The Importance of Differentiated Responsibilities' (2000) 49 Int'l & Comp. L.Q. 35.

Fukuyama, F., 'The End of History?' (Summer 1989) 16 *The National Interest* 3.

Gehring, T., 'International Environmental Regimes: Dynamic Sectoral Legal Systems,' in 1 Yearbook Int'l Envtl L. 35.

Ghébali, V.Y., 'La CSCE et la question de la protection des minorités,' in A. Liebich and A. Reszler, eds., *L'Europe centrale et ses minorités: vers une solution européenne?* (Paris: Presse Universitaire de France, 1993).

– 'The OSCE's Istanbul Charter for European Security' (Spring/Summer 2000) 48 *NATO Review.*

Guider, D.L., '1981 Italian Deposit Requirement' (1983) 14(3) *Law and Policy in International Business* 927.

Gupta, J., 'North-South Aspects of the Climate Change Issue: Towards a Negotiating Theory and Strategy for Developing Countries' (2000) 3/2 Int'l J. Sustainable Development 115.

Head, I., 'The Contribution of International Law to Development' (1986) Selected Papers on International Law: Contribution of the Canadian Council on International Law 59.

Heintze, H.J., 'The International Law Dimension of the German Minorities Policy' (1999) 68 Nordic J. Int'l L. at 117.

Helman, G.B., and S.R. Ratner, 'Saving Failed States' 89 *Foreign Policy* 3.

Hildyard, N., 'Foxes in Charge of the Chickens,' in W. Sachs, ed., *Global Ecology* (Halifax: Fernwood Publishers, 1993).

Hudec, R.E., 'GATT Legal Restraints on the Use of Trade Measures against Foreign Environmental Practices,' in J. Bhagwati and R.E. Hudec, eds., *Fair Trade and Harmoniza-*

tion: Prerequisites for Free Trade? vol. 2: Legal Analysis (Cambridge, MA: MIT Press, 1996) 95.

Hudnall, S., 'Towards A Greener Trade System' (2000) 29 *Columbia Journal of Law and Social Problems* 175.

Jones, W.B., 'The International Sea-bed Authority Without U.S. Participation' (1983) 12 Ocean Development and International Law Journal 151.

Kalu, O., *The Gods are to Blame* (Proceedings of the 6th International Congress on Ethnobiology, 1998, Whakatana, New Zealand).

Kaplan, R.D., 'The Coming Anarchy' *The Atlantic Monthly* (1994).

Keohane, R., and J.S. Nye, *Between Centralization and Fragmentation: The Club Model of Multilateral Cooperation and Problems of Democratic Legitimacy* (2001) John F. Kennedy School of Government Faculty Research Working Paper Series No. 01-004.

Khakimov, R.S., 'Prospects of Federalism in Russia: A View from Tatarstan' (1996) 27 *Security Dialogue* 1.

Killebrew, R.B., 'Force Projection in Short Wars' (March 1991) Military Review 30.

King Jr, J.E., *Civil Affairs: The Future Prospect of a Military Responsibility*, Operations Research Office CAMG Paper, No. 3 (June 1958).

Kofmann, M., 'The Danish Competition Act' [1998] E.C.L.R. 1.

Koh, H.H., 'Why Do Nations Obey International Law?' (1997) 106 Yale L.J. 2599.

Lal, D., 'Trade Blocs and Multilateral Free Trade' (1993) 31 *Journal of Common Market Studies* 356.

Lefeber, R., 'Creative Legal Engineering' (2000) 13 Leiden J. Int'l L. 1.

Luttwak, 'Toward Post-Heroic Warfare' (1995), *Foreign Affairs* 74 (May–June) 109.

MacCulloch, A., and B.J. Rodger, 'Wielding the Blunt Sword: Interim Relief for Breaches of EC Competition Law before the UK Courts' [1996] E.C.L.R. 393.

Maher, I., 'Alignment of Competition Laws in the EC' (1996) 16 *Yearbook of European Law* 223.

Manwaring, M.G., 'Limited War and Conflict Control,' in S.J. Cimbala and K.A. Dunn, eds., *Conflict Termination and Military Strategy: Coercion, Persuasion, and War* (Boulder and London: Westview Press, 1987) 59.

Markels, M., and R.T. Barbver, 'The Sequestration of Carbon Dioxide to the Deep Ocean by Fertilization' (2000) American Chemical Symposium on CO_2 Utilization & Sequestration, 20–24 August 2000, p. 1.

Mickelson, K., 'South, North, International Environmental Law and International Environmental Lawyers,' in J. Brunnée and E. Hey, eds. (2000) 11 *Yearbook of International Environmental Law 2000* [forthcoming in 2001].

Murphy, S.D., 'Biotechnology and International Law' (2001) 42 Harv. Int'l L. J. 47.

Mutua, M., 'Savages, Victims, and Saviors: The Metaphor of Human Rights' (2001) 42 Harvard J. of Int'l Law 201.

– 'What Is TWAIL?' (2000) 94 ASIL Proc. 31.

Myers, N., 'The Primary Source: Tropical Forests And Our Future (1984),' in *Rights Violations in the Ecuadorian Amazon: The Human Consequences of Oil Development* (Center for Economic and Social Rights, 1994).

Nader, L., 'The Anthropological Study of Law' (1965) 67 American Anthropologist 25.

O'Connor, T.S., '"We Are Part of Nature": Indigenous Peoples' Rights as a Basis for Environmental Protection in the Amazon Basin' (1994) 5 Colorado J. of Int'l. Env'tl. Law and Policy 193.

Okafor, O.C., 'The Concept of Legitimate Governance in the Contemporary International Legal System' (1997) 44 Netherlands International Law Review 33.

– 'The Global Process of Legitimation and the Legitimacy of Global Governance' (1997) 14 *Arizona Journal of International and Comparative Law* 117.

Packer, J., 'Autonomy within the OSCE: The Case of Crimea,' in M. Suksi, ed., *Autonomy: Applications and Implications* (The Hague: Kluwer Law International, 1998).

– 'On the Definition of Minorities,' in K. Myntti and J. Packer, eds., *The Protection of Ethnic and Linguistic Minorities in Europe* (Turku and London: Abo Akademi University Institute for Human Rights, 1993).

– 'The OSCE and International Guarantees of Local Self-Government,' in *Local Self-Government, Territorial Integrity and Protection of Minorities* (Strasbourg: Council of Europe Publishing, 1996).

– 'The Protection of Minority Language Rights through the Work of the OSCE Institutions,' in S. Trifunovska and F. de Varennes, eds., *Minority Rights in Europe: European Minorities and Languages* (The Hague: T.M.C. Asser Press, 2001).

Palmer, G., 'New Ways to Make International Environmental Law' (1992) 86 AJIL 259.

Paret, P., 'Continuity and Discontinuity in Some Interpretations by Tocqueville and Clausewitz' (1988) 49 *Journal of the History of Ideas* 1.

Peceny, M., 'Two Paths to the Promotion of Democracy During U.S. Military Interventions' (1995) 39 *International Studies Quarterly* 371.

Postema, G.J., 'Implicit Law,' in W.J. Witteveen and W. van der Burg, eds., *Rediscovering Fuller: Essays on Implicit Law and Institutional Design* (Amsterdam: Amsterdam University Press, 1999) 255.

Pritchard, K.H., 'Front and Center: The Army and Civil-Military Operations in the 21st Century' (December 1997) *Army* at 6.

Ratner, S.R., 'Does International Law Matter in Preventing Ethnic Conflict?' (2000) 32 N.Y.U. J. Int'l L. & Pol. 598.

Rodger, B.J., 'The Commission White Paper on Modernisation of the Rules Implementing Articles 81 and 82 of the EC Treaty' (1999) 24 E.L.R. 653.

Rodrik, D., '5 Simple Principles for World Trade,' *The American Prospect,* 17 January 2000.

Russett, B., *Grasping the Democratic Peace: Principles for a Post-Cold War World* (Princeton: Princeton University Press, 1993).

Sands, P., 'International Law in the Field of Sustainable Development: Emerging Legal Principles,' in W. Lang, ed., *Sustainable Development and International Law* (Boston: Graham and Trotman, 1995).

Schoonover, K.W., 'The History of Negotiations Concerning the System of Exploitation of the International Seabed' (1977) 9 International Law and Politics 483.

Shaffer, G.C., 'The World Trade Organization under Challenge: Democracy and the Law and Politics of the WTO's Treatment of Trade and Environment Matters' (2001) 25 Harv. Env'tl. L.R. 1.

Shultz Jr, R.H., 'The Post-Conflict Use of Military Forces: Lessons from Panama, 1989–91' (June 1993) 16 *Journal of Strategic Studies* 2.

Simmons, B., 'Money and the Law: Why Comply with the Public International Law of Money?' (2000) 25 Yale J. Int'l L. 323.

Smith, A.D., 'Ethnic and Nation in the Modern World' (1985) 14 *Millennium* 2.

Sommer, J., 'Environmental Law-Making by International Organizations' (1996) 56 Zeitschrift Für Ausländisches Offentliches Recht und Völkerrecht 628.

Spiro, P.J., 'New Global Communities: Nongovernmental Organizations in International Decision-Making Institutions' (1995) 18 Washington Q. 45.

Summers Jr, H.G., 'A War Is a War Is a War Is a War,' in L.B. Thompson, ed., *Low- Intensity Conflict: The Pattern of Warfare in the Modern World* (Toronto: Lexington Books, 1989) 27.

Symonides, J., 'The Legal Nature of Commitments Related to the Question of Minorities' (1996) 3 Int'l. J. on Group Rights 4.

Széll, P., 'Decision Making under Multilateral Environmental Agreements' (1996) 26 Envt'l. Pl. & L. 210.

Tanner, F., 'Conflict Prevention and Conflict Resolution: Limits of Multilateralism' (September 2000) 82 *International Review of the Red Cross* 839.

Toth, T., 'Competition Law in Hungary: Harmonisation towards EU Membership' [1998] E.C.L.R. 358.

van der Stoel, M., 'The Heart of the Matter: The Human Dimension of the OSCE' *Helsinki Monitor* 6:3 (1995).

Van Miert, K., 'Competition Policy in Relation to the Central and Eastern European Countries – Achievements and Challenges,' *Competition Policy Newsletter*, Issue 2, June 1998.

Wendt, A., 'Collective Identity Formation and the International State' (1994) 88 Am. Pol. Sci. Rev. 384.

Werksman, J., 'The Conference of Parties to Environmental Treaties,' in J. Werksman, ed., *Greening International Institutions* (London: Earthscan, 1996) 55.

Wessling, R., 'The Draft Regulation Modernising the Competition Rules: The Commission Is Married to One Idea' (2001) 26 E.L.R. 357.

Whitt, R.S., 'The Politics of Procedure: An Examination of the GATT Dispute Settlement

Panel and the Article XXI Defense in the Context of the U.S. Embargo on Nicaragua' (1988) 19 *Law and Policy in International Business* 603.

Wilks, S., 'The Prolonged Reform of UK Competition Policy,' in G.B. Doern and S. Wilks, eds., *Comparative Competition Policy: National Institutions in a Global Market* (Oxford: Clarendon Press, 1996).

Wolf, D., 'Perspektiven des Europaischen Kartellrechets' (Position paper, Frankfurter Institute- Stiftung Marktwirkschuft und Politik, 8 July 1999) [unpublished].

Wood, M.C., 'International Sea-bed Authority: The First Four Years' (1999) 3 Max Planck Yearbook of United Nations Law 173.

Wyatt, D., 'Foglia No.2: The Court Denies It Has Jurisdiction to Give Advisory Opinions' (1982) 7 E.L.R. 186.

Zinameister, U., and D. Vasile, 'Romania's New Competition Law' [1998] E.C.L.R. 164.

International Documents and Publications

Boutros-Ghali, B., *An Agenda for Peace: Preventive Diplomacy, Peacemaking and Peace-keeping*, 47th Sess., UN Doc. A/47/277/ S/24111 (1992).

Capotorti, F., *Study on the Rights of Persons Belonging to Ethnic, Religious and Linguistic Minorities* (UN Sales No. E.91.XIV.2, 1991).

Commission Notice of 23 December 1992 on co-operation between national courts and the Commission in applying arts. 85 and 86 of the EC Treaty, O.J.I. [1993] C39/6.

Commission Notice on co-operation between the national competition authorities and the Commission in handling cases falling within the scope of arts. 85 and 86 of the EC Treaty, O.J.I. [1997] C 313.

Commission of the European Communities Notice of 1997 October 15, [1997] O.J.I. C313/3.

Commission of the European Communities, *Green Paper on Vertical Restraints in EC Competition Policy,* [1996] C.O.M. 721.

Commission of the European Communities, *The Green Paper on Vertical Restraints*, 1996.

Commission of the European Communities, *White Paper on Modernisation of the Rules Implementing Articles 85 and 86 of the EC Treaty,* [1999] 5 C.M.L.R. 208, O.J. [1999] C 132/1.

Commission Regulation on Exclusive Distribution 1983/84, [1984] O.J.L. 173/1.

Commission Regulation on Exclusive Purchasing 1984/84, [1984] O.J.L. 173/5.

Communication from the Commission on the application of the Community competition rules to vertical restraints – Follow-up to the Green Paper on Vertical Restraints, [1998] C.O.M. 544.

Council of Europe, *The Protection of Minorities* (Strasbourg: Council of Europe Publishing, 1994).

CSCE *Charter of Paris for a New Europe* (Paris, 21 November 1990).

CSCE, Copenhagen Conference, *Document on the Human Dimension of the CSCE*, c. IV, (1990).

CSCE, Geneva Meeting, *Report of the Meeting of Experts on National Minorities*, c. II (1991).

CSCE, Helsinki Document of 1992, *The Challenge of Change* (1992).

European Platform for Conflict Prevention & Transformation, Prevention & Management of Violent Conflicts: An International Directory (1998).

General Agreement on Tariffs and Trade, *Basic Instruments and Selected Documents.*

Greenpeace International, *The Environmental and Social Costs of Living with Shell in Nigeria* (July 1994).

Hague Declaration on the Environment (1989), 1989 *ILM*, 28, p. 1308.

House of Lords Select Committee [Sub-Committee E] on the European Communitities, Session 1999-2000, Fourth Report 29 February 2000.

OSCE, Istanbul Summit, *Charter for European Security*, c. 3 (1999).

OSCE, Press Release 99/05, 'OSCE High Commissioner on National Minorities addresses Permanent Council on situation in the Former Yugoslav Republic of Macedonia' (12 May 1999).

Public Papers of the Presidents of the United States: The Public Messages, Speeches, and Statements of the President John F. Kennedy, 1962 (Washington, D.C.: U.S. Government General Printing Office, 1963).

Reg. 1215/1999 of June 10, 1999 amending Reg. 19/65 on the application of Article 81(3) of the Treaty to certain categories of agreements and concerted practices, [1999] O.J.L. 148/1.

Reg. 1216/1999 of June 10, 1999 amending Reg. No. 17: first Regulation implementing Articles 81 and 82 of the Treaty, [1999] O.J.L. 148/5.

Report of the Secretary of Defense to the Congress for Fiscal Year 1987 (Washington, D.C: US Government Printing Office, 1986).

Report of the UN Commission on Human Rights, Sub-Commission on Prevention of Discrimination and Protection of Minorities, 45th sess., E/CN.4/Sub.2/1993/34/add.4 (1992).

The Role of the High Commissioner on National Minorities in OSCE Conflict Prevention: An Introduction (The Hague: The Foundation on Inter-Ethnic Relations, 1997).

U.N.E.P., International Environmental Governance: Multilateral Environmental Agreements (MEAs) (2001) [unpublished].

UN Doc. A/55/305-S/2000/809, 21 August 2000, Annex III, Rec. 1(b).

UN Doc. S/RES/1244, 10 June 1999.

UN Doc. S/RES/794 3 December 1992.

UN Doc. S/RES/836, 4 June 1993.

UN GAOR, 54th Sess., 4th Plen. Mtg.,UN Doc. A/54/PV.420 (1999).

World Commission on Environment and Development, 'Our Common Future' (Oxford: Oxford University Press, 1987).

Newspaper Articles

Friedman, T.L., 'The Clinton Gamble,' *New York Times* (6 December 1995) A25.
'Max van der Stoel, Minority Man,' *The Economist* (11 September 1999) 36.
Nigerian Chronicle (14 August 1980).
Nigerian Daily Times (18 June 1974) 2.
Nigerian Daily Times (7 October 1974) 11.
Nigerian Tide (1 May 1 1974) 1.
'OSCE Minorities Chief Aims for Early Action,' *Financial Times* (19 May 2000) 3.
Re Sandhu, *The Times*, 10 May 1985.
'The Multiethnic State,' Letter to the Editor, *International Herald Tribune* (2 February 2000).
'Van der Stoel warnt vor Fundamentalismus,' *Frankfurter Allgemeine Zeitung* (23 November 1999).